D0200985

CODES OF EVOLUTION

CODES OF EVOLUTION

The Synaptic Language Revealing the Secrets of Matter, Life, and Thought

RUSH W. DOZIER, Jr.

CROWN PUBLISHERS, INC., NEW YORK

Copyright © 1992 by Rush W. Dozier, Jr.

All rights reserved. No part of this book may be
reproduced or transmitted in any form or by any means,
electronic or mechanical, including photocopying,
recording, or by any information storage and retrieval
system, without permission in writing from the publisher.

Published by Crown Publishers, Inc.
201 East 50th Street
New York, New York 10022.
Member of the Crown Publishing Group.
Random House, Inc. New York, Toronto, London, Sydney, Auckland

CROWN is a trademark of Crown Publishers, Inc.

Manufactured in the United States of America
Design by Shari DeMiskey

Library of Congress Cataloging-in-Publication Data

Dozier, Rush W.
    Codes of evolution : the synaptic language revealing the secrets of matter, life,
and thought / Rush W. Dozier, Jr. — 1st ed.
    Includes bibliographical references and index.
    1. Evolution.   2. Quantum theory.   3. Big bang theory.   4. Mind
and body.   I. Title.
B818.D69   1992
116—dc20   92-9087
                                                                         CIP

ISBN 0-517-58642-8
10 9 8 7 6 5 4 3 2 1
First Edition

Contents

CONTENTS

For my wife, Patricia,
whose love and intelligence
made this book possible.

Preface and Acknowledgments

ON APRIL 23, 1992, AT A PACKED SCIENTIFIC MEETING IN WASHINGTON, D.C., a team of scientists led by George Smoot of the University of California at Berkeley announced that it had detected the fingerprints of evolution at the birth of the universe.

"If you're religious," Smoot said, "this is like looking at God."

What the team had discovered were tiny fluctuations in temperature among the gigantic clouds of radiation, billions of light years across, that were created by ripples in space and time at the origin of the cosmos.

This is the most powerful confirmation yet of the big bang theory, which postulates that the entire universe began some fifteen billion years ago as a tiny seed, far smaller than an atom, that explosively grew into the behemoth we now see.

Until that day in April, there were serious questions about how the rich structures that populate today's universe could have evolved from such a strange beginning. The radiation clouds provided an answer. It is from these clouds that matter clumped together into galaxies, stars, and planets. When we look at these clouds, we are looking at the ancestors of everything in the universe, including matter, life, and thought.

Codes of Evolution will take you on a journey from the big bang that began the cosmos to the big brains within which human consciousness evolved.

I am deeply indebted to many people for assistance and counsel in the writing of this book. My wife, Patricia, has been my chief booster and intellectual partner in seeing through a project of this magnitude.

It has been my extraordinary good luck to have a superb editor, Richard Marek, who not only deeply believed in what I was writing but helped me express complex ideas in a much more accessible way. I would also like to thank the many others at Crown Publishers who have been involved with this book, including Laura Hildebrand, Andy Martin, Cameron Dougan, and Andrea Connolly.

A number of busy people generously took the time to read the manuscript of *Codes of Evolution* and offer their comments and suggestions. I would like to thank Jonas Salk of the Salk Institute, James Stigler of UCLA, Eric Kandel of Columbia University, David Gelernter of Yale University, Evan Balaban and William Lipscomb of Harvard University, Fang Lizhi and Henry Byerly of the University of Arizona, Robert Kaita of Princeton University, Stephen Libby of the Lawrence Livermore National Laboratory, Patricia Churchland of the University of California at San Diego, and Virginia Fox of Kentucky Educational Television. I would like to thank three old friends, Lillian and Leonard Press and Charles Alexander of *Time* magazine, not only for their interest in this project but for their affectionate support over many years. Carol Price has also been enormously helpful during this undertaking.

The opinions expressed in this book are my own, and I take full responsibility for any errors of fact or judgment.

I would like to specially note the unflagging support and enthusiasm of my mother-in-law, Thelma McHugh.

My mother and father, Patricia and Rush Dozier, took me to my first observatory, where I looked with wonder at the craters of the moon that floated high above in the Arizona sky. Their enthusiasm for life and learning set me on the quest that culminated in this book.

Finally, I would like to acknowledge a very talented writer, my nine-year-old daughter, Beverly, whose never-ending exploits, literary and otherwise, are a constant source of delight.

Introduction: Arizona Nights

ON A CLEAR NIGHT, THE SKY ABOVE SOUTHERN ARIZONA IS DARK AND deep, like a black satin pillow artfully strewn with diamonds and pearls. That magically transparent sky serves as the perfect setting for the oldest and most astonishing light show known to humans: the nightly wheeling of the moon, stars, and planets.

As a boy I often watched the night sky from the backyard of my home in Tucson, Arizona. My mother is from the West and my father is from the East. Both love their home ground and we alternated between them as I grew up. We moved to Tucson when I was five and for the next seven years I was captivated by the desert.

Tucson sits on the floor of a huge valley that stretches northwest to Phoenix and south to Mexico. The peaks of the mountains around the city offer the clear air and good weather that astronomers prize, and Tucson has become one of the world's foremost centers for astronomy.

My childhood interest in astronomy was stimulated by the swirl of scientific activity in the area. The local newspapers were full of stories about the discoveries made by the large telescopes that began to ring the city. Some of my teachers were intensely interested in

1

astronomy, and my parents took me to see the telescope at the University of Arizona, where I had my first close encounter with the surface of the moon. I remember my excitement one night as I went to sleep, knowing that my best friend and his father were going to wake me up a few hours later and take me out to watch a lunar eclipse.

What fascinated me most, beyond the cosmos itself, was the idea of infinity. I struggled to grasp what that meant. Did the universe really go on endlessly? How long had it existed? It was this struggle that led to a strange yet exhilarating experience that has haunted me ever since.

I was eight years old and had been reading my first books on astronomy. One night as I lay in bed before going to sleep, I began thinking again about the meaning of infinity. I stared at the ceiling and tried to imagine that I could see right through it to the sky above. I projected my thoughts deep into space, traveling on and on, wondering how I could ever reach infinity and trying to fathom the nature of such a mysterious universe.

Suddenly I experienced a bewildering and intensely powerful sensation. I felt as if I no longer existed as an individual but had somehow merged with the universe, with infinity itself. I had the most extraordinary feeling that all my questions had been answered—that I somehow understood the entire universe. Yet when I asked myself what it was that I knew, I was startled by the answer. It was knowledge unlike any other I had ever experienced. It was seamless, unbroken by any categories or divisions. The feeling I had is almost impossible to convey: somehow I understood the entire universe, yet part of this understanding was that specific questions no longer existed. Everything was a perfect whole. I felt a kind of ecstasy flood through me. My individuality was completely submerged in this perfection.

The experience did not last long. It was like a flash of illumination. I tried to prolong it, but it quickly faded into a vivid memory. I have had glimmerings of similar experiences since then, but never with the utter clarity of the original. I later learned that such feelings of illumination are not uncommon. Psychologists sometimes call them oceanic experiences. The individual seems to merge momentarily into the ocean of the cosmos.

Other thinkers have described experiences of illumination similar to mine.

"Still there are moments when one feels free from one's own identification with human limitations and inadequacies. At such moments, one imagines that one stands on some spot of a small planet, gazing in amazement at the cold yet profoundly moving beauty of the eternal, the unfathomable: life and death flow into one, and there is neither evolution nor destiny, only being," wrote Albert Einstein. [1]

I emerged from the experience confused and amazed. As I grew older, the memory of that night intensified my desire to rationally understand the universe that I had seemed to glimpse in a way that had transcended reason. Through study and reflection, I became convinced that there must be a fundamental unity underlying all things. I determined to discover its nature.

There were tantalizing hints of this unity wherever I looked. The universe seems to have had a single beginning at the big bang. Life appears to have emerged from the evolution of a single type of molecule: DNA. Consciousness seems to have its roots in a single type of cell—the neuron—and in the huge expansion of the human brain over the last million years.

Since my undergraduate years at Harvard University studying science and public policy and sampling the history of human knowledge and experience, my quest has taken me down many paths. I have been a journalist and city editor of a newspaper, a lawyer and general counsel to a governor, founder of a state council on science and technology, founder and chairman of a nationally recognized program for gifted students, and a government regulator and chairman of a national committee on finance and technology that oversees the nation's sprawling telecommunications and utility industries.

I have worked with Nobel prize–winning scientists and leading officials in the public and private sectors. All of them realize that we are in the midst of enormous changes because of our rapid mastery of nature. But because of the many scientific disciplines involved and their specialized and technical nature, few people are aware of the scope of the transformation that is taking place. I have searched for an understanding that would be accessible to any interested person, with or without a scientific background.

What I have concluded is that science in this century has discovered three hidden codes that unlock the secrets of the universe. Among the mysteries being revealed is the secret of consciousness itself. Using the knowledge provided by the codes, the human race has begun the greatest revolution in history—a revolt of the brain against the tyranny of the genes.

Since its inception, life has been completely at the mercy of the genes. If the genes of an organism determine that it is crippled or diseased or disadvantaged in some other way, there is no appeal. Yet by using our brain's ability to decipher the three fundamental codes, we have begun to overthrow the power of the genes. Through genetic engineering, we are beginning to tell the genes what to do. If they malfunction, we can fix them. We are even gaining the ability to enhance them. We are on the verge of an era in which the brain, for good or ill, will wrest from the genes control over our health, our longevity, our intelligence, and even the course of our own evolution as a species. Every educated person should become familiar with these codes and the evolutionary process in which they operate. Without this knowledge we will be unable as a society and as individuals to intelligently make the profound choices and pursue the phenomenal opportunities that are now beginning to present themselves and that will dominate the next century.

My book will take you on a journey of discovery. It not only reaches conclusions about the universe and our place in it, but it also explores the creative mechanism of scientific thought by which we reach those conclusions. This mechanism, I argue, is a form of evolution that involves the spinning out of varying ideas and theories, each of which is tested against observation and experiment. The ideas that pass these tests are selected and the others are discarded, at least temporarily. No scientific theory is perfect, and new concepts, new data, or a careful rethinking of existing information may bring an old idea roaring back or generate something brand new.

UNIFIED SELECTION

In the following chapters, I will put forward four major propositions that collectively comprise a theory of evolution that encompasses the origin and development of the universe and the emergence of the human brain. These four propositions contain conclusions that scientists have painstakingly teased out of their research as well as a number of original ideas of my own.

First, I argue that the process of evolution that Charles Darwin

4

used more than a century ago to explain the origin and diversity of living things should not be confined to biology. Instead, I expand it to include the realms of matter and thought as well. Darwin called his mechanism of biological evolution "natural selection." I propose that the evolution of matter, life, and thought has a common mechanism, which I call "unified selection."

Matter evolves. Life, which emerged from nonliving chemical reactions, is just one way that matter can evolve. Life, most scientists believe, is a by-product of the evolution of matter on Earth. The matter on each of the other eight planets in our solar system also has a unique evolutionary history, although none of these histories has as yet been found to include living things.

Ideas, too, evolve. Human culture has generated a flourishing thicket of ideas and behaviors that is as dense and rich as any rain forest. Every idea is subject to growth, change, mutation, and even extinction, just as is any species of animal or plant.

"In short, all is evolutionary process, and evolutionary process is the master key to modern science and all other human knowledge," writes Dennis Flanagan, former editor of the *Scientific American* magazine.[2]

Second, I argue that three fundamental codes are at the core of this grand scheme of evolution: the quantum code, the genetic code, and the synaptic code. Figure I summarizes the codes.

The quantum code, which has been painstakingly revealed by physics and chemistry, guides the evolution of matter. All things in the universe are built out of inconceivably tiny, indivisible quantities called elementary particles, which are glued together into larger structures by the four forces of nature: gravity, electromagnetism, the strong force, and the weak force. These elementary particles and fundamental forces come in discrete units called quanta and combine according to specific rules. An electron is an example of an elementary particle of matter, while a photon is a particle of electromagnetism, which includes visible light. As we shall see, the term particle is somewhat misleading because a quantum particle sometimes behaves like a tiny billiard ball but other times mysteriously behaves like a wave.

From quantum evolution emerge atoms, molecules, and ultimately stars, galaxies, and other colossal structures of matter and energy that pervade the universe. The interactions of elementary particles and the four fundamental forces create an alphabet and

THE MASTER CODES

Quantum Code Combines quantum fields into forms of matter, life, and thought. There are two basic kinds of fields: boson fields that convey the forces of gravity, electromagnetism, the strong force, and the weak force; and fermion fields that create the elementary quanta of matter—that is, quarks and leptons. Bosons are the glue that binds fermions into nuclei, atoms, and molecules. Unified selection is the mechanism of evolution and centers on the collapse of the wave function.

Genetic Code Combines four kinds of nucleotides in double-stranded chains forming the double-helix DNA molecule that can reproduce itself exactly with only a rare mutation or error. Specific sequences of three nucleotides (codons) on the chains are arbitrarily linked to one of twenty types of amino acids, the building blocks of proteins. Using another type of nucleic acid (RNA) as an intermediary, the information coded by genes, which are sequences of codons, is translated into proteins that interact to produce entire life forms.

Synaptic Code Combines synapses—that is, electrochemical connections among brain cells (neurons)—so that the pattern and strength of these synaptic connections create networks of circuits that form the basis of learning, memory, and behavior. Through association, these synaptic networks coalesce into models that allow humans to remember the past, interpret the present, and predict the future. Models of the modeling process itself are the source of consciousness. The NMDA receptor, a protein switch on the neuron, is in part responsible for establishing associative connections by selectively allowing calcium ions to enter neurons.

Figure I. The entire universe is constructed from the fundamental codes of matter, life, and thought.

a grammar for matter. Everything in the universe, including life and thought, is ultimately assembled from this quantum alphabet.

The genetic code, as we have seen, shapes all life on Earth. It consists of a four-letter alphabet made up of four different kinds of nucleotides. These nucleotides are the structural units that make up the DNA molecule. The sequence of nucleotides on the DNA molecule provides all the information needed to make a human being or any other organism. A word in this alphabet consists of a sequence of three nucleotides and is called a codon. Each codon-word stands for one of twenty different amino acids. RNA molecules, which are chemically related to DNA, read these codons and use them to construct proteins, which are long chains of amino acids. Proteins are the microscopic machines out of which living things are made.

Science is only now in the process of unlocking the mysteries of what I call the synaptic code, which is the fundamental code of the brain and nervous system. The synaptic code consists primarily of the interaction of one class of cells in the brain and nervous system. The cells are called neurons and the connections between them are called synapses. These cells have developed a method of electrical and chemical communication that allows the brain to record and process information about its environment. The synaptic code explains how the brain continually wires and rewires itself.

Most neuroscientists, as a practical matter, view the mind and brain as synonymous. A person's state of mind is seen as a reflection of the changing electrical and chemical state of the brain. This reduction of mind to brain is extremely controversial among philosophers (and some neuroscientists) but it is the only sensible way for a scientist to go about the day-to-day process of brain research. When a medical researcher designs a drug to eliminate depression, for example, the drug is intended to alter the physical state of the brain, including the responsiveness of its synaptic connections. Although knowledge of exactly what a drug does in the brain is usually incomplete, the assumption is that if the state of the brain is modified appropriately, then the unwanted state of mind—depression—will disappear. This book takes the position that the mind and brain are equivalent.

Third, I argue that every form of matter, life, and thought that exists today can trace its ancestry through a sequence of earlier forms all the way back to the big bang. The big bang, the echo of which we can still detect as the sea of microwave radiation that fills the universe, is the common ancestor of all things. Evolution began with the big bang. It created space, time, matter, and change: the basic ingredients of unified selection.

The theories of physics suggest that until the big bang there was no space and time as we comprehend the terms. There was no distinction between present and past, and all particles and forces merged into a single, primal field.

The perfect unity that existed at the moment of the big bang has unraveled over the eons. Since the big bang, the overall direction of change in the universe has been one-way: from order to chaos. With every passing moment, the universe becomes more disorderly. In the long run, more stars will burn out than burst into flame. The tendency toward disorder is part of our most mundane experiences, such as the tendency of our homes and offices to become messy and disorganized unless we make a concerted effort to keep things neat. It is also the reason we die.

New forms of order structured by the quantum, genetic, and synaptic codes do come into existence, but their creation is more than counterbalanced by the increase in disorder in the universe as a whole. The energy used by your muscles and brain to keep things organized is significantly greater than the order represented by your clean office or home. The general tendency to disorder is referred to by scientists as the second law of thermodynamics.

Fourth, and finally, I argue that the deepest implications of the quantum code are that the evolution of the universe is inherently uncertain and unpredictable. Particles of matter and force are not really clear-cut particles at all, like microscopic grains of sand. Instead, they are more like knots in a web or field of probabilities. Sometimes they behave like particles, and other times like waves. We call them particles for the sake of convenience. In reality, no one knows exactly what they are.

Physicists have discovered a profound theory to describe the probabilistic nature of reality. They call it quantum mechanics, because it is built on the basic insight that all things are made of microscopic quanta. Quantum mechanics provides a mathematical method of predicting the behavior of elementary particles and forces through the calculation of what is called a wave function. This wave function has an irreducible element of randomness and does not make exact predictions but only gives probabilities. Using the wave function, quantum mechanics supplies a model of the universe that predicts the behavior of phenomena at the subatomic level with unprecedented accuracy. If I fire an electron at a detection screen, for example, the wave function of the electron will give me the probability but not the certainty of finding the electron at any given point on the screen.

I shall argue that wave function is the fundamental organizing principle of the quantum code. Since everything in the universe is made of quantum particles, every object can be described by a wave function. Some physicists are even beginning to calculate—very crudely—the wave function of the universe as a whole. The wave function predicts the probabilities that quantum particles will be located in a particular place or organized in a particular way. If, shortly after the big bang, we could have calculated the wave function of the universe, it would have predicted a high probability that the elementary particles of matter would someday evolve into stars and galaxies.

To summarize the four propositions, I am arguing, first, that there is a fundamental mechanism of evolution—that is, unified selection—that governs the evolution of all things; second, that three fundamental codes are found at the heart of the evolution of matter, life, and thought; third, that everything in the universe has descended from the big bang; and finally, that the universe is structured in a way that prevents us from knowing the future with absolute certainty.

THE NATURE OF TIME

To understand the application of the wave function to unified selection, we must carefully distinguish between potentiality and probability. Potentialities are the possible future states the universe and everything in it may assume. They often represent contradictory alternatives. If some intelligence had calculated the wave function of the universe as it stood five billion years ago—just after the Earth was formed—that wave function would have contained two contradictory potentialities: the first, that life would arise on the cooling Earth; and the second, that it would not. When we say that life might arise, what we really mean is that a portion of the quantum particles on the surface of the Earth might evolve over time into forms that we label "life."

The wave function would then predict the comparative *prob-abilities*, under all the circumstances of five billion years ago, that one or the other of the two *potentialities* (life or no life) would come to pass. Assume that the probabilities or odds were sixty percent that life would evolve and forty percent that it would not.

Just as the universe evolves, so its wave function evolves over time. As it evolves, the probabilities that it yields for any given set of potentialities shifts, depending on the circumstances. If the newly formed Earth was broken apart by a hail of giant asteroids two hundred million years after the wave function yielded the first set of probabilities, a new calculation would be necessary because the wave function would have evolved to include these new circumstances. This new calculation of the Earth's wave function would yield very different probabilities for the potentiality of life evolving. The probability of life evolving might now be only five percent, while the probability of no life ever evolving would shoot up to ninety-five percent.

It is important to note that physicists have only been able to calculate the wave function of relatively simple systems involving a few elementary particles. The calculation of the wave function of large numbers of interacting particles, much less the universe itself, is far beyond their current mathematical abilities. Nevertheless, the principles of quantum mechanics seem to apply to all systems. So in principle this kind of calculation can be made, although we are limited to seeking ways of roughly estimating the probabilities.

The structure of quantum mechanics—and the universe itself—decrees that there is a genuine element of uncertainty about the future and this uncertainty is inherent in the wave function. We can, however, be certain about the present and past. While the future exists only as a set of potentialities, the present and the past exist in concrete reality. Once life actually evolved on Earth, one potentiality (life) came into existence as a fact while the other potentiality (no life) ceased to exist.

The notion that the future is uncertain, while the present and past are not, seems only common sense. Yet this idea has traditionally been rejected by many physicists, including, as we shall see in Chapter 2, Albert Einstein. Before quantum mechanics, physics had difficulty distinguishing between the present, past, and future, and many felt that our sense of the future's uncertainty was simply an illusion imposed by the limitations of consciousness. Even today the interpretation of quantum mechanics and the wave function is controversial. Many physicists view it merely as an extremely useful calculational tool that does not establish the reality of an uncertain future. Unified selection, however, treats the wave function as establishing a definite division between the present and past, on the one hand, and the future, on the other.

How does the universe move from future potentialities to present actuality? Quantum mechanics describes this process as the collapse of the wave function. The multiple future potentialities, with their varying probabilities, collapse into a single actuality that we call the present. In our life–no life example, at some point in the history of the Earth these contradictory multiple potentialities collapsed into a single actuality: life evolved at a moment of what was then the present.

What triggers the collapse of the wave function is another controversial question among physicists. Some argue that human consciousness alone precipitates the collapse of potentialities into actuality. Only when we are looking or doing experiments do the potentialities collapse into measurable concreteness, they contend. Not only does a tree falling in the forest make no sound if no one is listening, they would argue, but the tree itself does not exist unless someone is looking at it. From this perspective, there is no objective reality, only observer-created reality.

Unified selection proposes, however, that the collapse of the wave function does not depend on an observer but happens throughout the universe at every moment of the present. This collapse is a *selection* of an actuality from among the multiple possible potentialities. The selection of which potentiality comes into existence in the present is influenced by relative probabilities. Potentialities that have a higher probability are more likely to collapse into existence. Yet there is an element of genuine randomness in the collapse of the wave function. It may have been more likely than not that life would evolve on Earth. But it could have happened otherwise.

Unified selection contends that the constant collapse of the wave function of the universe from potentiality to actuality is built into the structure of the universe. The first collapse was the big bang itself, when the infant universe collapsed into existence from pure potentiality. Einstein's relativity theory warns us that there are no privileged frames of reference: clocks can run at different speeds in different frames of reference depending on the relative state of motion of two observers. Yet relativity also gives us the tools to translate every frame of reference in the universe into our frame of reference. When we do that, unified selection concludes that at the moment we call the present in our frame of reference, not only is our small part of the universe collapsing into actuality, but the universe as a whole is doing so as well.

RIDING THE BUBBLE

Think of the universe as an expanding bubble with the big bang at its center. The area inside the bubble represents the past, which has already collapsed into actuality. The area outside the bubble represents competing future potentialities that have yet to be realized. The skin of the bubble represents the present, constantly expanding into the area that was once pure potentiality. We live on that expanding boundary between the past and the future. It is the only portion of reality we experience directly. The past is accessible to us solely through memory, while our access to the future is limited to predictions based on our past and present experiences.

I will argue that wave function of the universe collapses from potentiality to actuality trillions of times per second. These slices of time are so small that we never notice them and reality appears to be smooth and continuous. A number of physicists have pointed out, however, that if we could examine space and time at the smallest level we would see not a smooth surface but a grainy, frothy structure. This illustrates what I believe is one of the deepest insights of the quantum code: neither space nor time is infinitely divisible. Both are constructed from incredibly tiny, indivisible units called quanta.

Each object in the universe, including every living thing, is associated with a wave function that defines its potentialities and the differing probabilities that these potentialities will come to pass. Every object has a tiny share of the wave function of the universe. As the wave function evolves through time, the probabilities it predicts change. For example, the particles of every living thing have the potential for entering a disorganized state we call death. The probability that a living thing will die increases as it ages. But the predictions of the wave function are always based on probabilities. We can never predict with absolute certainty the exact moment of death.

I shall argue that all living things have a set of potentialities that are defined by their wave function, and these potentialities are reflected in their genes. Similarly, certain living things have the potential for complex thought and behavior. These potentialities are expressed in their synaptic code: the mechanism by which the brain wires itself.

The universal evolutionary mechanism that I propose—unified selection—is the process of selection from among the multitude of potentialities as the wave function of the universe constantly collapses into the present. The mechanism is universal because all forms of matter, life, and thought ride along on the surface of the expanding bubble we call the present. The structure of matter, life, and thought at any given moment reveals the outcome of a long series of collapses from potentiality to actuality. The constant process of collapse leads to the evolution of new forms of matter, life, and thought and to the disappearance of old ones. But all are linked by their common descent from the big bang itself.

The universe of matter and energy rises like a chain of islands from a sea of quantum fluctuations, which can nudge the course of evolution in unexpected ways. Brain cells, which like everything else in the universe are made of quantum particles of matter and force, can discharge seemingly at random under the influence of these fluctuations. Random discharges can push the pathways of thought into new directions.

The study of the amplification of tiny fluctuations into large effects is an important part of the burgeoning scientific discipline of nonlinear dynamics, which embraces what is known as the theory of chaos. In a nonlinear system a small input can produce a very large output. Your car, for example, is nonlinear in that a slight turn of the key in the ignition starts an engine powerful enough to move a ton of metal. A slight push on the accelerator is amplified into rapid acceleration. The same sort of nonlinear process can amplify an insignificant squall in the southern Caribbean into a monstrous hurricane. Random fluctuations from the microscopic world of atoms and molecules are amplified into the larger universe and disturb the course of cause and effect. Slight variations in the initial conditions of complex systems like the brain can produce significantly different outcomes. In unified selection, amplification is an exceptionally important process.

In this book I contend that free will is a nonlinear phenomenon that has a sound scientific basis. The inherent uncertainty of the future allows individuals to change the probabilities that future events (potentialities) will occur (collapse into existence in the present). Individuals can sometimes change the course of history because their influence is amplified by circumstances. A frustrated, unemployed young art student in Vienna, Adolf Hitler, embraced a vicious racist philosophy and hastened the rise of fascism and terror in the heart of Europe. In contrast, an unemployed Polish electrician, Lech Walesa, decided to climb over a wall at the Lenin Shipyards in Gdansk in a seemingly quixotic effort to mold worker discontent into political action, a deed that helped bring down the Soviet empire.

Complex systems that are exquisitely sensitive to tiny differences in initial conditions are the bridge between the world of quantum fluctuations and the larger world that we live in. DNA molecules are one such complex system. As we shall see in Chapter 3, mutations in the genetic code carried by DNA can be caused by quantum fluctuations in the form of radiation. This is because a tiny change in the order of the information carried by DNA can cause a significant change in the organism produced by the genetic code. An accumulation of genetic mutations can lead, over time, to the evolution of an entirely new species.

In this book, I argue that the brain, with its billions of tiny interconnections, is a similarly complex system that is sensitive to initial conditions. Quantum fluctuations cause "mutations" of thought that take the form of variations in ideas and behaviors. These variations are the grist for the evolution of thought.

The common evolutionary mechanism that governs the development of matter, life, and thought provides a scientific basis for a comprehensive philosophical framework explaining the origin and unfolding of the entire universe and everything in it. This evolutionary philosophy fully integrates human beings into nature. The split between natural selection (produced by nature) and artificial selection (produced by humans) is false. The evolution of human beings, including their civilizations and ideas, is just as natural as the evolution of the behavior of any other living thing. The same principles of variation and selection that underlie the evolution of, say, popular music are shaping the evolution of life, although different types of evolution have far different consequences.

The process of evolution has been characterized as a mixture of chance and necessity. Five or six billion years ago, when our solar system evolved, it was not preordained that there would be nine planets with the precise orbits we see today. There could have been three planets, five, none, or many other combinations. These potentialities were winnowed down to the one we now see through the operation of chance and necessity in the form of unified selection. I argue that the infinite number of potential forms of life and thought are similarly shaped, sorted, and selected by unified selection.

Ever since the big bang, the universe has been evolving, first through forms of matter structured by the quantum code and now, on Earth, through forms of life and thought structured by the genetic and synaptic codes. It is the structure of the codes that determines the variations of matter, life, and thought that are produced at any particular time. These variations then either survive or disappear as they undergo selection by the environment. Because of the amplification of nonlinear subatomic fluctuations into the larger world, the exact direction that evolution will take can never be predicted.

There is a grand continuum in which the quantum code—forged in the big bang—evolved a series of subsidiary codes that govern what we call life and thought. The quantum code is the parent of the genetic code, which in turn gave rise to the synaptic code. Living things obey the genetic code but they continue to be governed by the quantum code as well. The thinking brain, which is a product of the synaptic code, obeys both the genetic and quantum codes. (See Figure II.)

The backbone of the quantum code is the wave function, which determines the probabilistic behavior of quantum particles. The backbone of the genetic code is DNA, the structure of which contains the genetic information needed to create and sustain a living organism. The backbone of the synaptic code is the synapse—the information processing connection among neurons—which allows the brain to map its environment and interconnect those maps to create synaptic models to guide its behavior. Both the quantum and synaptic codes, I contend, represent a subset of potentialities contained in the wave function of the universe.

Unified selection exposes the underlying symmetries, or unifying elements, hidden among the infinite forms of matter, life, and thought in the universe. Everything in the universe descended from

Time Line of Cosmic Evolution

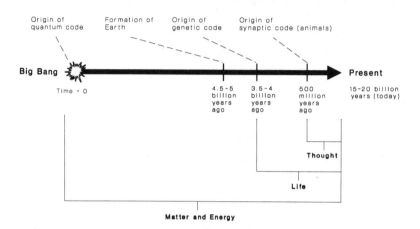

Figure II. The three master codes have come into existence at different times since the big bang. The quantum code originated with the big bang. The genetic code evolved about one billion years after the Earth was formed. The synaptic code is the baby of the group, only half a billion years old.

the big bang and is governed by the quantum code. All life is related through the genetic code; all thought through the synaptic code. Out of the bewildering diversity of matter, life, and thought, basic symmetries or unities emerge that form the cornerstone of the powerful and general scientific theories that we are employing to transform ourselves and our world.

Scientists who study the universe—known as cosmologists—often use the term cosmic evolution to describe the origin and development of the universe from the big bang to its present state. Rarely, however, do they extend their analysis to life and thought or propose a common evolutionary mechanism. Most biologists, on the other hand, resist efforts to broaden the Darwinian mechanism to the evolution of ideas or the evolution of the universe.[3]

In this book I fuse Darwinian natural selection with quantum mechanics to derive a single mechanism for both the evolution of the universe as a whole and the evolution of life and thought on Earth. That mechanism is unified selection.

The evolution of matter, life, and thought, I argue, is a succession of broken symmetries. At the moment of the big bang, matter and force were fused into a unified, indistinguishable whole. The expansion and cooling of the universe after the big bang broke this symmetry. Matter separated from force, and force itself broke apart into the four different fundamental forces we see today: gravity, electromagnetism, the strong force, and the weak force. Gravity dominates the large-scale organization of the universe into stars and galaxies, while the last three forces govern the shapes of atoms and molecules.

On Earth, more than three billion years ago, the first simple species of life evolved, probably from a single source. These species were based on DNA molecules, which are the carriers of genes. As the genetic information within the DNA molecules mutated, however, the symmetry of early life forms was broken. New species evolved and older ones became extinct. From mutating DNA molecules that produce variations in living things descended all the millions of species of life that have populated our planet over the last three-and-a-half billion years. The evolution of life continues. Any living species, including our own, is capable of producing new species, just as the early primate species from which we descended millions of years ago produced not only human beings, but chimpanzees, gorillas, and many other species as well.

One particular branch of primates—human beings—developed large brains capable of language and other feats of mental prowess. From the earliest forms of language have emerged thousands of different languages, many embodying very different ways of looking at the world. And within these languages ideas have evolved, mutated, and split into many different offspring. The study, thought, and speculation of the ancient world about the nature of the universe, for example, particularly by the Greeks, have evolved and descended into the impressive array of disciplines and ideas that constitute modern science.

The collective body of scientific knowledge is our greatest cultural achievement. Being ignorant of science in the twentieth century is like living 4,500 years ago in the shadows of the newly constructed pyramids of Egypt and not noticing. Of course everyone is aware of the products of science: the rapid advances in technology and the soaring skylines of our great cities. Yet the pyramids of the twentieth century have been constructed not with steel but with ideas.

NESTED BOXES

Like Chinese boxes nested one inside the other, matter, life, and thought are inextricably linked. The outer box is matter (which is interchangeable with energy), the quantum mechanical laws of which must be obeyed by all things in the universe. Life, the next box, was produced by a mutation of matter that permits the storing and reproduction of information in the genetic code. Thought, the innermost and newest box, was produced by a mutation of living tissue. (See Figure III.) Perhaps there is another box that has not yet been opened and a fresh code that we have not yet discovered. On other worlds there may be other codes that, while obeying the universal quantum code, are very different from the genetic and synaptic codes that have evolved on Earth. It is even possible that

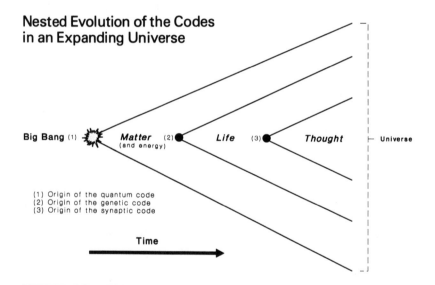

Figure III. This is a schematic representation of the evolution of the fundamental codes. At the big bang, matter and energy emerge. They are governed by the quantum code. From matter and energy in the form of complex molecules, the genetic code of life evolved on Earth. The genetic code, in turn, spawned the synaptic code of thought. Note, however, that the quantum code applies to the entire universe while the genetic and synaptic codes exist, as far as we know, only on Earth. If this figure were drawn to scale, the realm of the genetic and synaptic codes would be invisible in the vastness of the universal quantum code.

human beings will create a new code as we seek to produce synthetic forms of life and intelligence.

The principles of biological evolution, although taken for granted by the vast majority of the scientific community, still stir up controversy in some quarters. Regardless of one's point of view, the practical impact of the rapid growth of our understanding of the quantum, genetic, and synaptic codes must be reckoned with. The impact has been good and bad, as is the case with all powerful ideas. The discovery of the quantum code has produced both computers and hydrogen bombs. With the discovery of the genetic code has come genetic engineering, a technology that may be the key to curing many diseases, including cancer, by allowing us to insert healthy genes into unhealthy cells. But this same technology may make possible vastly more dangerous forms of biological warfare. Our embryonic understanding of the synaptic code could one day lead to the cure of most mental illnesses and the enhancement of our intellectual capacities. Yet it could also lead to frightening techniques of mind control and the synthesis of unbelievably addictive drugs.

Despite the risks, the rapid increase in our knowledge is an astonishing scientific triumph. The brain is especially fascinating. There is a growing body of evidence that the brain creates what I call synaptic maps and synaptic models. Synaptic maps and models are an internal representation of our experiences created out of synaptic connections among neurons in the brain. In the process of creating these models, new synaptic connections may be made between brain cells, or existing connections may be strengthened or weakened.

Synaptic maps of discrete aspects of reality are integrated into complex synaptic models of the past, present, and future. The neural pathways from the eyes into the brain are dotted with synaptic maps that record limited aspects of the shapes, orientations, movements, and colors of the things we see. Somehow this collection of specialized maps—all based on information gathered by a small patch of sensory neurons in each eye—is interconnected to form the vivid, detailed, continuously updated synaptic model of the world that we experience when we open our eyes.

These maps and models are created by the unique way the brain wires and rewires itself. We are beginning to understand the way this wiring works by studying the microscopic switches in

19

the neurons that turn it on and off. Two important components of the switching appear to be the NMDA receptor, a specialized protein molecule that is embedded in the cell membranes of many neurons, and the flows of calcium into and out of the neuron. The NMDA receptor and calcium cycling, along with a few other basic processes, appear to form the core of the synaptic code out of which synaptic models are constructed.

One of the most important conclusions of this book is that learning is modeling. We do not precisely and unerringly inscribe information into our memory like a computer. Instead, we create dynamic models that place facts in a context; models that continually evolve in response to experience.

Someone visiting New York City for the first time will usually find it confusing and have a hard time getting around. But if that same person gets a job in the city, he will soon become familiar with its layout and be able to find his way with comparative ease. A synaptic model or representation has been created in the individual's brain. This internal model is constantly updated by new experiences and insights.

Consciousness itself appears to be an integrated, constantly updated model of the world that draws on neural subsystems that map and model the past (memory), the present (awareness), and the future (extrapolations from the past and present).

There is evidence that the more powerful or significant an experience, the stronger and more numerous are the synaptic connections and the better we remember it. Traumatic emotional experiences leave vivid and persistent memories. Nearly everyone old enough to remember can recall exactly what they were doing when they first heard that President Kennedy had been shot or that the space shuttle *Challenger* had exploded. These memories are burned into the synaptic connections in our brains.

The act of creating synaptic models can stimulate emotions as well, through both the pain of the struggle and the pleasure of the insights and abilities obtained. Perhaps it was the effort I was making to create a model of the infinite universe that triggered my youthful oceanic experience.

The tremendous expansion of the human brain over the last million years has given us sufficient neural space to create extremely elaborate synaptic models, more elaborate than those of any other animal. Models of the past, present, and future reach a peak in the complex, counterintuitive models of science. Quantum mechanics, genetics, and evolution are all elaborate synaptic models that are created by and reside in the brains of scientists. They allow scientists to navigate their way through the complexities of the universe.

Nearly a century passed after the publication of Charles Darwin's *On the Origin of Species* before James Watson and Francis Crick in 1953 hit upon the double helix of the DNA molecule as the correct structure of the genetic code. Forty years after this discovery we are still wrestling with the subtleties of heredity. Physics labored for two centuries after the death of Isaac Newton before it produced the quantum code, which received its modern formulation in the 1920s. It has been a century since neuroscientists began to conclude that the neuron is the fundamental cell that makes up the brain and nervous system. There is as yet no generally accepted formulation of the synaptic code. But the progress of the past decade has been breathtakingly fast and I believe we are within sight of that goal, just as biologists knew in the years prior to 1953 that a breakthrough in understanding the genetic code was near at hand.

When neuroscience finally cracks the synaptic code and discovers the basic mechanism of thought, humanity will have realized one of its greatest achievements—if not the greatest. Yet even then, neuroscience will have decades, if not centuries, of work ahead of it to fathom the depths and intricacies of the synaptic code. The three master codes represent the pinnacle of modern science.

Understanding the three codes is only the beginning of the quest to understand our place as a species in the universe. Each code contains a message—often complex and puzzling—about who we are, what our purpose is, and where we are going. Our journey through the codes will begin to reveal these messages.

In our quest we are always in danger of seeking too much certainty in the scientific evidence. There are no final truths in science, only provisional theories subject to revision as new evidence warrants. Theories often have overwhelming support, but a good scientist always keeps an open mind to new ideas (although scientists can be as stubborn as anybody else). On the frontiers of science, where much of the work on the codes is going on, the normal state of affairs is turmoil and controlled chaos. In this book I can only give a flavor of this complexity.

SKYLINE

During a trip to Phoenix a few years ago, my wife and I took a side trip to spend the day hiking along the cliffs of the Grand Canyon. We stayed for dinner at the rustically elegant lodge perched on the canyon rim.

It was getting dark and we were tired as we drove toward Flagstaff on our way back to Phoenix. My wife reclined her seat to take a nap. Suddenly she froze and told me to pull the car over. The moonless night was clear and cold and there was no one in sight. It was my wife's first visit to the canyon and as she had begun to doze she had looked out of the car window up into the night sky and been struck with awe. We stopped the car and stood by the side of the road gazing at a Milky Way so vivid that it was almost preternatural.

The great cities of Earth are one of the summits of our civilization and we love to admire their majestic skylines at night. Yet as we watched the stars slowly wheeling I thought to myself that the Milky Way is our true metropolis—our mother city. It is our home galaxy and its hundred billion suns create a skyline that will never be equalled. Just as our brain has rebelled against the domination of the genes, so too it may one day rebel against its isolation on a single planet. Perhaps it is our destiny to explore this cosmic metropolis. To do so we will first have to master the intricacies of the three codes.

PART ONE

Code of Creation

*How wonderful that we have met with paradox.
Now we have some hope of making progress.*

—NIELS BOHR

*The paradox is now fully established that the
utmost abstractions are the true weapons with which
to control our thought of concrete fact.*

—ALFRED NORTH WHITEHEAD

Chapter 1

The Quantum Code

WHAT PRECISELY IS EVOLUTION? THE TERM IS OFTEN USED LOOSELY to describe development and change. But in my theory of unified selection I define it to mean a change in the forms of matter, life, and thought over time. Fifty years ago the big bang's major challenger for theory of the universe was something called the steady-state theory. According to this theory, the universe has always looked basically the way it does today, with stars and galaxies filling the sky. This has been the view of most human beings for thousands of years. The steady-state theory postulated that at places in the universe matter was constantly being created so that when stars burned out or galaxies dissipated there was always plenty of additional matter around to form new ones. There was *change* in the steady-state universe but not *evolutionary change* because the basic forms of matter—stars, galaxies, planets—never changed.

It is absolutely essential to understand the distinction between ordinary change and evolutionary change. If human beings and all the other species we see today had always existed since the inception of life on Earth, then there would be no biological evolution. There would be plenty of change because generations of animals and plants would have lived and died. Yet there would not be evolutionary change since the forms of animals and plants—humans, trees, bacteria—never would have changed. But this is not the case. The forms of life that we call species have changed dramatically over millions of years. Life evolves. If you believe in dinosaurs you believe in evolution. The overwhelming evidence that vastly different species have come and gone throughout the history of life on Earth is the reason scientists say that biological evolution is a fact and not a theory.

The remarkable revelation of twentieth-century science is that evolution in the strict sense of the word takes place on all levels, from the largest to the smallest. There has been a drastic change in the forms of matter since the origin of the universe. Not only were there no stars and galaxies shortly after the big bang, there also were no atoms and molecules. There was only a soup of elementary particles. Similarly, for several billion years after life began, not only were there no human beings, but for millions of years there were no organisms larger than a single cell. In addition, the types of ideas that populate the minds of human beings have changed radically since *Homo sapiens* emerged. We can be confident that early human beings had no inkling of quantum theories or symbolic logic. These ideas evolved over thousands of years.

What is the greatest challenge for the artist or the scientist? Finding the right questions to ask, I would say. The frontiers of knowledge are a series of important questions the answers to which will lead not only to profound insights into human existence and the nature of the universe, but also to more questions.

Truly fundamental questions are rarely obvious. For centuries, gifted thinkers fruitlessly pondered what kept the planets in their orbits. Only after Isaac Newton asked himself whether the fall of an apple and the orbit of the moon had something in common did the law of gravity finally reveal itself.

Our search for the fundamental unity of all things begins with a simple question. What are things made of, deep down and fundamentally, and how do they change? That question is at the core of physics and chemistry, where our search for the secrets of the universe begins.

This chapter will discuss the nature of the quantum code, a subject of some complexity. But this discussion is indispensable because it shows that the entire universe has evolved. The forms of matter and energy have changed radically since the big bang, from a single force to four different forces and from a soup of particles to a universe populated by galaxies, stars, and, on our planet at least, by life and thought as well.

In the empire of modern science, all things in the universe—everyone you have ever known, every object you have ever seen, the planet you live on, the air you breathe, the sun, the moon, the stars, your very body and brain—are made of different combinations of four fundamental forces and three families of particles. The forces are the glue that hold the particles together.

The description of these forces and particles and how they combine is what I call the quantum code, what physicists call quantum mechanics. It is the language of the cosmos and the code of creation.

From this perspective, the only difference between this book and its reader, or any object in nature, is the organization of their common components of forces and particles. Roughly ninety-six percent of the human body consists of carbon, hydrogen, oxygen, and nitrogen in different combinations. Yet the pages of this book are largely made from these same elements. How did these four elements come to assume two such distinctive forms? The answer is evolution, and the rules by which it occurs begin with the quantum code.

The four fundamental forces are gravity, electromagnetism, the strong force, and the weak force. Gravity bonds us to the Earth, and forms matter into planets, stars, and galaxies. Electromagnetism is the source of visible light and other kinds of radiation. The strong and weak forces determine the structure of the nucleus of the atom and affect radioactive decay.

All the fundamental forces have messenger particles that carry the force. The messenger particle of gravity is the graviton and the messenger particle of light is the photon. The strong force is carried by messenger particles called gluons, while the messenger particles of the weak force are called intermediate vector bosons.

Turning from forces to matter, each of the three families of matter is made up of three kinds of elementary particles. The three most important kinds of elementary particles are the electron and the up quark and down quark. They belong to the first family of matter and are the building blocks of atoms. (See Figure 1.1.)

Quantum Alphabet of Matter

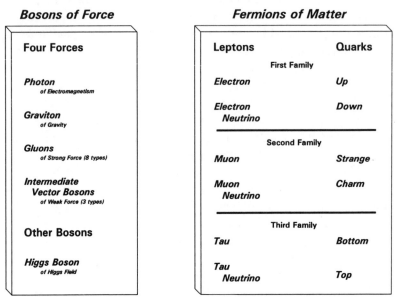

Bosons of Force

Four Forces

Photon
of Electromagnetism

Graviton
of Gravity

Gluons
of Strong Force (8 types)

**Intermediate
Vector Bosons**
of Weak Force (3 types)

Other Bosons

Higgs Boson
of Higgs Field

Fermions of Matter

Leptons	Quarks
First Family	
Electron	**Up**
Electron Neutrino	**Down**
Second Family	
Muon	**Strange**
Muon Neutrino	**Charm**
Third Family	
Tau	**Bottom**
Tau Neutrino	**Top**

Figure 1.1. Recent particle accelerator experiments have revealed that there are only three fundamental families of matter. Each family has two leptons and two quarks. To these elementary particles must be added the bosons on the four fundamental forces and at least one other particle that physicists believe is essential to the creation of matter: the Higgs boson, which is believed to be responsible for the different masses of the different types of elementary particles.

Electrons form the outer shells of atoms, while quarks combine to make the protons and neutrons in the nucleus of atoms.

The second and third families of matter contain heavier relatives of the electron and up and down quarks. These particles are highly unstable, however, and are rarely found in ordinary matter. Each of the three families of matter has a final type of particle—the neutrino—that also has virtually no effect on ordinary matter. Neutrinos pepper the universe and millions of them pass through us, unnoticed, every second and sail right through the Earth.

Physicists refer to the four forces and three families of matter as the Standard Model. For example, hydrogen, the simplest of atoms, is understood by the Standard Model to consist of three quarks (one down quark and two up quarks), which form a single proton in its nucleus, surrounded by a single electron. Knowing the elementary structure of the atom allows science to understand how atoms combine to form molecules. Two hydrogen atoms link with one oxygen atom to form a molecule of water, for example. The electrons of the three atoms form an electromagnetic bond that holds them together.

The quantum code can be compared to an alphabet in which the elementary particles of matter are the consonants and the four fundamental forces are the vowels. Just as vowels bind consonants into words, elementary particles of matter are bound together into atoms by the four forces. Each object in the universe is precisely described by the quantum language, just as each living thing is precisely described by the information contained in its DNA.

The quantum alphabet seems confusing at first, just as the English alphabet is confusing to someone who is just learning the language. Yet to have all the matter and energy in the universe explained by the interaction of a handful of particles is something of a miracle. The quantum code is truly a universal language.

COSMIC ROULETTE

For our purposes—searching as we are for the unity of existence—the most important fact about the quantum code is that it evolves. All the particles and forces we see today evolved from the big bang. At that instant of creation, the quantum code looked quite different than it does now, just as the earliest forms of life were different from those that exist today. The universe was infinitesimally small and unthinkably dense. Something that small and dense is also unimaginably hot. Most physicists believe that there was no distinction between particles and forces at the big bang. They all blended together into a unified, symmetrical whole.

Imagine a perfect sphere. No matter how you turn it, the sphere looks just the same. It is perfectly symmetrical in any rotation. The symmetry of particles and forces at the big bang may also have been perfect, although the kinds of symmetry involved are more mathematically abstract.

Physicists seek the hidden symmetries in nature, symmetries that have been "broken" in the cold universe in which we live. A bar magnet, for example, is asymmetrical. Each end of the magnet has a distinct charge, positive or negative. If the magnet is heated, however, a hidden symmetry is revealed. The magnetism in the bar of metal disappears. Since there is no distinction between either end, the bar now remains unchanged when its ends are reversed. When the bar cools, the magnetic poles return and this symmetry of rotation is again broken.

Symmetries like this have led physicists to look for hidden symmetries at the higher temperatures of the universe that existed shortly after the big bang. This search has led in recent years to a tremendous effort to unify the laws of physics. Many physicists believe that concealed in the inconceivable heat and density of the big bang itself is the ultimate symmetry from which the entire universe evolved. All particles and forces would be unified in this supreme symmetry.

The quest for unification helps explain the exceptional importance of particle accelerators in physics. By smashing subatomic particles together, these accelerators can recreate on a small scale the tremendous temperatures that existed shortly after the big bang. By giving physicists a glimpse into the distant past, accelerators allow them to test their unification theories.

Think of the universe as a spinning roulette wheel. The hotter the universe, the faster the roulette wheel spins. On the roulette wheel are balls representing the four forces and three families of matter. We first glimpse the roulette wheel at only 10^{-43} second after the big bang. This incredibly tiny fraction of a second is called the Planck time, in honor of one of the founders of quantum mechanics, Max Planck. The Planck time is associated with a temperature called, appropriately enough, the Planck temperature: 10^{32} degrees Kelvin (1 followed by thirty-two zeros). This is the farthest back physics can go without its equations self-destructing and producing nonsense. [1]

(Before we proceed any further, let me say a word about temperature. The Kelvin scale, named after a famous physicist of the late nineteenth century, measures the temperature above absolute zero. At absolute zero, a temperature that most physicists believe is unattainable, the motion of atoms would cease. For comparison, absolute zero is -459.67 degrees Fahrenheit or -273.15 degrees Centigrade. The Kelvin scale is designed to measure temperatures that are extremely cold or extremely hot.)

As I was saying, we meet our roulette wheel when the temperature of the newly emerging universe is 10^{32} degrees Kelvin, or 100 million trillion trillion degrees above absolute zero. As you can imagine, the roulette wheel is spinning at a fantastic rate. The roulette balls representing force and matter are whirling above the wheel in a uniform blur. We cannot pick out any distinct particles. The symmetry is perfect.

Suddenly we hear the clatter of a roulette ball falling into one of the wheel's slots. It is the graviton of gravity. Even at this high temperature the wheel has slowed enough for the graviton to become a distinctive particle. Gravity is the first of the four forces to split off from the others.

As the universe cools, the roulette wheel continues to slow. The strong force, weak force, and electromagnetism are still united, but as the temperature cools to 10^{27} degrees Kelvin, we hear another clatter as the balls representing the gluons fall into slots on the wheel. The strong force has split off from the remaining two forces. When quantum particles fall into slots on the wheel, they take on distinctive features, including a characteristic mass or weight.

Electromagnetism and the weak force continue to be indistinguishable until the temperature cools to 10^{15} degrees Kelvin. This is about seventy million times hotter than the center of the sun. As the wheel slows, the balls representing the photons of electromagnetism and the intermediate vector bosons of the weak force bounce into slots on the wheel. The evolution of the four forces is complete.

Meanwhile the particles of the three families of matter have also come to rest on the wheel. The evolution of the quantum code into the form in which we now see it is complete. The stage is set for the clumping of ordinary matter into stars and galaxies, the first step on the road to life and thought.

Today the roulette wheel is barely moving. The universe as a whole has cooled to an average temperature of 2.7 degrees above absolute zero. Stars and planets are tiny outposts of warmth in this immense and frigid landscape.

SECRETS WITHIN SECRETS

The quantum code gives science the secret of the universe and the key to the structure of matter. Without it, modern chemistry, genetics, and neuroscience are inconceivable.

Yet at its deepest level, the quantum code also presents a picture of the underlying reality of the universe that is extremely strange. Physicists are still bitterly divided over its meaning. Albert Einstein, for one, never accepted it. He longed for the certainties and determinism that had pervaded Newtonian physics.

The quantum universe is one ruled by probabilities rather than cause and effect. Particles, which sometimes behave like waves, pop in and out of existence without warning. The way we choose to observe phenomena affects their behavior. Somehow they seem to know we are looking at them. Yet, as we shall see in Chapter 2, the weird implications of the quantum code are essential to understanding such basic concepts as the nature of time.

The formulation of the quantum code, which emerged from the field of physics called quantum mechanics, is the result of a long, complex process of the variation and selection of ideas that stretches back to the Greeks. Democritus of Abdera, who died in 370 B.C., proposed that all matter is made up of tiny, indivisible particles called atoms. The atomic theory of matter was revived in the seventeenth century to explain new discoveries in chemistry and physics. In the twentieth century, scientists realized that atoms were not indivisible and could be divided into even smaller units. With electrons, quarks, and neutrinos we seem to have reached the final level of matter. They are called elementary particles of matter because they do not appear to be divisible into other smaller units.

Our window into this subatomic world is the particle accelerator, which accelerates streams of elementary particles to nearly the speed of light before smashing them together. The heat from these tiny collisions is far hotter than the sun and reproduces conditions that have not been seen in the universe since shortly after the big bang. Using this technology, science can tear matter apart and see how it puts itself back together. Particle accelerators are time machines. They take us back billions of years to show us what the universe was like just after its creation and how it evolved thereafter.

The fact that human beings have been able to devise such machines is amazing. Even more amazing, perhaps, is the fact that these machines and those who build and operate them are not more celebrated. Imagine if someone built a machine that could for a few fractions of a second recreate the dinosaurs. It would be an instant worldwide sensation. (In fact, as we shall see in Chapter 4, biologists have recently developed a kind of genetic time machine.) Yet important as they are, dinosaurs are just one of millions of extinct species that have evolved on a single small planet. With particle accelerators, physicists can recreate the early universe itself on a microscopic scale, reproducing conditions that determine the structure and fate of everything in the entire cosmos. This is quite an achievement for the inhabitants of a fragile blue planet.

Our knowledge of the structure of matter has emerged over the last few decades in a breathless and sometimes emotional competition of scientific ideas and experiments. One of the major questions has been how many families of matter there are. Particles belonging to three families had been discovered. Each family consisted of an electron or related particle, a neutrino, and two quarks. But some hoped that more particles and families would be found. These new particles might account for new forms of matter that had not yet been discovered but which some physicists nevertheless suspected might pervade the universe. Yet more than three families of matter would complicate physicists' calculations of the evolution of the universe and might call into question the big bang itself. Are there more than three families of matter? The answer came in 1989.

RACE FOR THE CODE

Carlo Rubbia is the director of the large electron-positron collider, known as the LEP, the most enormous scientific instrument ever built. It is a particle accelerator designed to discover the secrets of matter by smashing streams of subatomic particles together.

Just beyond his office outside of Geneva, Switzerland, at the headquarters of the European Organization for Nuclear Research (CERN), the accelerator's 16.8-mile-long octagonal tunnel begins. The tunnel is buried an average of 360 feet below ground and straddles the Franco–Swiss border. Inside and around it are 60,000 tons of hardware, nearly 5,000 electromagnets, four 3,000-ton particle detectors, 160 computers, and 4,000 miles of electrical cables. All this to generate temperatures high enough to unite electromagnetism with the weak force by creating what we might call tiny spinning roulette wheels of energy. It takes hundreds of Ph.D.'s to run a single experiment on this giant machine.

The huge stakes and large egos of high-energy physics were dramatically put on display in October 1989 when Rubbia's team was beaten in the race to formally announce to the world that there are only three families of elementary particles in the universe. The Italian physicist's arch-rival, Burton Richter, of the Stanford Linear Accelerator Center (SLAC), had called a press conference in California to make the same announcement on the day before CERN was to make its conclusions public.

The one-upmanship was doubly galling because the finding that there are only three families of matter, not more, was based on measuring the mass of the Z^0 particle (pronounced "zee zero" or "zee naught"), which is one of the messenger particles (the intermediate vector bosons) of the weak force. Rubbia had been awarded the Nobel Prize in 1983 for confirming the existence of this particle using a CERN accelerator.

Richter, too, is a Nobel laureate, having won the prize for finding a particle that confirmed the existence of quarks. But the fame both men had achieved in the physics community seemed only to make their rivalry more intense. Each has a reputation for being driven, demanding, and extremely competitive.

As Jack Steinberger, another Nobel laureate and one of Rubbia's lieutenants at CERN, put it:

"Competition in science is not always a pretty thing, but it's always stimulating and productive."[2]

Richter was particularly bold in challenging CERN in this race. The Stanford accelerator is unusual because it is not circular, as most traditional accelerators are. Instead, it fires streams of subatomic particles down a two-mile straightaway before separating them and smashing them together. Linear accelerators have not been able to reach the high energies possible with circular accelerators, which can whirl particles around and around thousands of times before shattering them. Yet Richter chose to try an untested design for overhauling his accelerator so that it could attain the energies needed to produce the Z^0 particles.

The Stanford overhaul, which cost about $115 million, was a bargain compared to the $1 billion CERN spent on building the large electron-positron collider, but it took two years of tinkering before Richter's team could get its accelerator to work properly.

The Stanford accelerator only began producing Z^0 particles on April 11, 1989. Meanwhile CERN was working feverishly to finish its accelerator. The LEP began producing Z^0 particles in August 1989. Two months later both teams were ready to make their announcements.

As a much larger accelerator, the LEP was able to manufacture thousands of Z^0 particles while Stanford was able to produce fewer than 500. That was enough to make them confident of their conclusions, but the disparity was reflected in the anger expressed by the CERN team after Richter's press conference.

"I guarantee our results are more accurate than Stanford's," Steinberger told the press. "The people at Stanford knew perfectly well that we were going to do this. They timed their press conference to get in ahead of us, even though we have ten times as much useful data. They've done some nice work, but I don't like it when they try to beat us by one day in this way."[3]

FINAL UNDERSTANDING?

Physicists are working more intensively than ever to refine and perfect the Standard Model. One major remaining problem is that gravity has not yet been fully integrated with the other three forces. Some physicists nevertheless believe that the final understanding of the structure of the universe is near at hand. Others are skeptical. But whether science plumbs the final secrets of the quantum code in ten years or a thousand, the knowledge that has already evolved has utterly transformed the modern world. It is at the core of our industrialized, technological civilization.

Using our knowledge of atoms and molecules, we have created an array of materials from plastics to synthetic fibers to metal alloys. With these materials we have built a broad range of machines, from computers to X-ray scanners—out of which modern economies have blossomed. Understanding that a flow of electrons produces electricity has allowed us to develop a source of power for these machines. Science has used modern technology to probe the universe and has vastly expanded our sense of the dimensions of time and space, from the unimaginably large to the unimaginably small. Scientists now operate comfortably in the realms of billionths of a second and trillionths of an inch as well as billions of years and trillions of miles.

The quantum code is the most complex and profound model ever produced by the human mind. Its usefulness is unlimited. By grasping the nature of atoms and molecules, physics provided the basic insight into understanding the genetic and synaptic codes. For the genetic code is constructed out of special kinds of atoms and molecules in the cell, while the synaptic code is formed by atoms and molecules in the brain.

Particles are not confined to the three families of matter. As I mentioned, each of the four forces has an associated particle as well: a messenger particle that carries the force. The messenger particle of electromagnetism, for example, is the photon. Just as electricity is a stream of electrons, light is a stream of photons. Like elementary particles, messenger particles are not thought to be divisible into other, smaller particles.

The essence of the quantum code, however, is not the elementary particles of matter and the messenger particles of force; it is the quantum fields of which these particles are manifestations. In the language of the quantum code, the smallest unit of a field is called a quantum. An electron is the quantum of an electron field, while the photon is the quantum of the electromagnetic field. It is these invisible fields and the interaction of their associated quanta, which are quite visible, that are the ultimate reality.

The concept of quantum field is at the heart of the quantum code, but it is a difficult and puzzling idea. Quantum fields are usually interpreted in terms of probabilities. The greater the intensity of the field at a given point in space and time, the greater the probability of finding the particle associated with that field at that point. Where an electromagnetic field is very intense, for instance, we are most likely to find a photon. The fact that the fields are manifested by quantum particles gives them a grainy quality. They only reveal themselves in tiny but discrete units, which are the quantum particles.

What is a field? An illustration is the simple experiment in which iron filings are sprinkled on a piece of paper which is then held over a bar magnet lying flat on a table. Under the influence of the magnetic force, the iron filings rearrange themselves in a series of loops, each of which starts at one pole of the magnet and curves around to the other pole. These loops are called lines of force and they trace out the shape of the electromagnetic field generated by the magnet. We never see the field directly, only its effect on particles represented by the iron filings. What we call the universe is a structure permeated, defined, and created by these invisible fields and their quanta. Quantum fields have many strange consequences that challenge the conventional view of reality. We will explore some of these consequences later in this chapter and in Part Four.

THE FUNDAMENTAL FORCES

The most familiar fields are those generated by the four fundamental forces, particularly gravity and electromagnetism. Fields generated by the fundamental forces are said to interact with objects by exchanging quanta with them. If the positive end of one bar magnet is attracted to the negative end of another, they are said to be exchanging photons, which are the quanta associated with the electromagnetic field. This is a bit like the coordinated movement of two athletes as they throw a basketball back and forth while running down the court.

Most physicists believe that at the unimaginably high temperatures of the big bang there was only one force, not four. As we illustrated in our roulette wheels example, the symmetrical unity of this single force broke apart as the universe expanded and cooled. First gravity split off as a separate force, followed by the strong force, electromagnetism, and the weak force. The most cherished goal of physics is to mathematically reconstruct this ancestral force and demonstrate how the four forces we observe today descended from it.

Gravity is the familiar force of attraction that holds the solar system and the galaxies together, and gives us weight. In the quantum code, the force of gravity is thought to result from the exchange of messenger particles—the gravitons. Gravity is produced much like the attractive force between the opposite poles of two magnets. The closer the magnets are held together, the stronger the attraction. But as the magnets are pulled apart, the attraction quickly becomes weaker. Gravity is generated by mass; the greater the mass, the greater the gravity. The closer we are to that mass, the more strongly we feel its gravitational field. Since all objects have mass, they all generate gravitational fields. Unlike the magnetic force, gravity always attracts; it never repels.

Gravity is by far the weakest of the four forces. Gravitons interact so weakly with matter that they have not yet been detected in the laboratory. But physicists infer their existence from the effects of gravity and the nature of the quantum code. When objects have a great deal of mass, like the Earth, their cumulative gravitational attraction is significant. Yet despite the fact that the gravitational force of the entire Earth is acting on each of us, we can walk about, pick up objects, and even find ways to leave the Earth and explore space. The Earth is estimated to have a mass equal to roughly 6.6 sextillion tons (a sextillion is 1 followed by 21 zeros). If gravity were even a small fraction closer to the strengths of the other forces, we would be crushed to the ground.

Gravitons are the messenger particles of gravity. At every instant, our bodies are exchanging gravitons with the Earth. This creates a flexible bond with the planet. As we move farther from Earth, the bond stretches and weakens but never completely breaks. Someone traveling far beyond the solar system would still have a slight gravitational bond with the Earth through the exchange of gravitons. But the effect would not be noticeable.

We exchange gravitons not just with the Earth but with all other objects in the universe. The sun, the moon, the planets, and the stars all generate gravitons that affect us and everything else in the cosmos, if only slightly. Because gravitation and gravitons have an infinite range, the universe is knitted together in a complex gravitational network.

This is not as strange as it sounds. Light forms a similarly complex web. When we walk outside in the daytime, the light from the sun and every object we see is affecting us and creating a network of complex light interactions. On a clear night, we can see light created by starlight that has, in the case of distant stars, taken thousands of years to reach the Earth. Just as a star generates a huge amount of light and other forms of electromagnetic radiation from the nuclear burning of the fuel in its core, massive objects such as stars and planets are intense sources of gravitons. Less massive objects, such as human beings, produce only a glimmer of gravitons in comparison. Since all mass produces gravity, the universe is flooded with gravitons, just as it is filled with electromagnetic radiation in the form of light.

Electromagnetism is the second fundamental force. The electromagnetic field generates all forms of radiation, including X-rays, microwaves, radio waves, and visible light. Like gravity, it has an infinite range. The messenger particle carrying the electromagnetic force is the photon. One of the greatest achievements of nineteenth-century physics was the realization that electricity and magnetism are different aspects of the same force. This culminated in the 1860s and 1870s with the publication by Scottish physicist James Clerk Maxwell of four equations definitively describing the electromagnetic force, and thereby beginning the age of electricity. Maxwell's equations were used to design giant turbines that produce electric power by spinning large magnets inside great coils of wire.

Light is a form of electromagnetic radiation. Maxwell predicted that other forms of radiation would be found that were not visible to the eye. Indeed, a whole spectrum of radiation has been discovered—from microwaves to X-rays—and put to use in science and technology. Unlike gravity, which is universally produced by all matter regardless of the state it is in, electromagnetism is only associated with charged particles of matter and energy, such as the negatively charged electron and the positively charged proton. The electromagnetic force can be either positive or negative. As with our magnet, like charges repel each other and unlike charges attract.

We live in a sea of photons carrying electromagnetic radiation to and fro throughout the universe. Our eyes can perceive a fraction of this radiation, but the majority of it passes around and through us unnoticed. We know it is there because we have built machines to detect it. Radios and televisions are sophisticated devices designed to respond to the information carried by certain frequencies of this electromagnetic radiation.

Electromagnetism is the second most powerful force, 137 times weaker than the strong force. Its most important effect is to bind negatively charged electrons to positively charged nuclei, creating atoms. It also governs the way atoms combine to form molecules and is, therefore, the key to chemistry. Its interactions provide the chemical rules by which huge collections of atoms combine and recombine to form the world of objects, including our own bodies. The basis of chemistry is the electromagnetic interaction between the clouds of electrons that surround atoms.

The third and most powerful fundamental force of nature is the strong force. It is the force that holds protons and neutrons together in the nucleus of the atom. The strong force is trillions of times stronger than gravity and 137 times stronger than electromagnetism. This force must be strong because protons are positively charged and two or more protons squeezed together in the nucleus of an atom exert a tremendous electromagnetic force of repulsion that must be overcome by the strong force if they are to be kept from flying apart. Since the nucleus of every atom contains an enormous amount of energy, the rapid release of the energy in the nuclei of only a small quantity of matter can create a huge "nuclear" explosion. If we completely converted one ounce of matter into energy, it would produce as much energy as burning 56,000 tons of gasoline.

The messenger particle carrying the strong force is dubbed the gluon because of its phenomenal stickiness. While gravity and electromagnetism have an infinite range, the strong force has a very, very short range, less than one ten-trillionth (10^{-11}) of an inch.

The final force in this quartet of fundamental interactions is called the weak force. It is much stronger than gravity but far feebler than the strong force or the electromagnetic force. It is about one-hundred-thousandth as strong as the strong force. Like the strong force, the weak force operates in the nucleus of the atom. Its range is even shorter than the strong force, less than one-quadrillionth (10^{-15}) of an inch. It is primarily known for producing the radioactive decay of elements like uranium and radium. The messenger particles that carry the weak force are called intermediate vector bosons (or weak bosons) and consist of three particles designated as W^+, W^- (pronounced "W plus" and "W minus"), and Z^0.

THE UNIVERSAL ALPHABET

Figure 1.1 lays out the quantum alphabet as we understand it today. It represents what physicists call the Standard Model of the subatomic world. The Standard Model gives us a picture of three families of matter particles interacting through four types of force particles to form the entire universe. (The Higgs boson is a special case that we shall examine later.) This model supplies the alphabet for the quantum code.

Albert Einstein discovered that energy and matter can be converted into one another—that matter can be thought of as a kind of frozen energy. Nuclear bombs explosively turn small amounts of matter into energy. Particle accelerators turn huge amounts of energy into tiny bits of matter. Some of the particles produced by these accelerators are found nowhere else on Earth, and in very few other places in the universe. That is because the particle accelerators produce temperatures that are routinely even greater than those found in the cores of stars.

We have already considered the division of the elementary particles that make up the universe into the four fundamental forces and the three families of matter. Physics divides the particles another way as well: into fermions and bosons. Boson is the general designation for the messenger particles of the four fundamental forces that we have been discussing: gravitons, photons, gluons, and intermediate vector bosons. Bosons are named after the Indian physicist Satyendra N. Bose, a pioneer in describing their properties.

Fermions are the elementary particles of matter. Atoms of matter are constructed from fermions such as electrons and quarks. Fermions emit or absorb bosons. This is how fermions "feel" the effects of the four forces and thus stick together to form atoms and molecules.

Fermions, named after the Italian physicist Enrico Fermi, are subdivided into two basic classes: quarks and leptons. Quarks—a name derived from a whimsical word used by James Joyce in his novel *Finnegans Wake*—combine to form protons and neutrons, the elementary particles that make up the nucleus of the atom. Leptons (from the Greek "leptos," meaning light in weight) are lighter particles than the quarks. The best-known lepton is the electron, which occupies the energy shells that surround atoms. All atoms and molecules are made up of combinations of quarks and leptons.

There are six kinds of leptons and six kinds of quarks arranged into three families of matter. The first family consists of the electron, electron neutrino, the up quark, and the down quark. The second family is made up of the muon (which is a heavier cousin of the electron), the muon neutrino, the strange quark, and the charm quark. The third family of matter consists of the tau (an even more massive cousin of the electron), the tau neutrino, the bottom quark, and the top quark.

The electron, muon, and tau are all negatively charged particles. While the electron is stable, the muon and tau are highly unstable. The muon, for example, decays into an electron in approximately two microseconds (millionths of a second). Each of these three elementary particles has a neutrino partner. These three neutrinos are light, stable particles with no electric charge. They interact so weakly with other particles that they have essentially no impact on the formation of atoms and molecules. Each family of matter contains two quarks. Their fanciful names have no intrinsic meaning but only refer to the different fractional charges they have that, as we shall see later, determine how they combine.

Of the three families of matter listed in Figure 1.1, only the first family is required to create the ordinary matter we see in the universe today. Up and down quarks form the protons and neutrons that combine to form the nuclei of atoms. Electrons occupy shells around the nuclei. Electrons, up quarks, and down quarks are all that is needed to form atoms of matter. Electron neutrinos appear to play a negligible role.

At the high temperatures of the very early universe, however, the leptons and quarks of the second and third families existed side by side with the first family. As the universe cooled, the second and third families were too unstable to continue in existence, so they essentially became extinct—except in our particle accelerator time machines. Even in accelerators, they can only be observed for a fantastically brief instant before decaying into the more stable leptons and quarks of the first family.

This seems awfully wasteful. Why have three families of elementary particles if only one is needed to create ordinary matter? If we threw out the second and third families of matter (and the electron neutrino as well), the universe would look pretty much the same.

Yet wastefulness is a sure sign of evolution at work. Despite popular misconceptions, evolution does not create optimal designs with a minimum of waste. On the contrary, evolution can be a sloppy, wasteful process that takes whatever is at hand and seeks to adapt it to the current environment. True, the human eye and the human brain are miracles of complexity, but at what cost. As we look back in time with our marvelous eyes and brain we find that more than ninety-nine percent of the species of plants and animals that have ever lived are now extinct.

The picture of the three families of elementary particles is not complete, however, without taking antimatter into account. Each of the twelve particles in the three families of matter has an antimatter equivalent, which is identical to the ordinary particle except for its opposite charge. The antimatter equivalent of the electron, which is negatively charged, is the positron, which has a positive charge. Antimatter is not normally found in the universe because when it interacts with ordinary matter, both disappear in a flash of energy. But antimatter can be created in particle accelerators. The CERN large electron-positron collider creates such high temperatures by smashing electrons into positrons.

To this picture of four forces and three families of matter, physicists have added another boson—the Higgs boson—which they theorize is responsible for giving the different kinds of particles their unique masses.

UNITY IN DIVERSITY

Just as the discovery of evolution and the genetic code allowed us to structure the baffling diversity of living things into separate species and show how they evolved from common ancestors over the last three billion years or so, the Standard Model has shown how the perplexing diversity of subatomic particles can be constructed out of only a few basic particles, and how these particles seem to have evolved from common ancestors in the 15 billion years or so since the big bang.

These, then, are the particles that serve as fundamental building blocks for the construction of a universe: four kinds of bosons, or messenger particles, and two kinds of fermions, or elementary particles of matter. The bosons are gravity's graviton, electromagnetism's photon, the strong force's gluon, and the weak force's intermediate vector bosons. The fermions—ingredients of atoms—are the quarks (which make up particles in the atom's nucleus or center), and the leptons, whose ranks include the electrons that form the shells of the atoms and the ghostly neutrinos.

Quarks are knitted into hadrons by the strong force. (Hadron is the general term for the class of heavy particles that includes protons and neutrons.) Hadrons and electrons, which are a type of light particle or lepton, are then combined into atoms by the electromagnetic force. Atoms are strung together in molecules (sentences) by the electromagnetic force. These sentences, when they take the form of DNA molecules, are complex enough to specify a human being. As large collections of atoms and molecules form, they come under the influence of gravity, which, by creating stars, provides the furnace for forging larger and more complicated atoms, such as carbon, from which more complex molecules essential to life can be constructed. The weak force, because it is weak, ensures that the nuclear reactions that power the stars and create the primary source of hot spots in the galaxies do not proceed too rapidly, thus giving evolution time to create complexity. The grammar of the quantum code is comprised of the rules of interaction of the fermions and bosons. Hydrogen can be compared to a word written in the quantum language. It combines the consonants (a proton and electron) with the vowels of the strong force—in this case the electromagnetic and strong force. A sentence would be "water," combining the words hydrogen and oxygen according to the grammar of the electromagnetic force.

The Standard Model provides important support for a basic tenet of my theory of unified selection: matter evolves. Clearly the evolution of matter occurs at levels other than the subatomic level. But the Standard Model gives us the key to understanding how this evolution occurs. I would argue that there are five basic levels of matter: quarks, leptons, nuclei, atoms, and molecules. As I mentioned, quarks combine to form nuclei of protons and neutrons that combine with electrons (leptons) to form atoms. It is the electromagnetic interaction among the electron shells of atoms that links them together to form molecules. Electrons give atoms their unique chemistry. The genetic code of life and synaptic code of thought have evolved from chemistry of atoms as they form molecules. Both the DNA of the genetic code and the neurons of the synaptic code are complex assemblages of molecules that lead to whole new levels of evolution.

In my view the five levels of matter lead to five levels of evolution: first, particle evolution, in which elementary particles and messenger particles (the three families of matter and the four fundamental forces) evolve from the big bang; second, atomic evolution, in which atoms evolve from elementary particles; third, chemical evolution, in which the electron shells of atoms interact to form molecules; fourth, biological evolution, in which molecules of DNA (orchestrating the creation and behavior of other sorts of molecules) create diverse forms of life; and finally, synaptic evolution, in which complex structures of molecules under the control of DNA form neurons or brain cells that, in turn, evolve dynamic synaptic links that are the basis of thought and behavior. Just as chemically interconnected atoms of matter are the building blocks of the molecules of life, synaptically interconnected neurons are, in a sense, the molecules of thought.

The Standard Model is an amazing milestone in the evolution of thought, but it is probably not the final formulation of the quantum code. The Higgs boson and the top quark have still not yet been observed in particle accelerators. If they are not observed, then the model will have to be revised. Physicists assume that the gravitational field is quantized as are the other three force fields, but so far no generally accepted theory of quantum gravity has been formulated. The best theory of gravity remains Einstein's theory of general relativity, but it is a classical, not a quantum, theory because it does not account for the action of gravity at the subatomic level. It is possible that new and more powerful accelerators may turn up new kinds of forces and particles that will have to be incorporated into the model. The Standard Model does not explain why elementary particles and messenger particles have the masses and coupling strengths that they do, which raises the possibility that someday a more profound theory will be able to answer these questions.

Although the Standard Model will undoubtedly continue to evolve, modern physics has clearly demonstrated that a quantum code does indeed exist and that we have plumbed many of its secrets.

The theories that describe the behavior of elementary particles are intensely mathematical. In modern physics, mathematics created by the mind describes phenomena that our senses are intuitively unable to grasp. In the absence of mathematics, we can begin to glimpse the power of the quantum code only by using crude analogies.

The quantum code is my term for the relativistic quantum field theories that physicists have come to accept over the last few decades as the Standard Model describing the interactions between subatomic particles. These theories are called relativistic quantum field theories because they incorporate both the quantum concept that revolutionized physics early in this century and Albert Einstein's special theory of relativity, which redefined our notions of space and time and described the peculiar behavior of particles traveling at or near the speed of light.

Quantum electrodynamics is the oldest of the three relativistic quantum field theories, and the most precise. It was developed in its modern form after World War II. It describes with mathematical precision how the electromagnetic force, which acts on all electrically charged particles, is transmitted by the exchange of photons. The best known of these charged particles is the electron, a very light and stable particle that is thought to be fundamental—that is, it cannot be broken down into further particles. The negatively charged electron or electrons in the shell of an atom bind with another charged particle, the positively charged proton, to form atoms, which are the building blocks of matter. The proton is found in the nucleus of the atom; the electron in the shell surrounding the nucleus. The number and distribution of electrons in the shell determines the chemical properties of the atom. Electrons of different atoms link together to form molecules and create the whole panoply of living and nonliving structures.

Quantum chromodynamics is the relativistic quantum field theory that describes how quarks exchange gluons to bind together and form protons, neutrons, and other heavy particles in the atomic nucleus. Physicists believe that there are six types (playfully called flavors) of quarks and have named them the up quark, down quark, charm quark, strange quark, top quark, and bottom quark. (These last two quarks are sometimes known as truth and beauty.) All but the top quark have been detected experimentally. Quarks, which have odd fractional electric charges, can form an unlimited number of heavier particles called hadrons. Hadrons are divided into baryons and mesons. It takes three quarks to make a baryon and two quarks (a quark and its oppositely charged counterpart, the antiquark) to make a meson. Protons and neutrons are baryons.

Quarks bind through a complex process of exchanging combinations of eight different kinds of gluons. Each of the six quarks is assumed to have "colors"—red, green, and blue—that are associated with the strong force. The gluons carry colors among quarks. Quarks form baryons by seeking stable arrangements that are color-neutral. Mixing equal parts of red, green, and blue produces white, which is the stable, color-neutral ideal (the use of colors in the terminology of quantum chromodynamics is purely metaphorical). A proton, for example, can be formed by a red up quark, a green down quark, and a blue up quark. The binding scheme in quantum chromodynamics is so complex that physicists must use computers to sort out the possibilities and solve the equations. But the theory provides a coherent scheme for analyzing the many different kinds of hadrons.

The electroweak theory was proposed in 1967–68 but not confirmed until 1983, when the intermediate vector bosons were observed by scientists using a powerful particle accelerator. This theory unifies the electromagnetic force of quantum electrodynamics with the weak force. It does this in a very unlikely fashion: by showing that the massless photon of electromagnetism is a close relative of the intermediate vector bosons, the three very heavy messenger particles of the weak force (W^+, W^-, Z^0). According to the electroweak theory, at the higher temperatures of the early universe, all four of these particles were massless. Only when the temperature dropped did the three intermediate vector bosons gain their heavy masses.

Like quantum chromodynamics, the interactions of the electroweak theory are complex. Basically, the intermediate vector bosons W^+, W^-, and Z^0 can change the flavors of quarks. They can also convert one type of lepton into another. This is why the weak force is associated with the radioactive decay of particles. If a strange quark is transformed into an up or down quark by interacting with an intermediate vector boson, the hadron in which the quark resides may become unstable and decay. The existence of the weak force means that of the huge number of quantum particles, only a few can resist the weak force and remain stable. These stable particles are the electron, proton, and neutrino. All unstable particles of matter will eventually decay into one of these stable particles. From this short list of stable particles are built all the stable forms of matter. (There has been some debate in recent years about whether the proton is stable. So far no convincing experimental evidence has appeared to indicate that it is not.) These particles produce radioactive decay by inducing quarks to change their charge. They can also cause leptons to decay.

ROULETTE REPRISE

Let us return once more to our roulette wheel example to sum up what we have learned about the evolution of particles and forces. This time we will start the roulette wheel at today's cold temperatures and move back in time to the hot temperatures of the big bang. Imagine that the roulette balls representing the four forces and three families of matter are cemented to their respective slots on the wheel with different types of glue, some stronger than others.

The roulette wheel moves slowly at the beginning, but as we cycle back in time the universe shrinks and becomes hotter, speeding up the wheel. As the temperature passes 10^{15} degrees Kelvin, the glue holding the photons and intermediate vector bosons melts and these particles fly out of their slots and clatter around the face of the wheel so that their distinctive features are blurred and we cannot tell them apart. This is the fusion of the electromagnetic and weak forces described by the electroweak theory.

The next important stage is reached when the contracting universe reaches a temperature of 10^{27} degrees Kelvin. The glue holding the gluons finally melts, and these particles come flying out of their slots to join the electroweak particles.

Finally, we reach the Planck temperature of 10^{35} degrees Kelvin, only 10^{-45} second from the big bang. At this point, the powerful glue holding the gravitons to the wheel finally melts and, many theorists believe, gravity combines with the other three forces and one symmetrical superforce emerges. The particles of matter will have also come out of their slots and the distinction between quarks and leptons disappears. These blended fermions of matter combine with the united amalgam of bosons of force into a single, primal quantum field. Theorists would like to build this field out of elegant mathematical symmetries. The successive breaking of these symmetries after the big bang explains the evolution of all particles and forces in the universe today. Theories that combine elementary particles, gravity, and the other three forces are called theories of everything.

Physicists hope that a theory of everything will explain why only a certain number of particles and forces evolved, and why they look the way they do. This will tell us the reason matter exists in the forms we see today and why gravity split off first from the other forces, followed much later by the separation of the strong force, the weak force, and electromagnetism.

A number of theorists have been formulating theories of everything based on what is known as the superstring concept. These theories take a radically different approach: particles are built not of points of energy but of ultra-tiny strings, usually in the form of closed loops. The elementary particles of matter and messenger particles of force correspond to the different vibrations of these strings at lower temperatures. At the Planck temperature all we would see would be a symmetrical soup of identical strings vibrating randomly. Theories using strings are called superstring theories because the mathematical symmetry they incorporate is known as supersymmetry.

Why do we see points and not loops? The theorists explain that the strings are so small that they look like points unless we focus in the tiniest scales, in the range of 10^{-35} meter, which is known, not surprisingly, as the Planck length. If you could draw a circle ten times smaller than the period at the end of this sentence, it would be indistinguishable from a point unless it was magnified significantly.

The attraction of superstring theory is that it neatly combines gravity with the other forces and has a mathematically elegant way of merging fermions, the elementary particles of matter, with bosons, the messenger particles of the four forces.

Because the Planck temperature at which the four forces are thought to merge is so staggeringly high, physicists are at a loss about how to test superstring theory. One estimate is that a particle accelerator big enough to generate this temperature would have to be at least ten light years long, more than twice the distance to the nearest star beyond the sun, Alpha Centauri. The only hope is that some indirect way will be found to verify the theory. String theorists are actively trying to come up with predictions from their theories that can be tested at far lower energies, for instance predicting the masses of the thus far elusive top quark and Higgs boson, or the length of the lifetime of the proton. Superstring theories also predict many new kinds of particles, but none has been found so far.

With its symphony of vibrating strings producing the music of subatomic particles, superstring theory bears a haunting resemblance to ideas put forward 2,500 years ago by some of the first mathematicians—the Pythagoreans—who, according to Aristotle, "saw that the modifications and the ratios of the musical scales were expressible in numbers [and] they supposed the elements of numbers to be the elements of all things, and the whole heaven to be a musical scale and a number."[4]

Superstring theory may be one more in a long line of failed attempts to unify the laws of physics. Einstein himself worked unsuccessfully for decades on a unified field theory. Yet many prominent physicists are excited by strings and think they are the best hope for a true theory of everything. If the string idea proves correct, it will take us beyond the Planck time, the current barrier in physics, all the way back to the instant of the big bang itself. We may discover why the universe was created; why there is something instead of nothing.

Because superstring theories are so complicated mathematically—they are often formulated in ten or more dimensions with the assumption that the extra dimensions are somehow hidden in the folds of the four ordinary dimensions of space and time—it takes physicists a long time to work through their implications. Many feel, however, that within a decade we should know whether string theories are on the right track to the final unification of the laws of physics.

In this chapter I have sketched the state of our knowledge of the elementary particles and messenger particles of the quantum code from which all matter and energy is constructed. It is important to recognize that the present low-temperature form of the quantum code evolved from the presumed unity and symmetry of the big bang. Equally important is the fact that the development of the quantum code—the first link in the chain from matter to life to thought—is one of human history's most potent examples of the evolution of ideas.

A brief account like this cannot convey the confusion, dead ends, missed opportunities, and out-and-out errors that accompany the search for scientific truth. The evolution of our understanding of the quantum code is a complex and continuing account of variation and selection producing a succession of contingent intellectual models seeking to better approximate the ghostly subatomic world.

Each theory and refinement is a variation placed before the body of physicists. The selection process is governed by both experimental results and aesthetic appeal. Other ingredients include luck (good and bad), accident, personal relationships, brilliant insights, mistakes, drudgery, and a thousand unpredictable circumstances. Far from being a calm, Olympian search for truth, it is a messy, confusing, serendipitous enterprise. In short, it exemplifies the actual human thought process operating at a very high level, rather than the contrived, smoothed-over accounts that are common in textbooks.

Yet there is much more to the quantum code than an account of the elementary particles and forces out of which it is created. The next chapter will explore some of the more mysterious aspects of this code of creation, aspects that illuminate the very structure of reality.

Chapter 2

Soul of the Universe

WHILE WORKING ON THIS BOOK I LIVED FOR A TIME ACROSS THE street from Princeton University, to which Albert Einstein fled in 1933 from the menace of Hitler's Germany and lived for the last twenty-two years of his life.

Einstein loved to walk the streets of Princeton with his friends and colleagues, discussing the deepest problems in physics. One of those friends was Niels Bohr, the famous Danish physicist who developed the first plausible model of the atom using the findings of quantum mechanics.

Einstein was a cordial, gentle man but he could be a tenacious intellectual opponent. Bohr loved quantum theory, with all its uncertainties and probabilities. He became one of its chief interpreters and defenders. Einstein hated it, though he had helped to give it birth. He preferred the clarity and certainty of the classical physics created by Newton. For more than thirty years, the two old friends debated the validity of quantum mechanics. It was a contest for the soul of the universe.

CHANCE OR NECESSITY

At bottom, the dispute between Einstein and Bohr was over the fundamental nature of existence. Does the universe exist objectively, independent of observation and measurement? Is the present completely determined by the past, and the future determined by the present, so that our sense of the uncertainty of the future is only an illusion? Einstein answered these questions affirmatively. Objectivity and determinism were the pillars of classical physics and Einstein passionately believed in them.

Bohr answered these questions negatively. He believed that probabilities and uncertainties are inherent in the nature of the universe. They are not the result of our ignorance. No one can ever know with absolute certainty the trajectory of an electron or any other quantum particle—not a superintelligence, not even God.

Classical physics is the name given to the pre-quantum physics created by Galileo and Isaac Newton and dominant until the evolution of quantum mechanics early in the twentieth century. Classical physicists believed that it was possible, in principle, to have complete knowledge of every detail of the universe: present, past, and future. Even though the amount of information this would require was, as a practical matter, impossible to obtain, there was always the hope that someday civilization would become advanced enough to make the necessary calculations.

Pierre Laplace, a noted physicist and mathematician of the late eighteenth and early nineteenth century, summarized the Newtonian dream in a famous declaration:

> We must regard the present state of the universe as the effect of its past and the cause of its future. Consider an intelligence which, at any instant, could have a knowledge of all forces controlling nature together with the momentary conditions of all the entities of which nature consists. If this intelligence were powerful enough to submit all this data to analysis it would be able to embrace in a single formula the movements of the largest bodies in the universe and those of the lightest atoms; for it, nothing would be uncertain; the future and the past would be equally present to its eyes. [1]

The uncertainty principle of quantum physics, introduced by Werner Heisenberg, destroyed the basis for the classical belief in absolute certainty. For pairs of attributes like position-momentum (knowledge of both a quantum particle's position in space and its velocity multiplied by its mass) and time-energy (knowledge of a particle's energy at a given moment), the measurement of one attribute of the pair becomes more and more uncertain as the other is measured to increasing degrees of accuracy.

To visualize the uncertainty principle, imagine that we know the exact position, direction, mass, and velocity of a space probe traveling to Mars. Using this information, we can predict exactly where it will be a second from now, an hour from now, or a year from now, as long as the probe does not fire its on-board rockets or do anything else to change its speed and direction. In the classical world view, our knowledge of the position and momentum of the probe can be as exact as our instruments are capable of measuring. There is no theoretical limit to the precision of our knowledge.

Quantum mechanics takes a different view. Position and momentum cannot be simultaneously known with unlimited accuracy. There is always a limitation on our knowledge. In the world of ordinary-sized objects this limitation is sometimes, but not always, slight. If our instruments allow us to determine the position of the space probe within a few inches or so, the degree of quantum uncertainty about its momentum, calculated by Heisenberg's uncertainty principle, is exceedingly small, about one part in ten billion trillion trillion (10^{-34}). An uncertainty so negligible can be effectively ignored, which is why NASA normally uses the classical mechanics of Isaac Newton to track its spacecraft without worrying very much about quantum uncertainty.

At the level of subatomic particles, however, uncertainty becomes dominant. A quart of water contains more than one trillion trillion (10^{24}) electrons. If the space probe were the size of an electron, our knowledge of its location and velocity would be very different. One way to understand this uncertainty is by imagining how we would try to determine the position and momentum of the tiny space probe. If we used a scanning tunneling electron microscope—the state of the art in microscopes—problems would crop up immediately. Such a microscope can photograph the surfaces of atoms. It uses a stream of energetic electrons from a tiny metal tip as a source of "light" for exploring the quantum world. By bouncing electrons off our subatomic space probe's surface, the microscope might be able to pinpoint its position. But the stream of electrons

5 4

would simultaneously alter the probe's momentum by the force of their impact, just as the momentum of a life-size space probe would be altered if it were struck by a swarm of meteors. At the minute scale of the quantum world the very act of observation alters the phenomenon we are observing.

It is vital to understand, however, that uncertainty is the very soul of quantum mechanics, and thus is at the core of its view of the universe. It is not just the product of the way we measure things. No particle will ever be measured with both an exact position and a momentum.

Classical physics and quantum mechanics present radically different views of time, particularly the future. Classical determinism asserts that the future already exists, as do the present and past. Everything that ever will happen has already happened. But for some unknown reason our minds can only experience the future a piece at a time, in what we call the present. Free will is an illusion. Although we can calculate certain aspects of the future—for example, the future dates of solar eclipses—current limitations on our ability to gather accurate data and analyze it prevent us from knowing the future in great detail. As our technology and mathematics improve, however, our knowledge of the future will increase.

Classical physics takes a rigorous view of cause and effect. If an experiment is performed under identical circumstances, it should produce identical results. Identical causes produce identical effects. For every cause there is one and only one effect, which under ideal circumstances we can identify with certainty.

In quantum physics we can never predict the future with absolute certainty. The future does not yet exist in a single definite state. There will always be a measure of uncertainty about it. The Laplacean ideal of knowing at an instant the position and momentum of every object in the universe is out of the question. The uncertainty principle forbids us from knowing the simultaneous position and momentum of even a single quantum particle.

Quantum uncertainty does not deny us all knowledge about the future. It gives us the tools to make predictions, but only in terms of probabilities.

To illustrate the vital difference between quantum physics and classical physics, let us take a highly simplified example. Imagine an experiment in which we fire an electron gun, like the one in every television set, at a detection screen. We divide the screen into three parts: X, Y, and Z. Classical physics would allow us, in principle, to determine the exact position and momentum of every electron emerging from the gun and therefore calculate the exact position at which it will strike the screen. The electron would be treated like a tiny billiard ball. If we calculated that an electron would strike region X of the screen, then every time we fired an electron with the same position and momentum, it would invariably strike region X. Identical causes (firing an electron with a particular position and momentum) would cause the identical effect (striking region X).

Quantum uncertainty denies us this precision, however, because we cannot know precisely the position and momentum of the electron at the moment it emerges from the gun. But the power of quantum physics is that it does allow us to make a precise prediction about the probabilities that the electron will strike any one of the three regions. Let us say we do the calculation and find that there is a sixty-percent chance that the electron will strike region X, a thirty-percent chance it will strike region Y, and a 10-percent chance it will strike region Z. When we perform the experiment over and over under identical circumstances, we find that our results match these predicted probabilities: for every 100 electrons, on the average, sixty strike region X, thirty strike region Y, and ten strike region Z. But for any one electron we are genuinely uncertain about where it will strike, other than predicting that it is more likely to strike region X than region Z.

Quantum physics clearly has a much looser view of cause and effect than does classical physics. Although, as in classical physics, cause always precedes effect (we never see the electron striking the screen before we have fired the gun), identical causes can have multiple effects. In our example, repeatedly firing the electron gun under identical circumstances results in three possible effects: striking either region X, Y, or Z.

In quantum physics, causes in the present have multiple potentialities in the future. In this sense, free will becomes possible. Our actions in the present are not absolutely determined by the past and will not inevitably result in a single outcome in the future. What we do in the present may have many outcomes in the future. We can calculate the probabilities of the various possible outcomes but we can never be absolutely certain about what will happen.

Heisenberg knew that the uncertainty principle meant the death of classical determinism with its ironclad law of cause and effect, because classical theory was built on the presumed ability, in principle, to know the exact position and momentum of every object in the universe, no matter how small.

At the end of his celebrated 1927 paper announcing the uncertainty principle to the world, Heisenberg wrote:

> But what is wrong in the sharp formulation of the law of causality, "When we know the present precisely, we can predict the future," is not the conclusion but the assumption. Even in principle we cannot know the present in all detail. For that reason everything observed is a selection from a plenitude of possibilities and a limitation on what is possible in the future. . . . Because all experiments are subject to the laws of quantum mechanics, and therefore to [the uncertainty principle], it follows that quantum mechanics establishes the final failure of causality.[2]

Einstein could never accept a universe ruled by chance rather than necessity. God does not play dice, he protested. In the late 1920s and early 1930s, he put forward a number of hypothetical experiments—what he called thought experiments—designed to show that quantum mechanics is flawed. Bohr took it upon himself to rebut Einstein's attacks on quantum mechanics. Physicist Léon Rosenfeld, a friend of both men, recorded one of these memorable clashes, when at a 1930 conference Einstein proposed a counterexample that demonstrated a basic flaw in the uncertainty principle:

> It was quite a shock for Bohr. . . . he did not see the solution at once. During the whole evening he was extremely unhappy, going from one to the other and trying to persuade them that it couldn't be true, that it would be the end of physics if Einstein were right; but he couldn't produce any refutation. I shall never forget the vision of the two antagonists leaving the club: Einstein a tall, majestic figure, walking quietly, with a somewhat ironical smile, and Bohr trotting near him, very excited. . . . The next morning came Bohr's triumph.[3]

Bohr successfully invalidated all of Einstein's attacks. In fact, quantum mechanics has withstood every assault for more than half a century. The overwhelming experimental evidence demonstrates that quantum physics is correct and classical physics is wrong. Quantum mechanics is the most successful theory of matter and energy ever created by human beings. Without it we would have no idea how atoms work, and the electronic age along with the computer and most modern technology would have been impossible.

The battle between classical determinism and quantum uncertainty waged by Einstein and Bohr was one of the greatest episodes in the history of the evolution of thought. Yet it was a wrenching experience for many physicists. Einstein's biographer recounts an incident involving Paul Ehrenfest, one of the most gifted physicists of his day: "In tears, Ehrenfest said that he had to make a choice between Bohr's and Einstein's position and that he could not but agree with Bohr."[4]

Eventually, Einstein admitted that he could find no inconsistencies in quantum mechanics. Yet he never stopped searching for a more comprehensive theory that would restore classical certainty.

Toward the end of his life, in a letter of condolence written after the death of one of his closest friends, he wrote: "Now he has departed from this strange world a little ahead of me. That means nothing. People like us, who believe in physics, know that the distinction between past, present, and future is only a stubbornly persistent illusion."[5]

A month later, in April 1955, he died.

On the morning of Niels Bohr's death in 1962, a drawing of one of Einstein's thought experiments was found on Bohr's blackboard.

THE TWO-SLIT EXPERIMENT

Quantum mechanics—or the quantum code, as I call it—not only provides the recipe for every object in the universe, in the form of combinations of the three families of matter and the four fundamental forces, it also provides the master principle of evolution: what I call unified selection. Werner Heisenberg referred to this principle in 1927 when, as we noted earlier, he stated that "everything observed is a selection from a plenitude of possibilities and a limitation on what is possible in the future."

In my view, unified selection is the process by which the multiple potentialities of the future become the single actuality of the present; for example, the multiple potentialities that an electron will strike region X, Y, or Z become the actuality of the electron striking only one of these regions. Understanding this mechanism of selection will require us to explore more deeply some of the thought experiments that Bohr and Einstein used to probe the nature of the quantum code. Although quantum mechanics continues to rule unchallenged as a theory of matter and energy, the interpretation of this theory is still extremely controversial. We will see the reasons for this controversy when we examine Bohr's famous two-slit experiment. We shall also meet Erwin Schrödinger's notorious cat, the central character in a thought experiment which, though he did not originate it, was one of Einstein's favorites. But first, a bit of history.

In 1900, Max Planck announced his hypothesis that electromagnetic radiation came in discrete segments, each of which he called a quantum, from the same Latin root as the word quantity. The quantum postulate violated the classical idea that energy was emitted continuously and set off an intellectual chain reaction. Physicists began to find that all sorts of important quantities in the subatomic world were divided into discrete quantities that could not be cut into smaller units.

In 1905, Einstein showed that light behaves not only as a wave, but also as a particle. It is absorbed and is given off not as continuous waves but as tiny packets of energy, or quanta, that were dubbed photons. Each photon is a quantum of electromagnetism. The notion that light behaves as both a wave and a particle struck most classical physicists as absurd. It is both ironic and a tribute to Einstein's genius that his theory of the photon was one of the seminal ideas in the development of quantum mechanics and the uncertainty principle, ideas that Einstein later disowned. To compound the irony, it was for this contribution, not his more famous relativity theory, that Einstein was awarded the Nobel Prize in 1921.

In 1913, Niels Bohr applied Planck's quantum to the emerging theory of the atom with startling results. He proposed that electrons occupy only certain discrete energy shells around the atom. When an electron moves to a different shell it simply disappears and reappears in the new shell, emitting or absorbing quanta of energy in the process.

As physicists grappled with the implications of Bohr's model over the next fifteen years, the modern discipline of quantum mechanics was born. Werner Heisenberg and Erwin Schrödinger developed mathematical formulations of the quantum effect. Both matter and energy were found to exhibit wavelike and particlelike behavior. Electrons could be diffracted, or bent, just as light is diffracted when it passes through a prism. Matter and energy seem to have a dual nature: part particle, part wave. Note that in this book I often simply refer to quantum particles. This is just a matter of convenience. We must never forget that each of the quanta we commonly refer to as particles (electrons, photons, and so forth) has both a particle and wave nature.

Heisenberg formulated his celebrated uncertainty principle in order to account for the wave–particle duality. The wave or wave function is interpreted not as an actual wave, like a water wave, but as a probability wave. The intensity of the probability wave at any point (its amplitude squared) reflects the probability of finding a particle at that point.

Niels Bohr proposed a series of thought experiments to illustrate the strange quantum behavior. (Thought experiments are hypothetical experiments performed in the mind to explore scientific principles. They may later be confirmed in the laboratory, as Bohr's thought experiment was.) There are several versions of this experiment, but for our purposes we will break the experiment down into three phases.

In the first phase, imagine a solid wall with two small slits that can be opened or closed separately. Now imagine a remote-control gun facing the wall, which has both slits open. The gun can be programmed to randomly fire bullets at the wall. Most of the bullets will be stopped by the wall, but some will go through the two slits. Behind the wall is a replaceable backstop the purpose of which is to make a record of the pattern of bullets that go through the slits. The bullets are fired slowly enough so that there is no danger of their interfering with each other. If they were fired too rapidly, one bullet might ricochet off the wall and strike the next.

With this arrangement we perform three separate tests, with a new backstop put in after each test. In the first and second tests, we open one slit at a time and randomly fire bullets at the wall. In the third test, both slits are opened at the same time. After each test we carefully measure the distribution of bullets that hit the backstop.

We find that most of the bullet holes are found in a limited area on the backstop. This is the area that the bullets hit if they pass cleanly through one slit or the other. A few bullet holes are made outside this area when bullets grazed the sides of the slit and were deflected into another part of the backstop. If we combine the two patterns of bullet holes made when the first slit and then the second slit was open, it is basically the same as the pattern produced when both slits were open at the same time. In other words, the probability distribution of randomly fired bullets striking the backstop when both slits are open is the same as adding the distribution of bullet holes when each slit is open separately. There is no surprise here.

PARTICLES AND WAVES

In the second phase, the wall with the two slits is immersed in water. The gun is replaced with a wave machine. The backstop is redesigned to detect the presence of a wave by recording the varying intensity of the water pressure on its surface when the wave strikes it. We perform the same three tests: for the first and second test, only one slit is open; for the final test both slits are open simultaneously. We send the waves one at a time toward the slits, letting the water calm before generating the next wave. The backstop measures the intensity of the portion of the wave that goes through either or both slits.

After performing all three tests, we find that the results from the first two stages are very similar to the bullet experiment. When one slit at a time is opened, the pattern of wave intensity recorded on the backstop closely resembles the pattern of bullet holes. In the third stage, however, when both slits are open, something very different happens. The intensity pattern diverges sharply from the pattern that would be produced by adding the patterns generated when each slit is open separately.

When one slit is open, a segment of the wave passes through the slit and then hits the backstop without further interference. Each point on the wave segment corresponds to a point where a bullet might have passed through the slit in the previous experiment. The portion of the wave that passed through the center of the slit is least obstructed by the wall and will have the greatest intensity when it hits the backstop. Consequently, the area of the backstop recording the greatest wave intensity at the one-slit stage of the second experiment corresponds to the area with the most bullet holes at the same stage in the first phase of the experiment.

Why do we get a different result from the bullet pattern when we open both slits? Portions of the same wave pass through each slit at the same time. After penetrating the slits, the crests and troughs of these wave segments interfere with each other before hitting the backstop. When the crest of one segment meets the trough of another, they cancel each other out. When crest meets crest and trough meets trough, they intensify each other. A wave behaves very differently from a bullet, or any other particlelike object, that can only go through one slit at a time and cannot interfere with itself. The intensity pattern recorded by the backstop in the final test of the second phase of the experiment is typical of a wave interference pattern. Again, there is nothing exceptional about the result and it is perfectly in accord with classical mechanics.

In the third phase, we shift to the peculiar world of subatomic particles. Here we use an electron gun, like the one we used earlier, to fire electrons at a barrier that has two small slits. Behind the barrier is a backstop wired to serve as an electron detector. Each hit by an electron is registered on a portion of the backstop and triggers an audible click, like the click of a Geiger counter. When the first two tests are performed, with only one slit or the other open, the patterns of electrons recorded by the backstop are identical to the distributions registered by the bullet experiment. Each electron seems to behave like a tiny bullet, either being stopped by the wall or shooting through a slit and hitting the backstop. But in the third test, when both slits are open at the same time, the distribution pattern recorded by the backstop is not that of a stream of particles. Astoundingly enough, it is a wave interference pattern.

To produce an interference pattern, the electron must be going through both slits at the same time in some sort of wavelike state. The wave segments that pass through the slits then interfere with each other, just as the segments of water waves did.

We can alter our experimental setup once more to try to determine what is going on. A source of light, perhaps a tiny laser, is placed in back of the barrier. A thin slice of light shines across the back of each slit. When an electron goes through a slit it must pass through the laser beam. We will know the electron is there because we can detect the scattering of photons that will take place when it passes through the light. If the electron is behaving like a particle, it will go through only one slit. If it is behaving like a wave, it will go through both.

First we turn on the electron gun and open both slits. The wave interference pattern appears on the detector screen. Yet when we turn on the laser detectors the behavior of the electrons changes completely. They again start acting like particles. Our lasers record each electron passing through only one slit, not both. The pattern on the backstop produced by the stream of electrons is identical to the pattern of bullet holes produced when both slits were open in the first phase. The wave interference pattern has vanished and the particle pattern has taken its place.

What if we dim our lasers so we can only detect some, not all, of the electrons passing through the slits? The wave interference pattern begins to reappear! The fewer electrons we can detect with our light beams, the more the backstop records a shift to the wave interference pattern. It is as if once the electrons are out of our sight, they transform themselves into waves and again begin passing through both slits simultaneously. No matter how cleverly we alter our experimental setup, we can never catch them in the act. We always measure them as acting as either waves or particles, never both. Many experiments confirming this result have been performed.

More than half a century after such puzzling behavior was first noted, many physicists still find it stunning and disturbing. How can an electron—a particle whose mass can be measured, whose tracks can clearly be seen in a cloud chamber—suddenly begin behaving like a wave?

Bohr and other leading physicists of the so-called Copenhagen School interpreted this paradoxical result as indicating that objective reality is an ambiguous concept at the quantum level. In physics, our knowledge comes only when we actually measure something, and even then the way we decide to perform the measurement affects the results we obtain. Asking the same question in different ways may give seemingly contradictory answers, but no single experiment will itself provide contradictory information. In other words, though some experiments will show electrons behaving like waves and in others electrons will show particlelike behavior, in no single experiment will electrons display wavelike and particlelike behavior simultaneously.

Bohr called this the principle of complementarity. Quantum mechanics leaves the observer uncertain about the actual nature of reality. Are they really waves or particles? We do not know and no experiment can tell us. Detecting one of the attributes automatically excludes knowledge about the other.

SCHRÖDINGER'S CAT

Erwin Schrödinger, another of the founders of quantum mechanics, was skeptical of Bohr's interpretation. Like Einstein, Max Planck, and other older physicists who helped found quantum mechanics, he objected to the more bizarre aspects of quantum theory. The Copenhagen interpretation sounded to him like observer-created reality.

Schrödinger devised a thought experiment to show that the rejection of objective reality was absurd and, if taken seriously, could lead to grotesque consequences in the larger everyday world. He imagined an unfortunate cat put into a sealed box, the cat's fate hanging by the thread of a quantum event. In one version of the thought experiment a small amount of radioactive material is in the box with the cat, along with a Geiger counter and a vial of poison gas. The apparatus is set up so that if the Geiger counter detects a particle emitted by radioactive decay, it releases the gas and kills the cat.

Let us say quantum mechanics tells us that the radioactive material has a fifty-fifty chance of emitting a particle every minute. Within the box, the Geiger counter is designed to switch itself on for one minute, then switch itself off. Only while it is switched on will it be able to detect a particle and release the gas.

What if we seal the box so that we have no way of knowing what went on inside and then run the experiment for one minute? What state is the cat in, Schrödinger asked, before we reopen the box to see if it has lived or died? The Copenhagen interpretation would seem to argue that prior to our opening the box and "measuring" the health of the cat, the animal exists in some twilight state of potentiality in which it can be considered both dead and alive. Or it might not exist at all in any meaningful sense until we have opened the box and performed our measurement.

Schrödinger, of course, thought this interpretation was nonsense since he, like Einstein, believed in objective reality and was certain that the cat was in a definite state—either dead or alive at every moment—whether we observe it or not. He implied that, contrary to the Copenhagen interpretation, the same must be true of elementary particles. An electron must always be in a definite state even when it is not being measured.

Is there a way around this paradox? I believe that there is, if we distinguish between the future state of the cat and the present state of the cat. I agree with Schrödinger that at every moment of the present, the cat is in a definite state: dead or alive. But while the cat exists in the present in a definite state, I also believe that the cat exists in the twilight state that Schrödinger objects to. How can this be? The cat simultaneously exists in a definite state in the present and in a twilight state of potentialities *in the future.*

This is perfectly consistent with the intuitive way we view the world. The present is definite but the future is indefinite. If I were sitting in that box with the cat, I would be keenly aware at each moment that I were alive. But I would also be painfully aware that at the next moment I might either be alive or dead. My future state is a mixture of potentialities—dead and alive—with the quantum behavior of the radioactive material determining what state I will actually be in when the next moment becomes the present. Two possible states can exist in the future, but only one of them can exist in the present. If there is no radioactive decay then my present state continues to be alive. If the Geiger counter clicks, then the cat and I share a terrible fate.

My theory of unified selection assumes that there are vastly more potential states of the universe than can actually come into existence at any one time. The quantum code, in principle, gives us the statistical tools for predicting the relative likelihood that each of these potentialities will actually come into existence. When a potentiality does become an actuality, the process irreversibly changes the state of the entire universe, even if only in a microscopic way. To echo Heisenberg, the emergence of a potentiality into actuality is a "selection from a plenitude of possibilities and a limitation on what is possible in the future." Such a selection is precisely what we see in the two-slit experiment. Prior to measurement, the electron has two possible future states: a wavelike state and a particlelike state. Only one of these can come into existence at any moment of the present. Quantum mechanics shows us how to calculate the relative probabilities for each of these two states, depending on the measurement arrangement we choose. If we use laser detectors we will obtain one set of probabilities, a particlelike set. If we eliminate the detectors, we obtain a wavelike set of probabilities.

THE WAVE FUNCTION

One of the most convenient ways in quantum mechanics to calculate relative probabilities of future potentialities is to use an approach developed by our old friend Erwin Schrödinger. His formulation of the quantum code is called wave mechanics and the equation that describes the evolution of quantum probabilities is called the wave function. The process by which the potentialities described by the electron become an actuality in the present is called the collapse of the wave function.

The quantum code supplies a formula for translating the wave function into a value for position and momentum, or any other pairs of attributes we care to measure. The formula usually involves Planck's constant, which is the measure of the granularity, or quantization, of the world of quantum fields.

If a physicist wishes to measure an attribute of an electron, the first step is to calculate the wave function of the electron in a proposed measurement situation—for example, a beam of electrons aimed in our two-slit experiment minus the laser detectors. Once the wave function is determined, then the physicist decides which attribute will be measured, in this case position or momentum.

The formula linking the wave function to the position of an elementary particle states that the square of the amplitude of the wave function gives the probability that an elementary particle will be found at a given location. Figure 2.1 shows what it looks like to square the amplitude of wave function to determine its position. If each point on the electron's wave function is thought of as a location where the electron might appear, then the square of the amplitude of the wave function at that location gives the probability that it will appear there. Squaring the amplitude is, mathematically speaking, how we collapse the wave function. The probabilities that we determine are the ones from which that quantum particle must select when it comes into existence.

It is easy to see in Figure 2.1 that the portion of the wave function with the largest amplitude will have the largest amplitude squared, and thus represents the location that the electron is most likely to be found. The wave function is not a static entity. It

Quantum Probability Waves

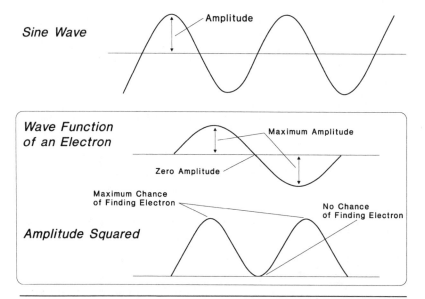

Figure 2.1. The sine wave is the standard wave that is used in the quantum code to represent the momentum of a quantum particle. The two waves in the box illustrate how a physicist calculates the likelihood of finding an electron in a given region of space. When the wave function of the electron (top) is squared, which involves squaring the amplitude of the wave function, the result is another wave (bottom) that gives the probabilities of finding the electron. (The amplitude is the distance of the wave's crest and trough from the baseline.) The points where that wave touches the baseline represent regions where the probability is zero, meaning the electron will never be found there.

evolves, and by studying how it evolves we can determine how quantum particles are likely to behave under all different circumstances.

As in our previous experiments, our physicist makes several calculations and concludes that the chance of finding an electron at location X on the detection screen is seventy percent, while for two other spots, represented by probabilities lower down on the curve, the chances of finding electrons at locations Y and Z are twenty percent and ten percent, respectively. The physicist then starts the experiment and uses an electron gun to fire electrons through the slits onto the screen. By performing the experiment, we are collapsing the wave function of the electron and forcing it to select a definite state from the multiple potentialities open to it. When the results are analyzed, the physicist finds that, indeed, about seventy percent of the electrons struck location X, twenty percent struck location Y, and ten percent struck location Z. The longer electrons stream through the slit onto the screen, the more exactly the distributions of electrons striking locations X, Y, and Z match the predicted percentages.

When a child draws a wavy line to represent a rippling surface of water, the child is drawing a sine wave (Figure 2.1). The track of a snake winding along a sandy desert floor is a sine wave. The vibration of a string on a guitar is a sine wave. In the quantum code, a continuous sine wave stretching out infinitely in both directions represents the momentum of an elementary particle. To measure momentum instead of position, our physicist would have to use standard mathematical techniques to break the wave function into sine waves. The sine wave is just one of many different kinds of waves contained in the wave function, each of which corresponds to a different attribute that a quantum particle may have.

The Schrödinger wave function supplies a compact mathematical representation of the potentialities contained by quantum entities, how they evolve through time, and the probability that they turn from potentiality to actuality during the collapse of the wave function. The wave function will play a key role in our final formulation of unified selection.

In classical physics the atom was considered impossible to explain because a classical electron, behaving like a tiny billiard ball, could not possibly circle the nucleus for long without losing momentum and crashing into the nucleus. But if we consider the electron to be not a particle circling the nucleus like a planet but a wave surrounding it, the atom suddenly begins to make sense. When our physicist calculates the wave function of the electron in the atom and squares the amplitude to discover where the electron is most likely to be found, the probability is zero where the wave function crosses the baseline (Figure 2.1). This zero probability corresponds to the chance that the electron will fall into the nucleus. Instead, the wave function shows that electrons are only likely to be found in certain specific layers around the nucleus. In this way, quantum mechanics is able to explain the stability of the atom.

Quantum randomness, as embodied by the wave function, has a vital function in the realms of matter and life. Matter, of course, is built on a quantum base. The decay of unstable elements such as uranium^{238} into more stable elements is mediated by the quantum randomness of the weak force. Radiation generated by radioactive decay is one way that genetic mutations are formed. It scrambles the sequence of information contained in the double helix of the DNA molecule. Thus quantum randomness supplies a steady stream of genetic variations.

How do living things use these mutations? It is to the operation of the code of life that we turn next.

Code of Life

The chess board is the world, the pieces are the phenomena of the universe, the rules of the game are what we call the laws of Nature.

—THOMAS HENRY HUXLEY

Chapter 3

The Genetic Code

ON SEPTEMBER 14, 1990, AFTER THREE YEARS, THREE MONTHS, AND two weeks of government review, the United States launched its first official experiment in gene therapy. Dr. W. French Anderson and his colleagues at the National Institutes of Health gave a blood transfusion to a four-year-old girl suffering from adenosine deaminase (ADA) deficiency, an inherited disorder that prevents her from producing an enzyme vital to her immune system. The transfusion contained millions of her own white blood cells that had been genetically engineered to replace the gene she is missing.

Since then, Anderson has reported that the girl's response has been extremely promising. A few cancer patients have begun to try gene therapy. Clearly this is only the beginning. The number of potential uses for the treatment is nearly limitless, including inherited diseases such as sickle-cell anemia, hemophilia, and cystic fibrosis as well as other conditions that may have a genetic component—certain types of heart disease, for example, and possibly Alzheimer's disease.

We are seeing the harvesting of benefits of an extraordinarily fruitful cross-pollination between biology and quantum mechanics that began, in large part, with publication by Erwin Schrödinger of *What Is Life?* in 1944. Buoyed by the outstanding practical success of quantum physics but somewhat weary of the debates about the theory's meaning, Schrödinger became intrigued by the ideas of another physicist, Max Delbrück, on the possible physical nature of inheritance. In those days, although biologists had developed a general understanding of genetics, no one knew how an organism passed the information in its genes from one generation to the next.

Schrödinger focused attention on the implications for biology of the realm that quantum mechanics had so spectacularly revealed: atoms and molecules. He suggested that structures of atoms within the cell could be arranged to carry a code, the master code of life. In *What Is Life?* he wrote:

> It has often been asked how this tiny speck of material, the nucleus of the fertilized egg, could contain an elaborate code script involving all the future development of the organism. A well-ordered association of atoms endowed with sufficient resistivity to keep its order permanently, appears to be the only conceivable material structure that offers a variety of possible . . . arrangements sufficiently large to embody a complicated system of "determinations" within a small spatial boundary. Indeed the number of atoms in such a structure need not be very large to produce an almost unlimited number of possible arrangements. For illustration, think of the Morse code. The two different signs of dot and dash in well-ordered groups of not more than four allow of thirty different specifications.[1]

Schrödinger's book helped trigger an exodus of scientists from physics to biology that contributed immensely to the unlocking of the genetic code of life. The fusion of quantum mechanics with biology produced a new discipline, molecular biology, which has been the key discipline in not only deciphering the secrets of the genetic code but also unraveling the mysteries of the synaptic code, another "well-ordered association of atoms" that is hidden within the cells of the brain.

Nineteen years after Schrödinger's prophetic words were published, the genetic code was broken. In 1953, James Watson and Francis Crick announced the structure of DNA (deoxyribonucleic acid). Watson, a gawky twenty-five-year-old with an irreverent sense of humor, wrote that after reading Schrödinger's book, he "became polarized towards finding out the secret of the gene." Watson was a protégé of Max Delbrück, whose ideas inspired Schrödinger. Although Schrödinger never left physics, Delbrück—like Schrödinger and Einstein a refugee from the Nazis—did. He settled in America and became one of the seminal influences in genetics.[2]

Crick, a Londoner and twelve years Watson's senior, was a former physicist who was self-taught in biology. Watson began his famous, gossipy book, *The Double Helix*, describing their discovery with the observation, "I have never seen Francis Crick in a modest mood."[3]

Crick did not yet have his doctorate when the two met, since his academic work had been interrupted by World War II, which he spent designing naval mines and mine detectors. Crick, too, had read *What Is Life?* and found it inspiring. "It suggested that biological problems could be *thought* about in physical terms—and thus it gave the impression that exciting things in this field were not far off," he said.[4]

The code that Watson and Crick uncovered is found in the large organic molecule DNA. This molecule, which is a form of nucleic acid, is organized in two long strands that wrap around each other in the famous double helix shape. (See Figure 3.1.) Once understood, the genetic code is simple and elegant, although its ramifications are exceedingly complex. Imagine the DNA molecule as a spiral staircase. The two railings of the staircase are constructed of sugar and phosphate molecules. These railings give the molecule its structure. The genetic information of the molecule, however, lies in the unique sequence of steps on the stairway. The steps are constructed from pairs of four bases: adenine, guanine, cytosine, and thymine. Adenine and guanine belong to a class of compounds called purines. They are abbreviated A and G. Cytosine and thymine are called pyrimidines. They are abbreviated C and T. The entire genetic structure rests on a simple chemical fact about these four substances: adenine always pairs with thymine and guanine always pairs with cytosine. The bonds are always A-T or G-C. (The bonds could also be described as T-A and C-G because the order of the bases in the pair does not make any difference.) Adenine and thymine are always found together as are guanine and cytosine. There are never bonds such as A-A, A-G, C-T, or G-T.

The Double Helix

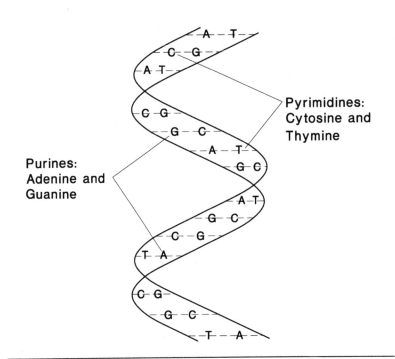

Purines:
Adenine and
Guanine

Pyrimidines:
Cytosine and
Thymine

Figure 3.1. The spiral staircase shape of the DNA molecule carries genetic information in the sequence of nucleotides linked together by purines and pyrimidines that make up its rungs.

Without the insights of quantum mechanics, the discovery of the secret of the double helix of DNA would have been impossible. The quantum code provided a detailed mathematical model for understanding how the atomic bonds that make up DNA are structured, and how they can be used to store, communicate, and reproduce information.

Each step on the DNA staircase is made up of two halves. One half may consist of any one of the four bases. But whichever of the four it happens to be, we always know which base the other half is made of because A always pairs with T, and G with C. As we walk up the DNA staircase, imagine that the right half of each step is engraved with one of the letters A, T, C, or G but the left half is covered with carpeting. Going from step to step we note the following sequence of letters: T, C, A, T, G, A. Once this sequence is recorded, we immediately know which bases make up the carpeted left half of each step. The right half of the first step is T. Since A and T always pair, the left half of the first step is made of A. The right half of the second step is C. Since C always pairs with G, the left half is G. This simple process of pairing A-T and C-G goes on up every DNA staircase, even if it is thousands of steps long. Our sequence T, C, A, T, G, A on the right half of each step is paired with a sequence A, G, T, A, C, T on the left half of each step.

Within this beautiful structure is the secret of the precise reproduction, or replication, of DNA. Every cell in our bodies has an exact copy of the unique DNA sequence that was in the single fertilized egg cell from which we developed. That cell and its descendants divide millions of times in the process of creating a complete human being. When a cell divides, its DNA staircase unwinds and divides right down the middle of each step. (See Figure 3.2.) In our earlier example of the DNA staircase, we would now have the right railing connected to the right halves of the steps with the sequence T, C, A, T, G, A and the left railing connected to the left halves of steps with the sequence A, G, T, A, C, T. From these two halves of the original staircase, the cell produces two complete staircases that are identical to the original. It supplies the missing half of each staircase by pairing a new series of bases (to which pieces of sugar-phosphate railing are attached) according to the rules A-T and C-G. When the cell divides, each new cell has a complete staircase. A three-stage quality control process, in which the pairing of bases is chemically proofread, keeps the error rate in DNA replications to only about one in ten billion.

Each base with its piece of sugar-phosphate railing is called a nucleotide. Each nucleotide is a letter in the genetic alphabet. Scientists discovered that a word in the genetic language consists of three successive nucleotides, called a codon. Francis Crick played a pivotal role in translating the genetic language; working with him was a young W. French Anderson, fresh from Harvard, who is now pioneering gene therapy.

Most codons code for one of twenty amino acids that are used to construct proteins, which are the building blocks of living organ-

DNA Replication

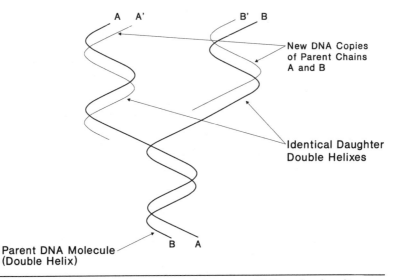

Figure 3.2. When the spiral staircase of the parent DNA molecule splits apart during replication, two new DNA molecules identical to the parent are formed because new complementary strands A' and B' are made using the simple A-T, G-C code.

isms. Since there are four letters in the genetic alphabet (A, T, C, G) and the letters are arranged in words three letters long, there are sixty-four different combinations of letters that can form the twenty amino acids. Most amino acids can be represented by more than one combination of three nucleotides. The combination of bases CAG codes for the amino acid glutamine. But glutamine is also represented by CAA. Some three-letter combinations are used as a form of punctuation. The order of these nucleotides on the DNA strand is crucial to their meaning. Whereas the combination CAG codes for the amino acid glutamine, the combination GAC codes for the amino acid aspartic acid.

A set of genetic instructions for a human being is approximately three billion nucleotide pairs long. These instructions are read through a process called transcription and translation. DNA is transcribed, nucleotide by nucleotide, into a related nucleic acid called messenger ribonucleic acid (mRNA). (See Figure 3.3.) This is then edited to make the final copy of the genetic message.

(Surprisingly, biologist Phillip A. Sharp at the Massachusetts Institute of Technology discovered in 1977 that much of the information on the DNA of more complex organisms does not code for proteins or any other product and is not used to construct the organism. It is this material, called introns, that is edited out of the RNA. Metaphorically speaking, an edited nucleotide sequence might look something like this: USE ~~GOOD~~ THESE ~~LOOK~~ NUCLEOTIDES TO ~~NOT THIS~~ MAKE INSULIN. The reason introns have accumulated in DNA is not yet understood, though there is evidence that some introns may be necessary for the proper transcription of genes. For example, certain stretches of introns, called teleomeres, seem to act as caps on either end of chromosomes, preventing any loss of genetic information.)

DNA Transcription

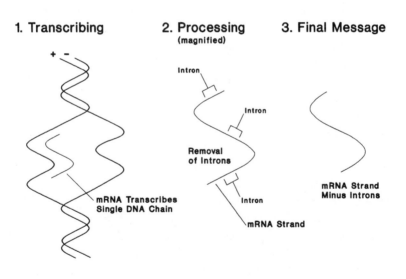

1. Transcribing   **2. Processing**   **3. Final Message**
(magnified)

+ −

Intron

Intron

Removal
of Introns

mRNA Transcribes
Single DNA Chain

Intron

mRNA Strand

mRNA Strand
Minus Introns

Figure 3.3. When a gene or set of genes is needed by the cell, the DNA staircase is split apart at the appropriate location and messenger RNA (mRNA) begins making a copy of the DNA sequence. Once the mRNA sequence is completed, it is edited to remove the nonsense intron sequences.

The letters in the RNA alphabet are slightly different from the DNA alphabet. Both have A, C, and G. In RNA, however, the base uracil (U) takes the place of thymine (T). So the RNA letters are A, C, G, and U. The relationship among the bases is the same in RNA as in DNA. Adenine (A) always pairs with uracil (U), instead of thymine; and cytosine (C) always pairs with guanine (G).

RNA generally comes in single strands that are shorter than DNA strands. The RNA forms a template or copy of the nucleotide sequence in the complementary strand of DNA, which is the strand opposite the one with the genetic code. If the coded strand of DNA has the nucleotide sequence TCA, which represents the amino acid serine, then the complementary strand will have the sequence AGT, like the negative of a photograph. When the RNA copies the complementary sequence AGT, its sequence will be UCA, or the same nucleotide sequence as the original DNA code except that RNA's uracil (U) has been substituted for thymine (T). The original photograph will have been reproduced from the negative.

One explanation for the substitution for thymine is that uracil takes less energy to synthesize. But since thymine is the more stable of the two, it makes sense that it has evolved to be the preferred pyrimidine, along with cytosine, for permanently storing the genetic information on the double helix.

Once any introns, or noncoding DNA, have been edited out of the sequence, the remaining information (called exons) is represented in the messenger RNA. The messenger RNA then leaves the DNA and goes to another part of the cell called the ribosome for translation into proteins. (See Figure 3.4.) In the ribosome, each sequence of three nucleotides or codon is matched by another kind of RNA called transfer RNA (tRNA). Each segment of transfer RNA has an amino acid attached to it. By matching each codon to its complementary segment of transfer RNA, the ribosome builds up long strings of amino acids, something like a string of beads. Thus proteins, which are long chains of amino acids, are constructed amino acid by amino acid from the genetic code. These proteins are the building blocks of the organism. Some proteins make up the physical structure of the body—muscles, blood, bone—and other proteins, called enzymes, regulate the chemical processes of the cell.

To summarize this brief sketch, the genetic code has three dialects. (See Figure 3.5.) The genetic information is permanently

DNA Translation Using RNA

1. Protein Synthesis: Overall View

2. Protein Synthesis: Detailed Analysis

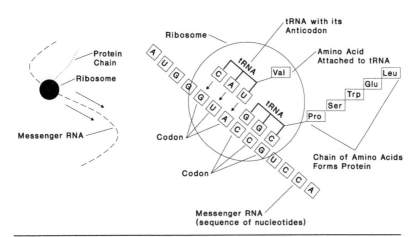

Figure 3.4. This is a schematic look at how sequences of messenger RNA (mRNA) are translated into chains of amino acids, the building blocks of proteins. The overall view shows the ribosome reading the mRNA and producing a long protein molecule based on the genetic instructions. The detailed analysis shows a simplified view of what is going on inside the ribosome. Each segment of transfer RNA (tRNA) has three-pronged anticodons that link up with the codons of the mRNA according to the code A-U, U-A. The tRNA anticodon is paired with a specific amino acid, which is attached to the tRNA. When the tRNA anticodon matches with the mRNA codon, the amino acid is released by the tRNA to be added as a link to the growing chain of amino acids being constructed from the genetic information. These chains of amino acids are the proteins, which build and maintain the body's biological processes.

stored in the sequence of bases that make up the steps of the DNA molecule. This is the code that is used to transmit genetic information when the cell replicates or reproduces. These sequences of bases with their sugar-phosphate attachments (nucleotides) are read by strands of RNA as words that are three nucleotides long (codons). This is the dialect of transcription, which is exactly the same as the replication dialect except for the substitution of uracil for thymine. Each word or codon represents one of the twenty amino acids that make up proteins, or some form of genetic punctuation. This is the dialect of translation. The codons are translated (primarily) into

The Genetic Code's Three Dialects

A. Replication
Adenine pairs with thymine (A-T or T-A)
Guanine pairs with cytosine (G-C or C-G)

B. Transcription
Adenine pairs with uracil (A-U or U-A)
Guanine pairs with cytosine (G-C or C-G)

C. Translation: The 20 Amino Acids and Their Codons

1. Alanine	GCU, GCC GCA, GCG	11. Leucine	UUA, UUG, CUU CUC, CUA, CUG
2. Arginine	CGU, CGC, CGA CGG, AGA, AGG	12. Lysine	AAA, AAG
3. Asparagine	AAU, AAC	13. Methionine	AUG
4. Aspartic Acid	GAU, GAC	14. Phenylalanine	UUU, UUC
5. Cysteine	UGU, UGC	15. Proline	CCU, CCC CCA, CCG
6. Glutamic Acid	GAA, GAG	16. Serine	UCU, UCC, UCA UCG, AGU, AGC
7. Glutamine	CAA, CAG	17. Threonine	ACU, ACC ACA, ACG
8. Glycine	GGU, GGC GGA, GGG	18. Tryptophan	UGG
9. Histidine	CAU, CAC	19. Tyrosine	UAU, UAC
10. Isoleucine	AUU, AUC AUA	20. Valine	GUU, GUC GUA, GUG

Figure 3.5. The genetic code has three components. First is the A-T, G-C code used by DNA molecules when they divide to form new molecules. Second is the A-U, G-C code used by messenger RNA to transcribe the DNA's information and use it as a recipe for making proteins. Third is the amino acid code in which arbitrary codons of three bases are linked to each of the twenty amino acids that are used to build proteins. Transfer RNA consists of a codon and the appropriate amino acid. Most of the amino acids are linked to more than one codon. The codon guanine-cytosine-adenine (GCA), for example, codes for the amino acid alanine—and so do three other codons.

long chains of amino acids that form proteins. The organism is then constructed from these proteins. As Francis Crick has said, the dogma of modern biology is "DNA makes RNA and RNA makes protein."[5]

A gene is the sequence of words that makes a single product like a protein. A typical gene is made up of a thousand or more nucleotides. Besides proteins, genes also make the various kinds of RNA that take part in the translation process.

Despite our understanding of the genetic code, the question lingers: what *is* life? Scientists have never really agreed on the answer. Some forms of very rudimentary organisms, such as viruses, seem to have little in common with more complex organisms, and do not seem to be alive in the same way. Viruses are not made of cells. They consist of DNA or RNA in a protein shell. They invade the cells of other organisms and take over the cell's machinery, forcing it to reproduce the viral DNA.

Virtually every other organism is built from cells, which are tiny chemical factories. Yet all forms of life, from viruses to human beings, use the genetic code based on adenine, guanine, cytosine, thymine, and, in RNA, uracil. I would argue that life simply describes those forms of matter that are organized by the genetic code. Since viruses use the genetic code, they are a form of life.

DARWIN AND MENDEL

The foundation of our ideas about evolution, genetics, and even dinosaurs were all products of the nineteenth century. In the 1840s and '50s, Charles Darwin was wrestling with his theory of evolution, which sought to explain the mechanism behind the origin of the diverse forms of life. A barrier to evolutionary thinking was the dogma that the Earth had existed for only a few thousand years. The traditional belief was that all species were specially created by God and did not change.

Beginning in the eighteenth century, however, geologists concluded from their studies of rock formations and fossil deposits that the Earth must be far older. The first dinosaur, a giant carnivore dubbed *Megalosaurus*, was described in 1824. The name *Dinosauria* was not coined until 1841.

Darwin published *On the Origin of Species* in 1859. In it he presented an impressive body of evidence supporting his argument that small, useful modifications in individual organisms can accumulate over generations and produce new species. Individuals with these modifications that are useful in a given environment tend to leave more offspring than less favored organisms. He concluded that this mechanism, which he called natural selection, operating over enormous lengths of time, produced all the diversity of life that we observe.

Darwin recognized that if every living thing reproduced at its maximum rate, all food and living space on Earth would soon be exhausted. There must be a mechanism that in each generation winnows the number of living things. He reasoned that every member of a species is a variation that is at least slightly different from every other member of the species. Some of these differences—swifter speed, better eyesight, greater cunning—may provide an advantage in adapting to the environment. Over the long run, Darwin theorized, the better adapted members of a species cope more successfully with environmental pressures. In this interaction between species and environment, the best adapted are more likely to live longer and produce more offspring. To the extent that their superior adaptations are genetic, they are passed on to their offspring. Darwin argued that over time this process of variation and selection should produce a changing array of species, which indeed we can clearly see when we examine the history of life over millions of years. The fossil record provides abundant evidence that whole groups of species, such as the dinosaurs, have evolved, flourished, and died out since life first appeared.

There is a striking similarity between life and thought. Just as there are more potential life forms than the planet can hold, there are more potential ideas than our minds can possibly absorb and remember. Natural selection generates evolutionary change by choosing from among the many potential forms of life and, I argue, thought as well.

Yet if we consider living things and ideas as different arrangements of the elementary particles that make up the body and brain, then the master evolutionary mechanism is found in the wave function of the universe, which guides the selection from among an infinite number of potential arrangements that the universe may assume from moment to moment. The structure of the universe one million years from now may contain the life forms we call human beings—or it may not. The way the universe travels from here to there is the process of evolution.

You will recall that unified selection describes the way the wave function of the universe evolves. The universe has many possible future states or potentialities represented by the wave function. In unified selection, the wave function is constantly collapsing into the present as the many possible states become a single state as the present unfolds and possibilities become actuality.

Unified selection requires a change of perspective from orthodox natural selection. In unified selection, we highlight the collapse of potentialities into actuality. How does this mechanism contrast with natural selection? When we analyze the evolution of a species, unified selection considers each member of the species that exists at a given moment in the present. The varying traits of these individuals are produced by the workings of the genetic code. Surrounding this population of individuals is a large set of potentialities, each of which is a future scenario containing different mixes of the individuals and their offspring. In one scenario or potentiality, the population might have more of the faster individuals; in another, the slower ones predominate. The nature of the genetic differences between individuals along with the circumstances of their environment determine the shifting probabilities that these competing potentialities will become actuality. For jaguars, the environment has favored scenarios dominated by the offspring of faster individuals; for sloths, scenarios with slower individuals have been favored.

Orthodox natural selection focuses on a population of individual organisms as it exists in the present. The individuals represent the variations. Selection chooses those that are best adapted to the environment. This is a source of confusion. Natural selection chooses from among a varying population of individual organisms. Unified selection chooses from a varying population of potentialities or future scenarios. In unified selection the act of selection takes place when competing future scenarios that have fluctuating probabilities collapse into the present so that only one scenario actually comes into existence.

Take our jaguar example. What will the population of jaguars look like a thousand years from now? There are many possible scenarios, but let's consider only four. The first scenario or potentiality is that the population of jaguars will be faster on average than today's jaguars. The second possibility is that they will be slower. The third possibility is that their speed will be about the same. And the fourth possibility is that jaguars will have become extinct. During the intervening years the probability associated with each of these scenarios will fluctuate as the circumstances change. If the jaguars' prey becomes faster, then the environment will put pressure on the jaguar to become faster as well. Faster jaguars will begin to leave more offspring because they can catch more food. The population will begin to change. A thousand years from now one of our potentialities will collapse into existence. If the jaguars have been able to adapt, the first scenario will become reality: the population of jaguars will be faster on average.

Note that we have not suddenly jumped to a population of faster jaguars. Future potentialities have been collapsing into the present throughout the thousand years. We can trace the intervening steps by which the jaguars became faster. Note also that in the real world there are many more traits than speed that affect survival and there are many complex factors in the environment and in the jaguars' genetic endowment that influence adaptability. Thus although in principle we should be able to calculate the wave function for the population of jaguars, in practice the mathematics is far too complicated to be solved by the current methods of analysis. Nevertheless, we can make very rough estimates of the jaguars' chances under different sets of assumptions.

Basically, I think the approaches of natural selection and unified selection are the same. Natural selection is really focusing on the reproductive potential of different individuals. When two individuals are compared in natural selection, we are actually comparing various scenarios involving the comparative reproductive success of the two. In one set of scenarios, individual A produces more offspring; in another set, it is individual B. When we conclude that natural selection favors one individual over another, what we are actually saying is that natural selection *tends* to favor one of the scenarios in which (say) individual A, who is better adapted, produces more offspring than individual B. In both natural selection and unified selection the variations are based on an analysis of potential scenarios, while selection involves a prediction of the relative probability of each potentiality.

Natural selection is a special case of unified selection that describes how genetic variations affect the long-term probabilities of reproductive success. Unified selection, in comparison, analyzes a much greater range of variations—including variations produced by the quantum code and the synaptic code—in its probability calculations of how the entire universe will evolve.

Two general lines of biological thought have been evolving since the time of the Greeks. Aristotle explored both of them in his long treatises on animals (his writings on plants have not survived). The first line focuses on the proper way to classify the diversity of living things, the science of taxonomy. The second focuses on the riddle of reproduction. The first gave rise to the modern theory of evolution. The second resulted in the discovery of DNA and the genetic code. These two lines of thought have now merged to form a comprehensive theory of the development of life on Earth.

The application of Aristotelian logic to living things by Carolus Linnaeus, the eighteenth-century Swedish naturalist, led to the modern classification system of biology. Linnaeus was a student of logic who was impressed by its exactness. The Linnaean system evolved into a hierarchical scheme in which the broadest classification is the kingdom (animals and plants make up two separate kingdoms) with the classifications progressively narrowing through the phylum, class, order, family, genus, and species, the narrowest classification. The Linnaean system gives every living thing a two-word (binomial) Latin or latinized name. The first word represents the genus and the second the species. Human beings are classified as *Homo sapiens* (homo meaning man and sapiens meaning wise). There are no other living representatives of the genus *Homo*. The two extinct species that are usually classified as members of this genus are *Homo habilis*, a species that appeared about 1.5 million years ago, and *Homo erectus*, a species that died out shortly after the appearance of *Homo sapiens*, about 250,000 years ago.

The Linnaean system had the twin advantages of precision and simplicity. It is much more precise than common names. The plant *Bidens frondosa*, for example, has many names in English, including bur marigold, rayless marigold, pitchfork weed, and sticktight. The Linnaean system is also much simpler than earlier systems. Prior to Linnaeus, there was little uniformity in naming, and species often had long descriptive names.

Darwin's great contribution was his insight that the species that Linnaeus had named were not immutable but had evolved over millions of years. Yet to the end of his life, Darwin never understood the principles of inheritance that play such an important part in his theory of evolution. He knew that organisms vary and that these variations could be passed on to offspring. He was unable, however, to discover the true mechanism of this inheritance. Darwin subscribed to a variety of theories of inheritance over the course of his career, including the common belief in his day in blending inheritance, which held that the traits of parents blend during reproduction, producing offspring whose inherited traits are somewhere in between those of the parents.

This is reminiscent of the continuous theory of matter and

energy held by classical physics in the nineteenth century. But just as the continuous world view of classical physics was overturned by quantum mechanics, which viewed the substratum of reality as made up of granules of matter and energy in the form of quanta, the blending theory of inheritance was overturned by a discontinuous theory based on granules of inheritance: the genes. Unknown to Darwin, the experiments establishing this theory were being done in what is now Czechoslovakia around the time *On the Origin of Species* was being written.

MENDEL'S PEAS

Gregor Johann Mendel carefully studied the process of inheritance and in his early research indicated the shortcomings of the theory of blending inheritance. In 1856 Mendel turned to the garden pea, *Pisum sativum*, and its related forms. Mendel had been particularly fond of physics in school, and he applied the quantitative methods of physics to the problem at hand, a cross-fertilization of physics and biology that has proved important time and time again in the history of science. Mendel used statistical methods. He identified seven clearly expressed pairs of traits of the peas—for example, whether the plants were tall or short, whether the flowers were yellow or white, whether the seeds were yellow or green. He then interbred plants with each trait (a tall plant and a short plant, for example) and observed which of these traits the offspring inherited. He then either self-fertilized the offspring or bred them with sister plants. He meticulously recorded the results of thousands of crossings carried through several generations.

The results he obtained were always the same. In the first generation, the offspring were all of one type. For tall plants bred with short plants, the offspring were always tall. For plants with white flowers bred with plants with red flowers, the offspring always had red flowers. For plants with yellow seeds bred with plants with green seeds, the offspring always had yellow seeds. But when the first-generation offspring for each of the seven traits were bred among themselves (tall offspring with tall offspring, and so on), something remarkable happened. In the second generation of plants, three out of four plants on the average had the same traits as their parents (tallness, red flowers), but the fourth plant would have the trait that was present in one of its grandparents (shortness, white flowers) yet had not been expressed in its parents.

In reflecting on his data, Mendel came to some historic conclusions. Each trait must be governed by a stable factor that does not change or blend as it passes through successive generations. These factors for each trait must come in pairs. Each plant must receive one factor for a particular trait (size, flower color) from each parent. In each pair of factors, one must be dominant and the other recessive. Whenever a dominant factor is present, its form of the trait (tall, red flowers) will be expressed.

Take flower color as an example. The original parents in Mendel's experiments were carefully selected to breed true. In order to constantly breed true for flower color, the pair of factors for flower color present in each red-flowering plant both had to be red (designated *RR*) and both factors for white-flowering plants had to be white (designated *ww*). So Mendel began his flower color experiment by breeding a *RR* (red-flowered) plant with a *ww* (white-flowered) plant. During sexual reproduction the two factors for flower color would separate and in each mating there would be a fifty-fifty chance that one factor or the other would be passed on to the offspring. For the red-flowering plant, the *RR* factor would separate into *R* and *R* and the white-flowering plant would separate into *w* and *w*. There are four possible combinations of these factors in the offspring if each parent contributes one factor. In this case, the four possible combinations are all the same: *Rw*. Hence for any four plants in the first generation, each will receive an *R* factor from the red-flowered parent and a *w* factor from the white-flowered parent. Since the first generation produces four offspring with pairs of factors for flower color that are *Rw*, *Rw*, *Rw*, and *Rw*, and assuming that red is the dominant color—which it turns out to be—then all the offspring will have red flowers, just as Mendel found.

If these first-generation *Rw* offspring are crossed with each other, then the mix of factors in the second generation will be somewhat different. Since the male *Rw* parent has a fifty-percent chance of contributing either the *R* or *w* factor, and the female has the same chance of contributing the same factors, we can summarize the factors that will be present in four randomly selected second-generation offspring. If the female contributes the *R* factor, then the male can contribute either the *R* or *w* factor. This would result in

RR or *Rw* offspring. If the female contributes the *w* factor, then the male again can contribute either the *R* or *w* factor and the resulting offspring are *wR* and *ww*. To summarize, four randomly selected second-generation offspring would most likely have the following pairs of factors: *RR*, *Rw*, *wR*, *ww*. Since red is the dominant flower color, any pair that has an *R* factor will produce a plant with red flowers. The first three plants have an *R* factor so their flowers will be red. (In traditional Mendelian genetics the *Rw* and *wR* pairs are treated as identical, though it has recently been discovered that for certain traits it does matter whether the gene comes from the male or female parent.) But the fourth plant has the two recessive factors (*ww*) in its pair without an *R*. Thus white flowers will appear on the *ww* plant after having skipped a generation.

In his classic paper, "Experiments on Plant Hybrids," published in 1866, Mendel summarized the results of the crossings that produced the second generation of plants:

> In this generation along with the dominant traits the recessive ones reappear in their full expression, and they do so in the decisively evident average proportion of 3:1, so that among each four plants of this generation three show the dominant and one the recessive character.[6]

Mendel's ratio of three to one is as important to the genetic code as $E = mc^2$ and the discovery of the atom are to modern physics. This ratio established once and for all that inheritance is based on the statistical combination and recombination of discrete particles. Mendel had discovered the basic unit of the genetic code: the gene. Each gene comes in different varieties, which are called alleles. In Mendel's experiment, the two alleles of the gene for color are red and white. In sexually reproducing species, genes for a trait such as color or height come in pairs, with one allele being contributed by the male and the other by the female.

Mendel's breakthrough was similar to the breakthroughs that led to the understanding of the quantum and synaptic codes. His work led to the fundamental insight that at the core of all living things are fundamental units that we have come to call genes. Similarly, physicists began to decipher the quantum code once they came to understand that all forms of matter are constructed from a few types of elementary particles. And, as we shall see in Chapter 5, the deciphering of the synaptic code began with the insight that the brain is built around two fundamental units: the neuron and its synaptic connections.

Building on Mendel's work, biologists identified the structure that contains the genes as the chromosome. A chromosome, which is made up of DNA, may have thousands of individual genes. In sexually reproducing organisms, chromosomes are normally paired. Human beings have forty-six chromosomes arranged in twenty-three pairs, with a total of 50,000 to 100,000 genes. During reproduction, these chromosomes in the reproductive cells divide an extra time so that the egg and sperm cell have only twenty-three chromosomes. This means that the mother and father each contribute one-half of their offspring's forty-six chromosomes.

As the egg and sperm cells form, the forty-six chromosomes of each parent are shuffled before twenty-three of them are placed in each sex cell. For instance, if the mother has eye color alleles for both blue and brown eyes (brown is dominant), the chromosomes containing these alleles will be distributed randomly among her egg cells. Some cells will have the chromosome containing the gene for blue eyes and others will contain the gene for brown eyes. Besides reshuffling of parent's chromosomes, portions of individual chromosomes can exchange places in a process called crossing over and genetic recombination.

When the egg is fertilized, the twenty-three chromosomes in the egg combine with the twenty-three in the sperm to produce the normal twenty-three pairs, or forty-six total chromosomes. With all this reshuffling and recombination it is clear why each human being, with the exception of identical twins, is genetically unique.

Unfortunately, as Mendel painfully discovered, the evolution of thought is shaped by contingencies that give it many strange twists and turns. Mendel's paper, considered one of the classics in all of science, was ignored for thirty-four years. It was published in the journal of the Brünn Natural History Society, Mendel's hometown journal (Brünn is now Brno, Czechoslovakia), and though copies of the journal were sent to most of the great libraries of Europe the paper went unread. Mendel himself sent copies of the paper to at least two renowned botanists and was met with a lack of understanding and indications of opposition to his ideas. Instead of being amplified and spread throughout Europe, as they were nearly forty years later, Mendel's ideas were effectively suppressed and almost forgotten. Since his paper was catalogued in many libraries, however, it remained in the pool of ideas that might be drawn on by enterprising minds.

Mendel gave up his biological studies in 1871 because of the administrative duties he took on that year on becoming abbot of his monastery. He died in 1884 at the age of sixty-two of a kidney infection, never knowing of the transforming effect his work would have on the world.

MENDEL REDISCOVERED

In the spring of 1900, biologists were surprised by one of the most stunning coincidences in the history of science. Three botanists—Hugo De Vries in Holland, Carl Correns in Germany, and Erich von Tschermak-Seysenegg in Austria—independently announced that they had discovered key laws of inheritance, and that in searching through the scientific literature they had discovered that Mendel had anticipated them by nearly four decades. With the rediscovery of his paper, Mendel's ideas were disseminated almost overnight. That began an increasingly feverish half-century of work culminating in the discovery by Watson and Crick of the genetic code.

(Another striking coincidence served up by the contingencies of history was that modern biology and modern physics began in the same year. For it was in 1900 that Max Planck proposed that electromagnetic energy was emitted not continuously but in packets of energy called quanta. The discontinuous nature of matter, energy, and life—measured in quanta and genes—was discovered [or rediscovered] in the same year. We shall note a further arresting parallel in Chapter 5: At about the same time as these advances in biology and physics were taking place, neuroscientists were proposing that the brain, too, is discontinuous and is made of separate cells called neurons.)

A complete review of the tangle of ideas that biologists sorted, shaped, and structured through variation and selection between 1900 and 1953 is beyond the scope of this book. I will simply touch on the career of one pivotal figure: Thomas Hunt Morgan.

Morgan, an embryologist by training who ultimately won the Nobel Prize for his pioneering work in genetics, will forever be linked to the tiny fruit fly, *Drosophila melanogaster*, which he studied for decades, first in his "fly-room" at Columbia University and later at the California Institute of Technology.

The years immediately after the rediscovery of Mendel's ideas showed that there were many types of inheritance that did not fit the simple garden pea model. Not all organisms reproduce sexually. Some simpler plants and animals clone themselves without the extensive reshuffling that sexual reproduction involves. Not all organisms have pairs of chromosomes; some have only one set of chromosomes in their cells, while others may have three or more sets of chromosomes. Not all traits are dominant or recessive. Some are only partially dominant. Through all the complexities, however, Mendel's central insight—that the factors controlling inheritance are found in nonblending particles in the organism—remained at the heart of all successful theories.

The task of Morgan and his colleagues was to flesh out this central insight into a full-fledged theory. By 1904, chromosomes had been identified in the cell and this discovery was combined with Mendel's ideas to produce the first chromosome theory of inheritance. When Morgan—born in Lexington, Kentucky, of a prominent family that produced the daring Confederate raider, John Hunt Morgan—began experimenting with fruit flies a few years later, this theory was still extremely controversial. In fact, Morgan himself strongly opposed it. The data from the fruit fly studies eventually changed his mind and by 1915 he and his colleagues in the fly-room had worked out a virtually complete theory of inheritance by chromosomes. This included an explanation of how the determination of the sex of an organism is linked to specific X and Y chromosomes. Females have a pair of X chromosomes while males normally receive an X chromosome from their mother and a Y chromosome from their father. Through a series of superb experiments, the Morgan group was able to pinpoint the specific locations of genes on the chromosomes. Maps of chromosomes were drawn up identifying the sites of specific genes.

Morgan's methods were those of Mendel: carefully controlled breeding experiments, meticulous quantitative analysis of the results, and incisive use of logic to deduce the underlying patterns and mechanisms. Both were fortunate in choosing organisms that yielded clear results with a minimum of complications.

The chromosome theory also tied mutations to chemical changes in the genetic material on the chromosome. Normally if genes are altered, the resulting organism will no more make sense (be free of crippling or fatal mutations) than a sentence will make sense if the words are randomly scrambled. Yet biologists ultimately concluded that an occasional mutation, like an occasional change in wording, will "make sense" to the organism and give it the flexibility to adapt to changing conditions.

Morgan was never a believer in natural selection. He believed that significant mutations alone could account for the origin of new species. But later biologists came to realize that most successful mutations have a relatively small effect on the organism. Mutations that alter many traits at the same time are almost always lethal. Through their reproductive process, species stockpile a whole variety of mutations (often as recessive alleles) that selective pressure can act upon. Over time the cumulative effect of these mutations on generations of organisms may be to alter the form of a species, or even bud off new species.

This concept is closely related to the idea of the gene pool—the pool of genetic variations or alleles, including mutations, that any interbreeding group has available to it. The frequency with which an allele is represented in the pool may change over time. If a population of organisms is living at a high altitude, then an allele that allows a more efficient use of oxygen will become more common in the gene pool over generations. Those that have this allele will have a slightly better chance of survival than others and will tend to leave more offspring, who may inherit the allele and pass it on to their offspring.

Once scientists began to pinpoint the location of genes on the chromosome, the question naturally arose as to their structure. Physicists, who asked the same question about the structure of the atom, were able to make progress more quickly than biologists. One reason for the delay in biology was that the quantum code needed to be better understood before biologists had the tools necessary to understand the complex organic molecules that make up living things.

As it turns out, DNA, RNA, and proteins are giants in the microscopic world. Most proteins consist of between 40 and 500 amino acids strung together. The DNA molecule is even larger, often consisting of chains of thousands of nucleotides. Although a strand of DNA is only several hundred millionths of an inch thick, a single DNA molecule can be several inches long when it is uncoiled in the laboratory. Molecules this large are much less subject to the quantum forces that cause so much strangeness at the subatomic level. But DNA is still affected by that quantum world in a very important way. Quantum forces are a major source of mutations in the sequence of nucleotides that make up the genetic code. Random mutations can be caused by high energy radiation, such as X-rays, cosmic rays, and radioactive decay. Chemicals can also cause mutations.

Mutations come in several varieties. A base can be added to or deleted from a nucleotide chain. These are very important mutations since bases are read in codons—that is, groups of three. If a base is added or deleted, then the wrong three bases will be read as a codon, making the genetic sequence meaningless. For example, the sequence of bases C G T A T C would normally be read as two codons: CGT and ATC. If a mutation adds a G to the beginning of this sequence, then it would completely change its meaning and since it would be read as GCG, TAT, C, the result would be to completely change the meaning of this stretch of code. In the initial coding we have the codon CGT, which codes for the amino acid arginine, and ATC, which codes for isoleucine. After the mutation, the bases would be read as GCG, which codes for alanine, and TAT, which codes for tyrosine.

Two other kinds of mutations are also important. One involves base substitution, in which one base in the chain converts into another (AGT becomes CGT when A changes to C). Another kind of mutation is known as transposition, in which stretches of DNA from one part of the nucleotide chain are inserted into another part of the chain.

UNSOLVED PROBLEMS

Although the discovery of the structure of DNA and the way genetic information is translated into proteins is essential to understanding life, it is not the whole story. The major challenge facing biology today is to comprehend exactly how the one-dimensional string of chemical words in the genetic code is transformed into a three-dimensional organism. Biologists understand much of the recipe for life (the information coded by the sequence of bases in the

DNA molecule), and how the ingredients are made (proteins are created from strings of amino acids as specified by the genetic recipe), but biologists do not yet understand how the ingredients are mixed and baked to create the fancy cake that is the final functioning life-form. This involves the complex interplay of highly folded proteins in cascades of interactions. A gene does not simply code deterministically for a single invariable trait. The same gene in different environments can produce many variations on the trait, and influence the expression of other genes.

Yet even short of a complete understanding of all genetic processes, the implications of our knowledge of the genetic code are vast. We can administer the kinds of gene therapy that W. French Anderson and others have begun. We can isolate individual genes and transplant them into different species. Human genes can be spliced into bacteria, for example, which can then be used to grow human hormones such as insulin. This is the new technology of genetic engineering. There is a vast potential for the genetic engineering of improved species of plants and animals to provide the agricultural products and livestock of the future, leapfrogging the generations of breeding that have historically been necessary to produce improvements.

The United States has begun a massive project, with international cooperation, to decipher all three billion or so pairs of nucleotides that comprise the human genome, a task that will probably be completed before the end of the century. The project, led until recently by James Watson, has staggering implications for human health. Since genes not only determine sex and genetic diseases, but affect behavior, intelligence, and longevity, this spectacular increase in genetic knowledge will have unlimited applications. Genetics has already provided new insights into diseases such as cancer, which seems to be caused by mutations in the nucleotide sequences in the DNA that control cell growth. Such mutations, which may only involve one nucleotide, unleash uncontrolled cell growth. Paradoxically, though they can ultimately destroy their host organism, cancer cells themselves seem to be immortal: they will continue to grow and multiply indefinitely as long as nutrients are available. In studying cancer we may learn the secret of enormously extending our own lives.

The most overwhelming implication of all is that as we understand how genetic instructions produce the final form of an organism, we will be in a position to alter our own form and the forms of all living things. The human body plan evolved in the unique circumstances of life on Earth. But it is not the only conceivable body plan. If we migrate into space, for example, a different plan might serve us better. Genetic knowledge will give us the option of directing our future evolution and the evolution of all life.

Chapter 4

Revolt of the Brain

WELLING UP FROM THE DEEPEST RECESSES OF OUR HUMANITY, A primeval conflict has exploded into revolution: the revolt of the brain against the genes. An ancient evolutionary order, billions of years old, is being overthrown. Using the tools of science, the human brain is winning ascendancy over the genes in the struggle to shape the future of all life on this planet, including our own.

In this new order, we—not our genes—will be able to select the sex of our children and influence their intelligence and health. We will be able to cure terrifying diseases like cancer and, perhaps, postpone death itself. We will be able to mix the genes of all living things, no matter how different, to create new forms of life that would be impossible under ordinary evolution. Through genetic engineering we have already inserted human genes into bacteria to produce an army of tiny living machines that manufacture insulin and other valuable substances.

The source of this revolt is the resentment and frustration human beings have felt since emerging into consciousness that so many must needlessly suffer and die from illness and disease, particularly children. Nature is often beautiful and harmonious, but to those with diseases such as muscular dystrophy or hereditary mental illness, it is cruel and painful.

Traditional Darwinian evolution operates through variation and selection over many generations. The best adapted organisms in any one generation are the ones that tend to survive and produce offspring. Their genes are overrepresented in the next generation, and over time this tends to adapt the population as a whole to its environment. Yet when a new disease or parasite attacks a population, this slow process can sacrifice millions of human beings in the search for the best adapted individuals.

Malaria, for example, is perhaps the worst scourge ever inflicted on mankind. It is estimated that nearly half of all human beings who ever lived have been killed by malaria or malaria-related illnesses. Among the first writings of the ancient Egyptians were accounts of the disease's high fever, shivering, and swollen spleen. Only in the last century was it discovered that this disease is caused by a single-celled parasite carried by mosquitoes.

The use of insecticides and other public health measures has basically eliminated malaria in the industrialized world. But malaria remains the world's number one killer because of its prevalence in less-developed tropical countries. Up to 300 million people are afflicted with the parasite and two to three million die every year. More than a million of those are children.[1]

Our genes provide our bodies with an immune system centered in the bone marrow that protects us from most diseases. White blood cells are designed to attack and destroy invading organisms. But parasites such as malaria can evolve ways of evading the immune system. Since everyone's immune system is slightly different, some are more resistant to malaria than others. Over thousands of years of evolution, people with greater resistance are more likely to survive until child-bearing age. They will produce more offspring than those who are less resistant. Eventually the human population will be dominated by those with genes that code for immune systems capable of fighting off malaria. Yet while genetic evolution slowly does its work, the slaughter of innocents is chilling.

Charles Darwin himself was appalled by the inefficiency of the evolutionary process:

"What a book a devil chaplain might write on the clumsy, wasteful, blundering, low, and horribly cruel works of nature," he wrote.[2]

Even when evolutionary solutions evolve, their side effects can be deadly for some. The sickle-cell gene has evolved in certain African populations as a defense against malaria. If the gene is inherited from one of the parents it makes abnormally shaped red blood cells that resist infection by the malaria parasite. Unfortunately, if the child receives the gene from both parents, these oddly shaped cells can also clump together and damage internal organs, causing a painful and sometimes fatal illness: sickle-cell anemia.

Today the malaria-infected tropics are in a crisis because the most deadly of the four types of malaria parasites has developed a resistance to the drugs that have kept the disease in check. The intervention of the human brain is necessary if the slaughter is not to escalate. After years of failure to develop a vaccine, the science of genetics appears to be on the brink of short-circuiting the slow evolutionary process and developing a workable way to inoculate people against the disease. Through genetic engineering, researchers have produced an experimental vaccine that stimulates the immune system of mice to resist malaria. They hope that a human vaccine may not be too far away.[3]

Malaria has affected evolution and genetics in many surprising ways. Darwin was forced to publish his theory of natural selection, in part, because of a malaria attack suffered by another biologist, Alfred Russel Wallace. Wallace had spent years exploring the tropics and collecting specimens. In 1858, during a severe bout of fever brought on by malaria, Wallace had a vision: "There suddenly flashed upon me the idea of the survival of the fittest," he later recounted. Filled with excitement, he spent the next two days writing a paper summarizing his ideas. He sent it off to a biologist he greatly admired: Charles Darwin.

Darwin had delayed publishing his theory for nearly twenty years, fearing the reaction of religious opinion to such a materialistic theory. Wallace's paper came as a shock, and after agonized consultation with his colleagues, Darwin presented Wallace's paper along with a paper of his own at a scholarly meeting in London in July 1858. The next year *On the Origin of Species* was published.

Ninety years later, Linus Pauling revolutionized medicine by introducing the idea that a mutation of a gene could cause a specific illness. The illness was sickle-cell anemia, which is caused by the victim's inability to produce normal hemoglobin. Pauling was the man who had already revolutionized chemistry by applying the precise methods of quantum mechanics to the chemical bonds that join atoms into molecules. Pauling, one of the few people who have won two Nobel Prizes, showed that these bonds tend to assume the forms that require the least energy to maintain. Chemists could for the first time visualize the shapes of molecules. Pauling's interest in molecules attracted him to the study of proteins, and it was this research that led to the finding that a single gene for a specific protein was the cause of sickle-cell anemia. This discovery was the first bold step on the road to genetic engineering, a turning point in the revolt of the brain.

HARNESSING THE BRAIN

Genetic engineering harnesses the brain's knowledge of the genetic code of life, which evolved on Earth from a group of large molecules that include DNA, RNA, and proteins. The "central dogma" of genetics, according to Francis Crick, codiscoverer of the double-helix structure of DNA, is that DNA makes RNA, and RNA makes protein. This statement expresses the rigid, one-way flow of information from DNA to organisms. DNA tells the RNA what to do, and RNA tells the proteins what to do. It is the tiny protein machines that assemble and operate all living organisms according to the genetic instructions they receive.

Yet the brain is not the first living form that has rebelled against the domination of the genes. Perhaps millions of years ago, a type of virus called a retrovirus partially reversed the dogma by evolving an amazing enzyme called reverse transcriptase that can use RNA to make DNA. The genetic material of the retrovirus is carried as RNA instead of DNA. When the retrovirus invades a healthy cell it takes over the cell's genetic machinery and uses its own RNA as a template to make new DNA. The retrovirus genes, now coded in DNA, are inserted into the host cell's chromosomes, which then become a factory for reproducing the retrovirus.

When molecular biologists discovered this phenomenon in 1970, they realized that by replacing retrovirus RNA with RNA of their own choice, the retrovirus could become a scalpel for redesigning the genes within a cell. Genetic engineering was born. The revolution against the central dogma begun by the retroviruses was completed by human beings. Proteins in the form of the brain selected RNA to be turned into DNA, which became the source of new genetic instructions for the cell: proteins made RNA, and RNA made DNA.

Now we begin to see the profound nature of our revolt. Evolution has unexpectedly produced an organ of the body that uses the accumulated experiences of a lifetime to communicate directly with DNA. Like all other organs, the brain is constructed by the genes using proteins. But it has evolved an independent code—what I call the synaptic code—that allows it to process and store information independently of the DNA. The brain can then use its stored information to modify the body's DNA through genetic engineering.

For example, if I decide (using my brain, naturally) that I am unhappy with a gene I have inherited that predisposes me to diabetes, genetic engineering will very soon become sophisticated enough to allow me to have that gene replaced with a healthy gene. I may even be able to engineer my germ line DNA—the DNA I pass on to my children—so that they, too, will never have the defective gene. In this way the central dogma of genetics has been turned upside down and the lowly proteins, in the form of the brain, have usurped the exclusive power that genes have wielded for the three-and-a-half billion years that life has existed on Earth. That is a truly astonishing revolution.

The brain's dominance over the genes reached new heights with the development in 1985 of the polymerase chain reaction (PCR) technique for amplifying slight traces of DNA into billions of copies that can be easily studied and manipulated. PCR takes place in a small machine that manipulates temperature and chemicals so that the DNA strands split apart and are used as templates to form more strands. The uses of PCR are limitless, from the so-called genetic fingerprinting of criminals and the pinpointing of genetic diseases to the amplification of DNA traces found in ancient plants and animals.

PCR is becoming to biology what the particle accelerator is to physics: a time machine. Already researchers have studied genetic material from a 12,000-year-old mastodon and a 17-million-year-old magnolia leaf preserved in shale.

It is genetic engineering and related techniques that are moving us to an era in which evolution will be dominated not by the genes but by the human brain. This revolutionary change, I believe, is part of an even larger revolution in which human beings in this century have uncovered the secrets of matter, life, and thought.

The brain not only is able to control life, it has also acquired the ability to manipulate matter. And it is beginning to be able to scientifically modify its own intelligence and its emotional states as well.

Gene-centered Darwinian evolution will never be eclipsed, but with the rise of brain-controlled evolution I contend that a new evolutionary synthesis is needed. The synthesis I propose is called unified selection and it extends the principles of evolution beyond the realm of life to the realms of matter and thought as well. Just as life evolves, I contend that ideas, planets, and all other forms of matter and thought evolve through a similar process of variation and selection.

The revolt of the brain caps centuries of scientific progress. Yet like all revolutions, it introduces enormous risks as well as great benefits. Our newly won control over matter, life, and thought can be used not only to heal and enhance but also to destroy and enslave. Nuclear weapons never could have been built without breakthroughs in understanding the quantum code. Our more recent ability to manipulate the fundamental character of minds and bodies poses even risks that are at least as sinister. They must be minimized, or instead of raising us to new heights this revolution could sweep us into extinction.

DARWIN'S LEGACY

What are the evolutionary chains that we are in the process of throwing off? Darwin was the first person to study them and systematically formulate their principles. In the *Origin of Species* he advanced four major propositions: first, that life evolves; second, that living things have a common ancestor; third, that evolution proceeds gradually, step by step; and, fourth, that the mechanism of evolution is natural selection.

When Darwin asserted that life has evolved, he meant that the world of life is not constant and stable but continually changes in accordance with understandable processes. New species bud off from older ones. Over time, most species become extinct.

To the Victorians, the most shocking implication of this idea was that humans and apes descended from the same stock. Darwin was mocked and caricatured mercilessly for daring to make such a ridiculous suggestion. Again, genetics has thoroughly vindicated him. Nucleotide-by-nucleotide comparisons of DNA sequences in chimpanzees and man have shown so few differences—less than one percent—that biologists wonder why the two species appear as different as they do. The latest studies indicate that chimpanzees are genetically closer to humans than they are to gorillas.

Darwin believed that every significant evolutionary adaptation could theoretically be traced through a series of steps in which the cumulative changes at each step served as the basis for further changes. As change accumulates in an organism, new adaptations become possible. Step-by-step evolution explains how organisms and their often extraordinarily complicated structures are cumulatively built up through a sequence of smaller changes. Eyes, wings, lungs, and human beings as a whole, for that matter, could no more have emerged in one step than a thoroughly mixed deck of cards could spontaneously order itself by suits after a few shuffles. But the emergence of biological structure can plausibly be understood as the end result of a long series of changes encompassing many, many generations.

Those who still find it difficult to believe that complex human beings could evolve from simple one-celled organisms should consider for a moment their own gestation and birth. Thanks to the information accumulated in human DNA over millions of years, a single fertilized egg cell evolves into a complete human being in nine months.

The marvelously complex human eye is the result of the elaboration of the photoreceptors in early one-celled organisms that helped orient these organisms in their environment by detecting the presence of light.

Human lungs, each of whose intricate branching structure enfolds a surface area of roughly seventy square yards, appear to have evolved from simple lunglike structures in fishes that lived in swamps, marshes, and similar environments with stagnant, poorly oxygenated water. Such simple lungs allowed these fish to take an occasional breath of air to supplement the oxygen produced by their gills. These fish gave rise to amphibians, which could live both in and out of water. Lungs supplanted gills in the land animals that evolved from amphibians. (In modern groups of fish that also descended from partially air-breathing fish, these simple lungs evolved into swim bladders, which have nothing to do with breathing. Swim bladders are oxygen-filled sacs that allow a fish to stop swimming and hover in the water. Sharks, a successful species that does not have this adaptation, must swim constantly or sink.)

The wings of birds appear to have originated with the small dinosaurs that were the birds' ancestors. All small animals have a high surface-to-volume ratio, which means they lose more heat than larger animals do and thus find it difficult to keep warm. In some small dinosaurs, scales appear to have evolved into feathers, which are very efficient insulators. In some of these animals, their feathered forelegs happened to become strong enough with respect to their body weight to permit gliding or short flights. We can speculate that such animals had a survival advantage in both escaping from predators and catching their prey. If so, they would have left more offspring than those animals that had feathers but could not fly at all. Thus the evolution of a new species—birds—began. Wings are an example of an important evolutionary principle: structures that evolve for one function, in this case to provide warmth, can be opportunistically adapted for another function, such as flight.

In recent years there has been a debate about the pace of evolution. One group of biologists who support a theory called punctuated equilibrium maintain that when new species are being formed the pace of evolution is very rapid in geologic terms—sometimes measured in thousands of years rather than millions. They contend that once a successful new species evolves, a long period follows in which it remains basically unchanged. Critics argue that these views are not significantly different from the views of many traditional biologists, who recognize that rapid evolutionary spurts can and do occur in some circumstances, but that most evolution is an eons-long process. In any event, both camps agree that evolutionary change proceeds in steps, not in miraculous leaps, whether those steps take millions of years, thousands of years, or even less time.

CREATIVE EVOLUTION

For Darwin, natural selection was the creative force in evolution. He argued that natural selection explains the changes in living things over time, including the emergence of new species, the persistence of older ones, the modification and extinction of still others, and the general tendency of organisms to adapt to their environments. Natural selection focuses on reproductive success.

Darwin made the crucial point that every organism is different, if only slightly, from every other. Many of these differences may be irrelevant to survival. But if a difference offers even a slight advantage in the ability to survive—swifter speed, keener eyes, more cunning camouflage—then that organism will have a better chance of leaving offspring, and more of them, than organisms without the advantage. If the advantageous trait can be inherited by the offspring, then they, too, will tend to be more successful. Over many generations, the adaptive trait will become widely dispersed among the members of the species because the more prolific forebears who originally had the trait will have more descendants represented in succeeding generations.

Natural selection is a purely mechanical explanation of evolution. It involves no grand purpose or design. Variations are produced at random with respect to their survival value. There is no necessary tendency toward progress. Organisms may become more complex, as did the evolutionary line leading to human beings, or remain simple, as with bacteria. Organisms may even lose complicated organs as they move into new environments. This is particularly true of parasites. The tapeworm, for example, has lost its digestive system, which it has no need of since it lives in the digestive system of its host.

Since the organisms best adapted to their particular environment are most likely to survive and produce offspring, it is not surprising that after thousands of generations of evolution we observe an amazingly good, but not perfect, fit between an organism and its environment. When the environment changes, however, selective pressure is applied to the species to change as well.

If the prey upon which a particular species feeds becomes faster and harder to catch, there will be strong selective pressure on the predator to compensate. Through natural selection, the predatory species may become faster as well, or more cunning. In every generation of predators, there will be a relatively small number of individuals that are slower than average, a similarly small number that are faster than average, and the majority whose speed falls somewhere in the middle. This distribution is described by the familiar bell-shaped curve. If there is a premium on speed, the faster members of the species will tend to catch more prey and, therefore, be in better health and produce more offspring. If greater speed has a genetic basis, then these offspring are more likely to be speedier than the offspring of slower parents. Over many generations the descendants of the faster animals will be heavily represented within the species and the genes for speed will be far more numerous in the species' gene pool. The bell-shaped curve for the species' speed will shift to the right, meaning the average speed of the species will increase, better adapting it to the demands of its environment.

Notice that the adaptation to the environment is not a certainty but only a tendency. It is probabilistic, like quantum mechanics, and does not provide clear-cut predictions for individual cases. Given two animals among the predators we have been discussing, one relatively fast and the other relatively slow, the faster animal is likely to leave more offspring. But chance may intervene and prevent this. The faster animal may be involved in an accident or be struck by an unexpected disease. Evolution only predicts that among a large number of animals over many generations, all other things being equal, the faster ones (in this example) will leave more offspring. In individual cases, the contingencies and uncertainties of history may prevent this from happening. In reality, there will be many traits—not just speed—interacting in complex ways. A faster animal with low intelligence might be less successful than a slower animal with high intelligence, for example.

Sometimes a number of organisms leave the main group to exploit a new habitat, the way amphibians left the water to live on land. If in adapting to the new environment the descendants of the breakaway population become so different from the parent group that they are unable to reproduce with members of that group, then a new species has been formed.

The fit between an organism and its environment is never perfect. Evolution does not adapt an organism from scratch. It can only work with the structures that are available. The basic body plan of all mammals includes four limbs. Natural selection has adapted these limbs in many ways, but it has not added a fifth (although the tail in some mammals has evolved to be almost a fifth limb). In man, the forelimbs have become versatile arms and hands. In bats, these limbs have become wings. In whales, they have become flippers. Yet the characteristic mammalian structure can be identified, bone by bone, in all these adaptations. The hind limbs and pelvis of humans have been adapted for upright posture rather than life on four legs, which is the rule for most mammals. But this adaptation has left us vulnerable to disorders of the knees and lower back.

These kinds of adaptations and imperfections are the telltale signs of natural selection at work, opportunistically adapting whatever structures are available. They are invaluable to biologists in tracing the pathways of descent among species. In designing new forms of life, time and natural selection are resourceful but not flawless.

By seeing clearly that living forms change through time and by proposing a mechanism to account for that change, Darwin transformed biology into one of the most dynamic of the sciences, a dynamism that has increased manyfold with the integration into Darwinism of the other great tributary of evolution: genetics. The combination of Darwinian evolution and Mendelian genetics has produced the magnificent synthesis that is one of the brain's most powerful weapons in its struggle to free itself from the domination of the genes.

"ARTIFICIAL" SELECTION

Through variation and selection, minds have created an extravagant array of new forms of matter, life, and thought. Yet Darwin tended to distinguish natural selection from "artificial" selection, which is the term for the efforts of human beings to shape evolution. This leaves the implication that humans are somehow outside of nature. My theory of unified selection combines natural and artificial selection, viewing human beings as a product of nature and human activities as eminently natural.

To buttress his arguments for evolution, Darwin referred to the successes of artificial breeding in producing strikingly different varieties of dogs, pigeons, and garden and agricultural plants. If breeders could succeed in generating such a rich variety of life in a relatively short time, he argued, then nature could surely produce the diversity of life on Earth over enormous stretches of time. Darwin was careful to point out, however, that breeders had only succeeded in creating varieties of plants and animals, which could normally continue to interbreed with parental stock, and not true species, which are reproductively isolated.

With the genetic breakthroughs of the past forty years, geneticists are now capable of creating new forms of life by combining the genes of widely different species. It appears likely that in the twenty-first century human-directed evolution will become the most important means of evolutionary change on Earth.

This process will not be limited to living things. By understanding the fundamental codes around which all contingent forms evolve, scientists are creating new forms of matter and thought. We have already seen a whole generation of new materials, from plastics to superconductors. And as we will see in Chapter 7, scientists have begun to significantly alter the functioning of the brain, using sophisticated new drugs and other techniques.

Colon cancer research has discovered one particular gene—the p53 gene on chromosome 17 (each of the twenty-three pairs of human chromosomes is given a number)—that also turns up in mutated form in many of the most common and deadly forms of cancer, including cancer of the lung, breast, skin, brain, and liver. The p53 gene (the name refers to a molecular weight of 53 kilodaltons) normally codes for a protein that controls the growth of cells. A mutation of a single nucleotide on the gene, however, can produce a malformed protein that pushes the cell into wild and uncontrolled growth, the hallmark of cancer. There is growing optimism that if ways can be found to correct or neutralize the mutation of the p53 gene, many forms of cancer might be cured.[4]

Once a malfunctioning gene is identified, what can be done about it? This is where genetic engineering is beginning to come to the fore. Geneticists are perfecting techniques for replacing defective genes with healthy genes using retroviruses, the small viruses that enter a cell and insert their genes in the cell's chromosomes. The most infamous retrovirus is the one that carries acquired immune deficiency syndrome (AIDS), which inserts genes into the victim's white blood cells that fatally depress the immune system. Yet some retroviruses do little damage because they do not carry such dangerous genetic cargo and, unlike other viruses, they do not destroy the cells they infect. Researchers have been able to remove most of the genes from certain retroviruses and replace them with other genes of their choosing. The custom-made retrovirus then becomes a vehicle—what scientists call a vector—for inserting the desired genes into the cell.

W. French Anderson used this technique to treat the young girl with inherited ADA deficiency mentioned on page 73. Since her body does not produce the adenosine deaminase gene that is essential for normal immune system functioning, the gene has been artificially inserted into retroviruses by Anderson. These retroviruses are mixed with her white blood cells, which in a matter of hours are infected with the healthy ADA gene. She then receives a blood transfusion containing the genetically engineered cells.[5]

Theoretically any gene could be inserted in a cell using this technique. Researchers have already reported successfully replacing the gene that causes cystic fibrosis—a severe lung ailment that is one of the most common genetic diseases among Caucasians—with a healthy gene in laboratory experiments. Despite these successes, extensive testing will be necessary to ensure that these kinds of treatments are safe and effective for human beings.

Many technical problems remain in ensuring that genetic engineering can introduce the right genes to the right cells in such a way that the genetic illness is cured. In addition, genetics itself has proven more complicated than researchers had thought. Mendel assumed that it was immaterial whether genes for the same trait were inherited from the mother or the father. But recent discoveries indicate that certain genes can have a different effect depending on from which parent they were inherited. Individuals who inherit the gene for Huntington's disease (a degenerative brain illness) from their father sometimes develop a more severe case at an earlier age than those inheriting the gene from the mother. This phenomenon is called parental imprinting and seems to involve genes from different parents reacting differently to the transcription and translation process in the nucleus.

Genetic engineering raises many ethical questions that will have to be answered as the technology evolves. Some are concerned that widespread genetic screening will lead to gene-based discrimination. Employers, insurance companies, and others might shun those considered to have unfavorable genes that might lead to illness or death.

A fundamental issue in the debate is the difference between germ cell and somatic cell genetic engineering. Germ cells are the reproductive cells in the body—the sperm and the egg. If the genes in these cells are manipulated, then the genetic endowment is permanently changed for all future generations. The individual conceived from the engineered sperm and egg will pass those genes to his or her offspring. In contrast, somatic cell therapy involves fixing the bodily cells but not the sex cells of an individual by splicing in a gene, for example. These changes are not inherited by the person's offspring. Most experts accept the need for somatic cell therapy but are just beginning to grapple with the implications of germ cell therapy. Should we merely seek to correct the gene for Huntington's disease in an individual or try to eliminate the gene from the germ cell so that no one will ever again inherit the disease? If we manipulate our germ cells, we will truly be controlling our own evolution, but the complexity of the human body and the uncertainty of evolution make the outcome of this control difficult to foresee.

Another of the many issues raised by genetic engineering is whether it should be used only to correct genetic problems or to enhance genetic fitness. It is conceivable that genes will be discovered that tend to increase intelligence, longevity, athletic ability, and so forth. Should these genes be spliced into the genome? Such a practice raises the specter of the kind of eugenics espoused by the Nazis. Yet the competitive pressures to seek this kind of therapy will be great. Laws limiting the availability of genetic enhancements would be difficult to enforce. Consider the widespread abuse of steroids and human growth hormone by athletes seeking a competitive edge, despite the illegality and obvious dangers.

These are not mere academic issues. We have already reached the stage where a couple can choose the sex of their child. British researchers recently announced that they have discovered the gene that determines whether a human embryo will develop into a girl or a boy. They identified the genetic switch—dubbed the testes-determining factor gene—that precipitates the development of testes rather than ovaries in the embryo.[6]

Meanwhile, another British team reported screening the embryos of five couples at risk of producing children with X chromosome-linked genetic defects including mental retardation. Fragile-X syndrome, the most common type of X-linked mental retardation, almost always occurs in males and has a frequency of approximately one in every 1,250 male births. Males are susceptible to genetic defects on the X chromosome because they have only one X chromosome along with their Y chromosome. As we have seen, females have two X chromosomes, one from each parent, and often one of these chromosomes will have a healthy copy of a gene that is defective in the other chromosome. The couples in Britain wanted to limit the risk of passing on X-linked genetic disorders by ensuring that their children were females. A number of eggs were removed from the women and fertilized in the laboratory. When one of the women's fertilized eggs had divided into six to eight cells a small amount of DNA was checked. Female embryos were identified and one of them was reimplanted in the woman's uterus. The rest were discarded. Within a six-month period, two of the five women became pregnant with normal female twins. [7]

This approach can be used to genetically screen the embryos not only for sex but for any other genetic trait. Theoretically, as more becomes known about the human genome, a couple could have a number of eggs fertilized in the laboratory and then pick the one with the preferred genetic endowment (or even a genetically engineered endowment) for reimplantation. The ethical issues are plainly enormous.

Just as genetics has illuminated the beginnings of life, it has begun to clarify the reasons for death. Genetic research may eventually lead us to treat aging and death like any other genetic ailment for which a treatment might be found. The result could be an enormous extension of the human life span, a development that would pose boggling problems for population control and the allocation of scarce resources.

Control of infectious diseases, better food and medical care, and improved sanitation have already lengthened life expectancy everywhere as compared with the turn of the century, and nearly doubled it in the developing world. The result is a rapidly growing world population that by 2001 is expected to grow by nearly one billion from its 1990 level of around 5.3 billion. If there are breakthroughs in research on aging, how will the planet support an even longer-lived population?

There are two basic theories of aging. One contends that aging is under genetic control; the other blames the accumulated wear and tear experienced by the cell as leading to its demise. The truth is probably a mixture of the two, but there is a growing body of evidence that the genes do have a role in programming death. The evidence comes in part from a paradox of medicine: the healthy cells of a human body are mortal, and naturally die after a specified period. Yet the body's unhealthiest of cells—cancer cells—are immortal. Somehow cancer cells have freed themselves from the normal constraints of growth and survival. This undisciplined growth is one reason cancer cells are so deadly. They crowd out normal cells.

By immortal, I mean that if we have a population of cancer cells in a laboratory dish (this is true of most, but not all, types of cancer) and we regularly nourish them, the cells will divide and replenish themselves indefinitely. The population of cells can theoretically live forever. But if we put a population of normal human cells in the dish and nourish them, they will divide about fifty times and then spontaneously die out (scientists call this senescing). The normal cells of every type of organism have a characteristic number of divisions they go through before dying. There are exceptions to this rule, however. Neurons, as we shall see in Part Three, do not divide at all during the human lifetime and can live as long as we do.

The longer the life span of the species, the more divisions its cells undergo. It is as if a biological aging clock were at work. Humans are an unusually long-lived species among vertebrates. Tortoises are the only documented vertebrate species that lives longer. Their cells divide about ninety times before dying out.

When we say that a person is seventy years old we do not mean that every one of the roughly ten trillion cells in his body has lived seventy years. They have not. Most cells live only a few days or weeks before dying and being replaced. What is critical for survival is that the cells reproduce accurately before they die. If they do, then the offspring cells can continue to do what the parent cell did and the total organism will not be affected. In the extreme case of cancer, cell reproduction goes out of control, threatening the existence of the entire population of cells that comprises the person.

An important part of aging seems to be a lack of accuracy and efficiency in reproducing new cells that take over when older ones die. Theoretical immortality for a human being would be achieved when accurate, robust cell division could continue indefinitely. The cells in such a person's body would be replaced many times, but the successor cells would be just as efficient at their tasks as the earlier ones were. For complex organisms, therefore, the concept of immortality applies to the continued functioning of the population of cells that make up the body, not endless survival of individual cells.

The only well-recognized method of significantly extending life span among animals is to adopt an extremely low-calorie diet, from sixty to sixty-five percent of normal food intake. In rats and mice such a diet can increase life span by fifty percent. Experiments are under way to see if this effect can also be found in primates. If so, human beings could theoretically extend their maximum life expectancy to 165 years from about 110. Investigators have not yet uncovered the reason for the longer life. Theories range from a possible reduction in the accumulation of damaging proteins and other molecules in the cell, to a slowing of cell division or a deceleration of some unknown genetic process.

Certain rare diseases seem to speed the aging process. The most ghastly is progeria or Werner's syndrome, a hereditary disease that affects children. By the time they are twelve, which is roughly their normal life expectancy, victims have the body of someone in his eighties or nineties. Science has not yet uncovered the genes that cause progeria, but the disease is a possible indication that elements of aging are under genetic control.

It is a supreme irony that one of our deadliest and most dreaded killers—cancer—may teach us the secret of immortality. The mechanism of aging probably involves not one gene but several interacting genes. Two recent studies of cancer cells have indicated that some of these genes may be found on human chromosome 1 and chromosome 4. In the first study, a population of cancerous hamster cells was combined through genetic engineering with the twenty-three human chromosomes. Most of the populations of immortal cells began to die after this fusion. The only exceptions were those populations that did not have copies of chromosome 1. Their immortality was unaffected.

In other words, in every combination of previously immortal cancer cells and chromosome 1, the cancer cells began to stop reproducing and die off. But when cancer cells were combined with all the other human chromosomes except chromosome 1, the immortality of the population of cancer cells was unaffected. The researchers concluded that a senescence gene or genes that causes cells to stop reproduction and die must be located on chromosome 1.

Another study found that chromosome 4 had a similar senescing effect on one kind of cancer—a line of cervical cancer cells—but not on other types of cancer.[8]

The greatest immediate practical use of an aging gene would not be to make humans immortal but to make cancer mortal. If we could somehow turn off cancer's unrestrained growth, the cancer cells would eventually die out and the body might recover.

Most cancer cells are immortal, but one price they seem to pay is that they are unspecialized. A liver cell that becomes cancerous loses its identity and functionality as a liver cell. It is not clear how mortality and specialization are linked, but it may be that a body that became immortal would be transformed into a blob of unspecialized cells. However, if cells could be coaxed into retaining their specialization while extending their life span (the number of divisions they undergo before senescing), then human life expectancy might substantially increase.

This is not some wild speculation, but a distant goal of sober scientists. One of the researchers in the chromosome 4 study expressed her hope that she would one day understand the genetic basis of the senescence of normal cells because "maybe then we will be able to intervene not just in the laboratory but in aging people."[9]

Genetic engineering is our most awesome tool for cutting free, at least in part, from the genetic chains that bind us. For millions of years the genes have ruled. As Richard Dawkins so trenchantly pointed out in his book, *The Selfish Gene*, "A body is the genes' way of preserving the genes unaltered."[10]

Genes struggle among themselves for survival using bodies as temporary vehicles. Once human beings have reproduced their genes, they become expendable. Many evolutionary biologists believe that bodies are designed to senesce and die after the prime reproductive years are over. A successful gene is theoretically immortal and can live for millions or billions of years in a succession of many bodies. Aging bodies are not worth the genetic cost of keeping them up.[11]

The evolution of the synaptic code, however, has allowed the lowly proteins that make up the brain to begin equalizing their relationship with the genes. By creating maps and models of the world and exchanging ideas with other minds, the brain has developed the means to tame the genes and put them at its service. But as with every revolution, if the revolutionaries are not willing to take up their new responsibilities in a vigorous, thoughtful, and humane way, the revolution will quickly collapse into chaos or tyranny and the new order will be worse than the old.

Under the old regime, we left it to the genes to decide whether a child would be normal or retarded, healthy or diseased, whether it would live or die. Now we—the collective minds of this world—must begin making these decisions.

Yet to responsibly exercise this new authority, we must clearly understand where we are and how we have gotten here. That is the purpose of this book: to point out that the human race in this century has achieved its greatest triumph by uncovering the three master codes of nature: the quantum code, the genetic code, and the synaptic code operating through evolution. With this triumph, enormous power is flowing into human hands, power that was once exercised by the genes and now will be wielded by the brain. We must prepare ourselves for the difficult and exhilarating choices that lie ahead by integrating a much deeper appreciation of science and its consequences into the population at large.

In this new era, human purpose and design must be fully integrated into our view of nature. I will argue in the next few chapters that purpose and design are something new in nature, at least on this planet. We can see their rudimentary functioning in other life-forms, but the culmination has come with the evolution of the human brain. Purpose and design result from the brain's ability to create a model of the environment in which it lives. This model can be used to test alternative courses of action and weigh consequences.

The fact that human beings have evolved the capacity for purpose and design as an extremely effective adaptive strategy does not imply that there is purpose and design in the larger universe. On the contrary, the evidence suggests that the brain and its capacities evolved through the purposeless mechanism of unified selection. It would be a mistake to project our sense of purpose on the universe as a whole.

Our capacity for purpose and design can be exaggerated in order to distinguish human beings from the rest of the natural world. Some argue that there is a major difference between works of nature and the works of human beings. Nature is opportunistic and must work with whatever is at hand in adapting organisms to their environment, even if the adaptation is not the optimal solution. Human beings, by comparison, can junk the old designs and start fresh in building their technology.

In reality, the theory that human beings can start from the beginning is an illusion. Our efforts to create designs and solve problems face limitations, just as the rest of nature does. One barrier is the limited pool of ideas from which we can draw to accomplish our tasks. We might call this our synaptic pool of ideas and behaviors: the brain's counterpart of the gene pool. If the ideas in the synaptic pool are inadequate to the problem and no new ideas are forthcoming, then the problem will not be solved or will be solved in an inefficient way. The new ideas that we might dream up are constrained because they are variations on the pool of old ideas.

A scientist or engineer in the early days of the nineteenth

century who sought to harness a new form of energy or find a mobile form of transportation could not be expected to invent the electric dynamo or the automobile, even though something was known about electricity and engines. It would be nearly half a century before James Clerk Maxwell would link electricity and magnetism in a way that suggested how the force could be harnessed on a large scale. And it would be at least that long until the principles of the internal combustion engine would be thoroughly understood. The need for energy and transportation at the beginning and end of the nineteenth century was basically the same; but the structure of ideas available in these two periods was much different.

The pool of ideas is a reservoir of variability available to our species to meet adaptive challenges. It grows through variation and selection, and as it grows the kinds of problems we can solve grow, too. The pool has been lavishly endowed with the legacy of the rational inquiry since the time of ancient Greeks. It has now become broad and rich enough to begin fathoming the seat of rationality itself—the mind—and to unlock the mind's fabulous secret: the synaptic code.

PART THREE

Code of Thought

Men ought to know that from the brain, and from the brain only, arise our pleasures, joys, laughter and jests, as well as our sorrows, pains, griefs and tears. Through it, in particular, we think, see, hear, and distinguish the ugly from the beautiful, the bad from the good, the pleasant from the unpleasant.

—ATTRIBUTED TO HIPPOCRATES, FIFTH CENTURY, B.C.

The Synaptic Code

THE FLOW OF UNDERSTANDING AS YOU READ THESE WORDS—AS YOU see the symbols printed on this page and translate them into meaningful concepts—reflects the miracle of the synaptic code. To someone with a brain injury affecting the ability of the code to function properly, these words would simply be so many meaningless squiggles. Imagine waking up one morning to find that all your books, newspapers, and memoranda were written in some incomprehensible script. This is exactly what happens to someone who has a stroke in a part of the brain necessary for reading comprehension.

As your eyes scan this page, an electrochemical system is at work. The photons of light reflected from the page are being detected by sensory cells, called rods and cones, in the back of your eyes. These cells, among other things, discern the shapes of the printed letters. A series of electrical and chemical signals is being sent from the rods and cones through a network of neurons to the visual cortex at the very back of the brain. The visual cortex, through its synaptic circuits, continually correlates the signals and produces a coherent image of what the eye is seeing. (This is why a blow to the back of the head can cause blindness.) The image is then transmitted via multiple processing pathways to the frontal lobes of the brain, which coordinate comprehension. Once the words are understood, the frontal lobes send signals, using motor neurons descending from the lobes, that tell the eyes to move to the next line. All this—detection, signaling, processing, and responding—happens in a fraction of a second.

The fundamental unit of what I call the synaptic code is the synapse, which is a highly specialized communications link sprouted by a type of information-processing cell that is unique to animals: the neuron. Synapses wire together the neurons in the brain. Over the last thirty years the one essential conclusion reached by most neuroscientists is that the secret of the brain's functioning resides in the pattern of synaptic wiring among neurons and the way this pattern dynamically changes during learning and memory. Neurons process information received from synapses and then use other synapses to pass on messages to other neurons. Synapses connect the billions of neurons in the brain into circuits that transmit both electrical and chemical messages, and the synaptic connections between neurons can strengthen or weaken as the brain learns and remembers.

"The essence of nervous organization is the establishment of synaptic circuits," as one leading neuroscientist puts it concisely. [1]

There is intense controversy about the precise mechanisms that underlie the synaptic network. Nevertheless, over the last decade neuroscience has made rapid progress in deciphering the synaptic code.

SYNAPTIC SIGNALING

The human brain is believed to have at least 100 billion neurons, each of which sends out an average of about 1,000 synaptic connections to other neurons and receives even more than that in return. When we try to calculate the different ways the neurons in a single brain can be linked together, the numbers quickly become astronomical—in the trillions—far greater than the number of stars in our galaxy. This staggering complexity is further revealed by the lavish amount of genetic information required to create the brain: of the approximately 100,000 genes needed to produce a human being, perhaps 30,000 code for aspects of the brain.

Human beings are born with all the neurons they will ever

have. Unlike most other cells in the body, which last only a few weeks before dying and being replaced, neurons are built to last a lifetime. Why is this? Many neuroscientists believe that since learning and memory are stored in the pattern of connections among neurons, the constant death and replacement of neurons would erase these patterns and force us to constantly relearn ideas and behaviors that are important for survival.

Yet a constant population of neurons does not imply a static brain. For the synaptic connections among these neurons are dynamic and constantly changing. As we learn and remember, new synapses can form and old ones disappear. The existing synaptic connections between particular neurons can grow stronger or weaker.

Figure 5.1 shows a schematic illustration of the synaptic con-

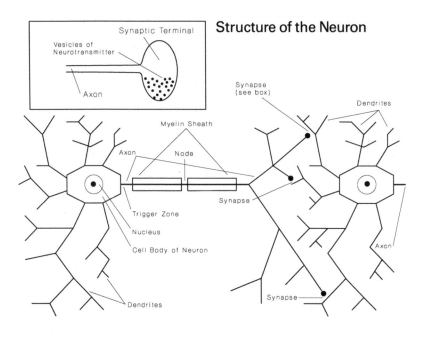

Figure 5.1. Two stylized neurons are shown with their axons and dendrites forming synapses. If the trigger zone on the axon of the neuron on the left is depolarized sufficiently, it will send an action potential through its axon to the neuron on the right. This action potential will trigger the release of vesicles of neurotransmitter in the synaptic terminals that stud the branches of the axon.

nections between two neurons. The typical neuron communications system includes a single sending wire, called an axon, over which messages are sent to other neurons, and a bushy antenna system made up of what are called dendrites. Although the axon starts off as a single projection from the main body of the neuron, it, too, branches out so that it can send messages to many neurons. The connection point between the axon sending wire and the dendrite receiving antenna is called the synapse. Synapses can also bypass the dendrites and form on the cell body of the neuron.

In the illustration, the neuron on the left is sending its axon to the dendrites of the neuron on the right. The axon carries an electrical impulse and in many cases is insulated with a substance called myelin. Within the brain, axons are usually short, but an axon that communicates with other parts of the body may be several feet long. The electrical signal is renewed at nodes or gaps between the myelin. A myelinated axon can carry an electrical signal at speeds of up to 400 feet per second, while the speed in an unmyelinated axon is less than two feet per second. Among other things, myelin allows the precise coordination of muscles that are a long distance away from the microscopic neurons in the brain. This is why multiple sclerosis and other diseases that attack the myelin sheath around axons are so devastating to muscle coordination.

You can see the three synaptic connections between the axon of the neuron on the left with the dendrites of the neuron on the right. The tips of the axons that make these connections are tiny bulbs called synaptic terminals. In an electrochemical synapse such as this, the terminals do not actually touch the dendrites. There is a microscopic gap called the synaptic cleft, as Figure 5.2 illustrates. The electrical signal in the axon does not jump to the dendrites as might be expected, but in most synapses it stimulates the release of chemicals called neurotransmitters into the synaptic cleft. There are about two dozen neurotransmitters, including serotonin, dopamine, and glutamate, and many more chemicals that affect their potency. After being stimulated by the electrical signal, neurotransmitters, which are contained in tiny sacs in the synaptic terminal, burst through the terminal membrane and flood across the synaptic cleft. They are detected by microscopic protein structures called receptors, which trigger electrical and chemical reactions in the receiving neuron.

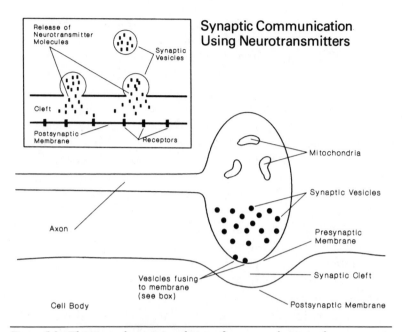

Figure 5.2. This is a schematic rendering of a synapse between the presynaptic terminal of an axon and a postsynaptic membrane. The axon is the signaling portion of the sending neuron and the postsynaptic membrane is the receiving portion of a second neuron. When the terminal is stimulated by an action potential (a kind of electrical impulse), tiny bubbles of neurotransmitter called vesicles fuse to the terminal wall and release their contents into the synaptic cleft. NMDA receptors and other kinds of receptors are embedded in the postsynaptic membrane and the chemical neurotransmitter may stimulate these receptors, prompting an electrical, chemical, or genetic response in the receiving neuron.

The elaborate structure of the electrochemical synapse permits complex networks to be set up among neurons. The messages that can be sent through these networks are exceptionally varied. Messages can vary depending on which neurotransmitter is used, how much is released into the synaptic cleft, how long it remains in the cleft, and what kind of receptors are detecting it.

This chapter and the two that follow will put forward a theory of the brain, building the higher functions of thought out of the elaborate interconnections of neurons and synapses. I argue that synaptic connections form electrochemical circuits among neurons, which are the most basic units for processing information in the brain. The mechanism underlying the formation of synaptic circuits is still being uncovered but it virtually always seems to involve the flow of calcium ions into the neuron. Calcium ions (Ca^{2+} or Ca^{++}) are simply atoms of calcium that are missing two electrons and thus have a positive electrical charge of $+2$.

Neuroscientists have come to believe that the process of memory-formation goes something like this: when the synapses of one or more neurons signal a target neuron strongly and repeatedly, calcium flows into the target neuron, beginning a series of biochemical changes that culminates in turning on a certain set of genes in the target neuron. These genes produce proteins that can permanently enhance the synaptic connections between the neurons. There is also evidence that, in some cases, the calcium flow is enhanced in the signaling neurons as well, which increases the flow of neurotransmitters across the synapse. Through this interaction between electrical, chemical, and genetic signals, long-term memories are formed.

The flow of calcium and other chemicals in and out of the neuron is controlled by tiny receptors and other protein structures embedded in the outer membrane of the neuron. These structures act as switches, turning on and off the chemical, electrical, and genetic machinery in the neuron as well as establishing, strengthening, weakening, and breaking the synaptic connections between one neuron and another. In Chapter 6 we shall examine in detail one of these switches, the NMDA receptor, which appears to be essential in many forms of learning and memory.

As the brain interacts with its environment, synaptic circuits combine to form synaptic maps of the world perceived by the senses. These maps describe small segments of that world—such as shape, color, and movement—and are scattered throughout the brain. As the brain's synaptic network evolves, beginning in earliest childhood, these maps process information simultaneously and in parallel, and their output coalesces into synaptic models that combine the fragments of perception into coherent wholes. The human brain, which has doubled in size to about three pounds over the last million years, has evolved the most sophisticated synaptic model of all: consciousness and its handmaiden, language.

Neuroscientists have marveled at the way the brain maps its

environment. As the leading neuroscience text, *Principles of Neural Science*, observes:

> The most striking feature of the organization of sensory systems is that the inputs from the peripheral receptor sheet (the body surface, the cochlea [ear], or the retina [eye]) are systematically mapped onto structures of the brain. These maps do not correspond point for point with the size and shape of the periphery but reflect the relative importance to perception of a particular part of the receptive sheet. Thus, the tips of our fingers have a large representation in the brain, whereas the skin on our back has a small representation.[2]

In calling my theory of brain function the synaptic code, I am making an explicit analogy with the genetic code. Just as the structure of an organism is translated into a population of genes contained in the DNA, the structure of the world is translated into a population of synapses contained in the brain. The human brain has evolved the capability to use the information recorded by the synaptic network to construct the maps and models we call learning, memory, and consciousness.

The existence of a synaptic code is virtually certain. But the precise structure of the code is still controversial. I believe we are now in the same stage of creative ferment today that existed in genetics during the decade prior to 1953, when Watson and Crick discovered the structure of DNA. The reader should be aware that there are many alternatives to the ideas I will be presenting in these chapters, and there is an enormous amount of information that remains to be learned about the brain. Nevertheless, I am confident that the final formulation of the synaptic code will resemble the theory that I have sketched above and will discuss more fully in the following pages.

GOLGI V. CAJAL

The crucial insight that the neuron is the primary information-processing element in the animal nervous system required a long and difficult intellectual struggle that took most of the last century and part of this one. The story began with the discovery that living organisms are made up of cells. This was a by-product of a seventeenth-century technological advance in grinding glass into curved surfaces. From these lenses the microscope and telescope were created, instruments that would forever change our ideas about the very small and the very large. In the 1830s, using evidence gathered from their microscopes, two German biologists—Matthias Jakob Schleiden and Theodor Schwann—proposed the cell theory, which states that all living things are constructed from cells, either single cells or populations of cells.

As the cell theory was accepted, scientists wondered if the brain and nervous system are also organized around cells. The question was maddeningly difficult to answer because nervous tissue is so tangled with synaptic connections that even under a microscope it is not clear whether it is one continuous substance or divided into discrete elements.

The question remained unresolved until a struggling Italian physician, Camillo Golgi, while working in his kitchen in 1873, found a particular kind of stain that makes the entire structure of individual nerve cells visible, down to the finest filament. His discovery was generally ignored until fifteen years later when the Spanish anatomist, Santiago Ramón y Cajal, began using the same method and publicized his findings in a torrent of brilliant publications. The study of the nervous system was transformed. Cajal has left a memorable record of his first impressions on looking at a neuron stained using the Golgi method:

> Against a clear background stood black threadlets, some slender and smooth, some thick and thorny, in a pattern punctuated by small dense spots, stellate or fusiform. All was sharp as a sketch with Chinese ink on transparent Japan-paper. And to think that that was the same tissue which when stained with carmine or logwood left the eye in a tangled thicket where sight may stare and grope for ever fruitlessly, baffled in its effort to unravel confusion and lost for ever in a twilit doubt. Here, on the contrary, all was clear and plain as a diagram. A look was enough. Dumbfounded, I could not take my eye from the microscope. [3]

Yet even when they are stained, the problem with neurons, as Cajal indicated, is that they sprout a thick underbrush of branches that are exceptionally difficult to untangle when looking at more than one or two neurons at a time. This led to decades of debate over whether neurons are separate cells or part of a mass of inter-connected tissue. Golgi believed that neurons were illusory—that they were not separate but were parts of one continuous mass of nerve tissue. Cajal strenuously argued that neurons were indepen-dent cells and through his unceasing efforts, and the efforts of many others, the neuron doctrine came to be an accepted corollary of cell theory. According to the neuron doctrine, neurons are the primary information-processing cells in the brain and nervous system. There is one other major type of nerve cell, the glia, but they are subsidiary to the neuron.

When Golgi and Cajal shared the Nobel Prize for Physiology or Medicine in 1906, the debate over the neuron doctrine was still raging. Golgi, in fact, never fully accepted the structural autonomy of neurons and criticized the neuron doctrine in his Nobel lecture. Nevertheless, with the identification of the neuron the stage was set for a great drama that is still going on: the deciphering of the syn-aptic code.

Just as physics was revolutionized by Einstein and Planck at the dawn of the twentieth century and biology was transformed by the rediscovery of Gregor Mendel's work in genetics at about the same time, neuroscience also entered the new century in the middle of a revolution. It is fascinating to note that each was based on a fun-damental particle: the quanta, the genes, and the neurons. In the 1890s, while Cajal was struggling to establish the existence of the neuron, he and a number of researchers wondered how these neu-rons were integrated into a functioning nervous system. It was Cajal himself who proposed that changes in the strength of connections among neurons might be the key to understanding the nervous system.

Painstakingly, biologists began to distinguish between two types of structures that sprout from the cell body of the neuron, the central part of the cell that contains the nucleus. The first, as described above, is a single thin axon that shoots out toward other neurons, often sprouting branches on its far end. The other is the bushy dendrites that surround the cell body and are in contact with axons from other neurons. While a neuron can have only one axon, it may have hundreds of dendrites.

Observers like Golgi believed that axons and dendrites were physically connected to other neurons, making the nervous system one large complex organ, something like an oversized spider web crumpled into a ball. Cajal and other researchers who were convinced that the nervous system, like other organs, is constructed out of autonomous cells, argued that there must be a special way neurons connect with each other. In 1897 an English physiologist, Charles Sherrington, made a proposal:

> So far as our present knowledge goes, we are led to think that the tip of a twig of the arborescence [of a neuron] is not continuous with but merely in contact with the substance of the dendrite or cell body on which it impinges. Such a special connection of one nerve cell with another might be called a *synapse*.[4]

Synapse is derived from the Greek word *sunaptein*, which means to fasten together. It is the synapses that knit neurons together into the circuits that process information and determine behavior. The more intensively neurons are studied, the more similarities biologists find between neurons and the other cells of the body. The one quality that has remained unique, however, is the synapse. No other kind of cell uses this structure. Hidden within its intricacies is the key to the synaptic code and the solution to the riddle of intelligence and consciousness.

I would argue that just as any organism based on the genetic code is a form of life, any organism using the synaptic code to process information is engaging in thought. The thoughts may be rudimentary, but they are nevertheless primitive examples of the kinds of information processing that goes on in our brains. As we shall see, there is an enormous difference between rudimentary thought and consciousness, but consciousness evolved out of the simplest kinds of synaptic processing, just as complex forms of life evolved from simpler ones. Thus the origin of thought coincides with the origin of the synapse.

Synaptic communication seems to have originated about 500 million years ago with the evolution of the fast-moving multicellular organisms we call animals. Organisms made of many cells require a means of coordinating the activities of those cells. But the newly evolving animals made far greater demands on this communication system than did plants and other older forms of life. It is instructive to contrast synaptic communication with a more ancient method of communication, signaling through hormones, that evolved in multicellular plants.

HORMONE COMMUNICATION

Any biological communication system, whether the nervous system or the endocrine system, must be able to detect a stimulus, generate a signal, process the signal, and respond. Even simple organisms like the common intestinal bacteria *E. coli* have evolved such a system. A single-celled *E. coli* orients itself so that it moves toward favorable regions and away from potential threats. It does this by constantly sampling its environment with thousands of receptor molecules that are built into its cell membrane. Once a receptor is stimulated by something in the environment, say sugar, a signaling chemical is released inside the *E. coli* cell. This signaling chemical is called a second messenger, and it diffuses in the cell fluid to the portions of the cell that process information.

This processing is a kind of voting. All the messages from all the receptors are continuously being summed up: the second messengers that signal favorable environmental chemicals are netted against those signaling less favorable or even dangerous chemicals. Using this kind of arithmetic, the *E. coli* remains aware of the nature of its environment, and sends electrical signals to its flagella (tiny propellerlike organs) directing them to adjust their orientation so as to propel it toward the most favorable part of its environment, which may contain a source of food.

E. coli are procaryotes, a class of organisms that lack a well-defined cell nucleus. They are among the earliest forms of life on Earth. Yet in this simple life-form are the rudiments of two different communication systems: chemical and electrical. Most plants, using hormones, evolved a variation of the chemical system. Using neurons and synapses, animals added an electrical system to supplement chemical communication.

Hormones are specialized chemicals that when released by certain cells diffuse through an organism's body fluids, influencing the behavior of other cells. The target cells must have a way of detecting these chemicals. Some hormones, such as small-molecule steroids, are made of fatty substances that can ooze through the cell's outer membrane and interact directly with its internal machinery. Other hormones are made of larger molecules and cannot penetrate the cell membrane. They must be recognized by the cell through an elaborate set of receptors embedded in the membrane, which act as chemically activated switches. These receptors, made of protein, protrude out of the cell membrane and have special areas that are shaped so that specific hormone molecules fit into them, just as a key fits into a lock. When a hormone molecule triggers a receptor, the receptor changes shape, activating some additional process in the cell: the receptor may start a chemical reaction in the cell or open a channel in the membrane that lets outside substances into the cell. By activating receptors, hormones can control the cell's internal machinery, even turn specific genes in the cell on and off.

Control through hormones is an ingenious method of orchestrating the activities of millions of cells. As a system of communication, however, hormones are slow.

Unlike plants, which usually make their food from sunlight and water, animals are predators that feed on other organisms. They must find their food or starve. A more rapid communication system was required.

Evolution rarely starts anew, with no regard to what has gone before. It opportunistically builds on whatever variations are available. No organism can escape history. All the twists and turns of an organism's evolutionary past provide both opportunities for and constraints on its future development. Animals continued to use hormones as the basic communication system for activities such as growth and digestion. All the while a parallel communication and control system—the nervous system—was evolving that yoked the speed of electrical impulses with the subtlety of chemistry. As the nervous system evolved so did a new type of cell, the neuron, and a new mechanism by which neurons use the receptors on other cells both to communicate with them and control their behavior. That mechanism was the synapse.

Every animal's body performs a delicate ballet between the nervous system and the endocrine system (it is the endocrine glands that secrete hormones). When an animal's nervous system senses danger, for instance, the adrenal glands pour the hormone adrenalin into the bloodstream. Adrenalin turns off nonessential muscles, such as those in the digestive system, and redirects their blood supply to the muscles that control movement. The endocrine system thus prepares the muscles for the rapid action that will be required by the brain as it calculates how best to meet the danger.

One-celled organisms that move through the environment had developed methods of responding to their surroundings using both chemical and electrical signals. In fast-moving, multicellular organisms, this evolved into a new system—synaptic communication—that harnessed rapid electrical impulses with complex chemistry.

There are dozens of chemicals that are active in the brain, with more being discovered all the time. Perhaps fewer than twenty of these are true neurotransmitters that are released from presynaptic vesicles into the synaptic cleft. The others have complex and subtle effects on such factors as the sensitivity of receptors and the extent of neurotransmitter release. Some chemicals are slow-acting, others are fast-acting.

Brain chemicals did not appear out of nowhere. Evolution, ever opportunistic, recycled many chemicals that are used elsewhere in the body to control the functioning of cells. Outside the brain, the body uses an array of hormones to control cell behavior, including the functioning of genes with the cell. The hormone system controls digestion and many other automatic bodily functions. Substances that function as hormones elsewhere in the body serve different but equally important roles in the brain.

Hormones and neurotransmitters rely for much of their effect on receptors, which are the switches in the cell for turning on and off many kinds of chemical changes. The two creative masterpieces of evolution on Earth are the genetic code and the cell. Yet the control of the cell's machinery through receptors is nearly as impressive. The receptor strategy is used throughout the body. Receptors in the immune system identify dangerous organisms that must be destroyed. Hormones accomplish much of their control through activating and deactivating receptors. In the brain, receptors that are sensitive to the same neurotransmitter may have completely opposite effects on the cell. What is important, therefore, is not so much what neurotransmitter is being used but exactly how the receptor changes the cell after it is switched on by the transmitter. It is like turning on two identical light switches and finding that one controls the living room lamp while the other turns off the heat. In a real sense, the brain has a receptor code rather than a chemical code, and this code is modeled on the receptor principle that operates throughout the cells of the body.

KEYBOARD OF THOUGHT

The crucial component in the neural network is the neuron's cell membrane. The cell membrane is the delicate skin of the cell. Within it is the cell's watery protoplasm and nucleus. Yet aside from the genes themselves, the membrane is one of the most versatile structures in the realm of life. The membrane of the neuron is so versatile it is almost magical. There is nothing else like it on Earth. The cell membrane gives the neuron its distinctive shape, often with luxuriously branching patterns of dendrites and axons. It is the neuron's membrane that conducts an electrical impulse. Although all cell membranes have an electrical potential, only the cell membrane of the neuron has evolved a special structure—the synapse—to use this impulse to communicate among nerve cells. The synapse is the specialized contact point between the cell membranes of two neurons.

To use a rough metaphor, the neuron's cell membrane is like the keyboard of a tiny but sophisticated computer. Embedded in the membrane are special receptor proteins that might be compared to the keys on a keyboard. Synapses are the hands that reach out from other neurons to type messages on this keyboard of receptors. The fingers on these hands are often chemical neurotransmitters, which press the keys with infinite subtlety—more like the carefully modulated playing of a piano than the typing of a typewriter. Just as pressing the keys of a computer keyboard sends signals to the core of the machine for processing, so chemical fingers typing on the receptor keyboard send signals that are processed inside the cell. Receptors do not turn on and off like light switches. They constantly flicker by the millions between on and off states. This makes them a particularly sensitive system for amplifying minute fluctuations, including quantum fluctuations.

Once the synaptic code is completely understood, we will be able to decipher the messages that are transmitted via the cell membrane's receptors and understand how the messages change the internal chemistry of the neuron, often making it more or less receptive to future messages.

The organization of the brain, like the organization of the universe itself, is not neat and simple. It is messy and variable. This variability is reflected by the fact that there is no truly typical neuron. They are all different in ways that range from subtle to significant. But as Figure 5.1 illustrates, there are certain basic characteristics we can identify. The neuron has a nucleus that contains the full complement of the genes the organism was born with. Only a subset of genes operates in each cell, allowing cells to differentiate and specialize. The cell is surrounded by a membrane that contains receptors and ion channels, made of protein molecules. These are essential to the functioning of the synaptic code.

The structures that the membrane forms on its surface are what make the neuron unique. Since the neuron can generate an electrical signal, it often has a long, thin extension leading away from the cell body. This is the axon. Bundles of axons form nerves and may be several feet long as they wire the brain with all parts of the body.

The neuron's antennae of dendrites are often covered with smaller spiky branches called spines. These spines are particularly important for information processing and form smaller circuits within the larger circuits created by the axons.

There are two basic kinds of synaptic connections between neurons: electrical and chemical. In the electrical connection, the axon terminal (called the presynaptic site) almost touches a patch of membrane on the dendrite (the postsynaptic site). In fact there may be tiny filaments actually connecting the two. This contact is so intimate that flows of ions can jump across it with comparative ease.

Yet by far the greatest number of synapses in the brain are chemical, not electrical (remember that a human brain is thought to have about 100 billion neurons and each neuron may have a thousand, ten thousand, or sometimes even more synapses). At a chemical synapse, the axon terminal (or terminal bulb) is somewhat farther away from the membrane of the neuron with which it is communicating than with an electrical synapse, although the distance is still tiny. The axon manufactures sacs of neurotransmitters that are transmitted to the membrane and burst into the synaptic cleft (the process of exocytosis). The molecules of neurotransmitter then drift across the synaptic cleft and are registered by the appropriate receptors in the postsynaptic membrane. The receptor may change shape on contact with the neurotransmitter and open a channel that allows ions to flow through the cell membrane. Based on the summation of thousands of these chemical contacts, the neuron decides whether to fire a burst of electricity called an action potential or whether to remain silent.

Electrical synapses are used for very rapid communication, because there is no chemical threshold that must be crossed and electric charges can move rapidly from cell to cell. They are linear communications points. These kinds of connections are often used for reflexes that are important to the survival of the organism.

If you have ever tapped the side of a goldfish bowl, you may have seen the fish dart away. The tail-flip mechanism has been found to be controlled by a large neuron in the fish's brain stem that receives sensory signals via electrical synapses. When the signals exceed a threshold, the tail flips and the fish darts out of danger. The response is automatic and predictable.[5]

Unlike the all-or-nothing response of electrical synapses, chemical synapses are capable of exquisite control in the processing of information. Their response to a signal can be strong or weak or somewhere in between. Chemical communication is nonlinear. Its signals are not necessarily proportional to the inputs. Chemical synapses amplify information, by releasing more neurotransmitters, or inhibit it by releasing less. It is through the web of nonlinear chemical communication that higher brain functions have developed. This is why the human brain has so few electrical synapses. Complex thought must be adaptable, not automatic.

All cells maintain concentrations of chemicals and stores of electrical charges that are out of equilibrium with their surroundings. To a cell, sustained equilibrium means death. Since molecules are constantly entering and leaving, the cell must expend energy to reestablish the original differential concentrations. Positive ions may have to be pumped out of the cell or certain chemicals pumped into the cell. This requires working against the thermodynamic forces that seek to push the cell to equilibrium, and this is an energy-draining process. An estimated thirty to forty percent of the energy used in a resting human body goes to maintaining the unequal electrical and chemical concentrations in the cells. That percentage is even higher in the brain.

The cell membrane of the neuron is constructed from a double layer of phospholipids, a kind of fatty molecule. Embedded in the cell membrane are a wide assortment of protein molecules that serve as selective gateways into and out of the cell. These membrane proteins are like tiny machines that enable cells to accomplish an amazing variety of tasks, including the thought process itself. A striking characteristic of membrane proteins is their exceptional variety of shapes. Some proteins can even change their shape when exposed to certain molecules. Evolution has seized on these shapes for many different purposes.

Membrane proteins perform five major functions: they serve as channels, pumps, receptors, enzymes, and structural proteins. As channels and pumps, certain uniquely shaped membrane proteins form mechanisms for allowing specific atoms and molecules to pass back and forth through the cell membrane. Other than small lipid molecules such as steroids, substances cannot pass through the phospholipid cell membrane unless they pass through these protein gates. In this way the cell selects for its own purposes only a few of the chemical variations present in its environment.

Receptors are protein molecules with a portion of their structure protruding from the cell. This protruding structure has been compared to a lock. It has a particular shape into which only a certain molecule fits (the key). When the proper molecular key finds its way into the receptor lock, the membrane protein changes shape, causing further changes in the cell. The three-dimensional surface structure of a protein is crucial to its biological activity.

Enzymes in the membrane produce important chemical reactions. Enzymes are catalysts that are not changed in the reactions they stimulate. Most enzymes are proteins and many have the ability to take on more than one shape. Shape-changing enzymes are termed allosteric. In one particular shape, an allosteric enzyme may be inactive. But if it changes shape, the same enzyme becomes active in stimulating chemical changes.

The membrane's structural proteins maintain the configuration of the cell. They also attach to other cells to form larger structures—organs such as the heart and the brain, and, ultimately, the body itself.

These five functions are not mutually exclusive. A membrane protein may be both a pump and a receptor, for example.

The simplest kinds of protein channels pierce the membrane and allow specific atoms and molecules that have the proper shape to squeeze through. The channel may also have an electrical charge that facilitates the flow of the correct ions and repulses others. Most cells maintain a high internal concentration of potassium ions. To keep this concentration from becoming too high, special protein channels in the cell membrane allow potassium ions to slowly diffuse out of the cell.

Still another kind of cell membrane structure particularly important to the synaptic code is the gated channel. Here, the membrane protein serves as a gate through the cell membrane that can be opened and closed. There are two general varieties of channel: voltage-gated channels and chemically gated channels.

The voltage-gated channel is formed from a protein molecule that is extremely sensitive to changes in the voltage, or electrical charge, in the surrounding membrane. The reason for this sensitivity is that crucial parts of the protein molecule are themselves electrically charged. When the voltage of the membrane changes, the electrically charged parts of the channel are affected, through electromagnetic attraction and repulsion, and cause the protein molecule to change shape. This change in shape has the effect of opening the channel and allowing specific ions—usually sodium (Na^+), calcium (Ca^{2+}), potassium (K^+), or chloride (Cl^-)—to pass in or out of the cell. Voltage-gated channels enable neurons to generate electrical impulses. Neuroscientists have found many kinds of these channels, each of which allows the neuron's electrical impulse to be altered in a distinctive way. The membranes of different kinds of neurons are studded with different densities and different varieties of voltage-gated channels.

Voltage-gated potassium and calcium channels are thought to have evolved about 1.4 billion years ago at the same time a new kind of cell evolved: the eucaryotic cell. Until that time, the single-celled bacteria that dominated the Earth had a simple cell structure that contained no well-defined nucleus and no tightly bundled chromosomes. DNA in these organisms is scattered throughout what is called the procaryotic cell. Eucaryotic cells, in contrast, contain a well-defined nucleus that holds the DNA. There are other structures within the cell, including mitochondria, which are tiny energy-producing factories. Eucaryotic cells with their chromosomes made sexual reproduction possible, which provided much greater genetic variability in offspring. Procaryotic cells normally just clone themselves. All complex multicellular forms of life are built from eucaryotic cells.

About 500 million years ago, voltage-gated sodium channels evolved. These channels, as we shall see, are essential for the rapid communication of electrical signals and were essential to the evolution of animals.

The chemically gated channel, in contrast, is opened by neurotransmitters and other chemicals rather than electrically. When the channel's receptor—the portion of the membrane protein that is protruding from the cell (the lock)—makes contact with a properly shaped neurotransmitter (the key), the configuration of the protein changes, opening the gate and allowing certain ions to enter the cell. The neurotransmitter key unlocks the gate into the cell.

Neurotransmitters are released at the synapses and are detected by these receptors. The flow of ions through chemically gated channels may either change the electrical charge of the membrane, affecting the voltage-gated channels, or activate a second messenger, which results in chemical changes in the interior of the cell.

Second messenger systems are very common throughout the body, but are particularly important in the brain. The neurotransmitter is the first messenger, which triggers the receptor, changing the shape of the membrane protein. This change in shape either causes the release of a second messenger substance inside the cell or opens a gate that allows a second messenger to enter the cell. The critical distinction is that the first messenger does not enter the cell; it only activates a receptor, which changes the shape of the membrane protein and causes other chemicals to do work inside the cell. The first messenger sends its message into the cell via the second messenger. Second messenger systems may be highly complex, involving many steps that bring cascades of changes within the cell that neuroscientists are only beginning to understand. Returning to our keyboard metaphor, the first messenger presses the protein key on the cell membrane, sending a signal into the heart of the cell in the form of a second messenger.

Neuroscience has revealed a large number of neurotransmitters that stimulate receptors on the surface of the cell membrane. Yet there seem to be relatively few second messengers that act within the cell. The same second messenger, however, can have different effects in different cells depending on the precise chemical composition of the cell.

With respect to learning and memory, calcium is the most important second messenger. Evidence is rapidly accumulating that the flow of calcium ions into the neuron serve as the impresario of thought, coordinating the wiring of synapses.

CHAIN REACTION

The dynamic electrical activity of the neuron membrane is generated by the varying concentrations of inorganic ions: potassium, sodium, calcium, and chloride. Most cells, including neurons, have a greater concentration of negatively charged ions within their membranes than in the outside fluid. The imbalance gives them a net charge of roughly -65 millivolts with respect to their surroundings. This "resting potential" is the neuron's charge when it is not being disturbed by ion inflows or outflows. This seemingly tiny charge is actually a very strong electrical force given the microscopic thinness of the membrane. Unlike other cells, neurons have evolved a way to use this electrical charge for communication.

The electrical imbalance across the cell membrane is responsible for the action potential, the neuron's most characteristic method of signaling. The action potential is the electrical signal that propagates down the axon. The action potential is an all or nothing phenomenon. Once the electrical charge at a crucial portion of the neuron's membrane called the trigger zone is reduced sufficiently—depolarized—the neuron fires the action potential.

To depolarize the membrane means to make it less negative with respect to the outside of the cell (for example, reducing the negative charge from -65 millivolts to -55 millivolts). When the membrane becomes significantly less negative, a chain reaction is set off, and the result is the action potential. To hyperpolarize the membrane is to make it more negative (for example, increasing the negative imbalance from -65 millivolts to -75 millivolts). This makes the firing of an action potential less likely.

This seems more complicated than it is. Basically when the synaptic connections to a target neuron result in a net increase in the neuron membrane's positive charge—by allowing sodium ions (Na^+) to flow into the cell, for example—then the neuron is likely to fire an action potential. On the other hand, if the net effect of the synaptic connections is to make the neuron more negative—by allowing chloride ions (Cl^-) to flow in, for example—then the membrane is moved farther away from the firing threshold and an action potential is less likely. Adding a positive charge excites the neuron; adding a negative charge inhibits the neuron from firing an action potential.

When a synapse releases its neurotransmitter across the synaptic cleft to a target neuron, those neurotransmitter molecules can change the electrical charge of the target neuron's membrane by opening or closing ion channels into the membrane. These electrical changes caused by the release of neurotransmitters at synapses are called synaptic potentials.

The distinction between synaptic potentials and action potentials is crucial to grasping the nature of the synaptic code. Synaptic potentials are the passive currents that flow through the membrane as receptors open ion channels in response to neurotransmitters. Synaptic potentials result from the fact that the cell body and its dendrites are studded with many synaptic connections—often thousands. Many or all of these may be stimulated in a fraction of a second. The response to this stimulation at each postsynaptic site (remember, the postsynaptic site receives the signal while the presynaptic site generates the signal) can be either depolarization, making the axon more likely to fire, or hyperpolarization, making it less likely. The neuron is constantly adding up these contradictory signals to see whether the threshold for firing has been reached. This is one of the most basic ways the neuron processes information.

An action potential is generated when the process of netting the positive against the negative synaptic potentials results in a sufficient electrical flow to depolarize (make more positive) the trigger zone, which is the portion of the membrane at the base of the axon. (See Figure 5.1.) When the trigger zone's threshold of about -55 millivolts is reached, an electrical impulse is generated from the zone down the axon to the terminal bulbs. At a chemical synapse, this causes the terminals to release packets of neurotransmitter—called sacs—into the synaptic cleft.

The long-distance transmission of an impulse down the axon is accomplished through an increased concentration of sodium ion (Na^+) channels along the axon membrane. These are special channels because they are voltage-sensitive. When these channels are opened there is a positive feedback, or self-amplification, mechanism that opens more channels, because the flow of electrical current of positively charged sodium ions depolarizes additional channels. If the net amount of inflowing sodium ions (attracted by the negative cell interior) exceeds the outflow of other ions, there is an explosive but brief influx of sodium ions which propagates down the axon as the action potential. This is called a wave of depolarization, because the positive sodium ions temporarily reduce the negative charge inside the membrane. It resembles a row of falling dominoes as one voltage-gated channel after another opens up, allowing the influx of sodium ions down the axon. The number of sodium ions crossing the membrane is relatively small, but it is sufficient to depolarize the membrane from -65 millivolts to about $+55$ millivolts. When the roughly $+55$ millivolt level is reached, the sodium ion channels are suddenly shut off. The total time the channels are open is only a few thousandths of a second. (See Figure 5.3.)

The action potential is a form of amplification, somewhat similar to the amplification role played by a transistor in an electrical circuit. The impulse generated by the action potential appears as a

The Action Potential

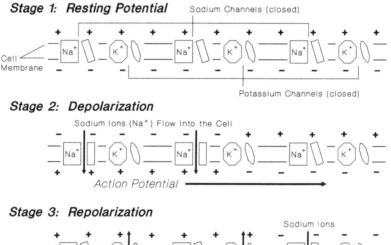

Figure 5.3. At the resting stage, the sodium and potassium channels in the cell membrane are closed. The inside of the membrane is relatively negatively charged with respect to the outside. Depolarization begins in Stage 2 as the voltage-sensitive sodium channels open, letting sodium ions flow into the cell, briefly changing its charge to positive with respect to the outside of the membrane. As the explosive action potential proceeds from left to right in Stage 3, the potassium channels begin to open, allowing potassium ions to flow out of the cell, returning it to the resting potential.

spike on an oscilloscope. The amplitude of the spike remains the same all the way down the axon. This wave of depolarization is followed by a wave of repolarization, in which potassium ions are pumped out of the axon so that it is ready for another action potential. Some neurons can spike several hundred times per second. Although basic electrical characteristics of the cell membrane have been known for almost forty years, the detailed molecular biology of action potentials (spiking), synaptic potentials, and related phenomena was not worked out until the 1980s.

The term "action" refers to the fact that the impulse is much stronger than the current of synaptic potentials that fired the impulse at the trigger zone; the action potential is nonlinear. To fire the action potential, the synaptic potentials merely have to reduce the membrane's negative charge from -65 to -55 millivolts. Once this is accomplished, however, the explosive influx of sodium ions that constitutes the action potential makes the membrane's charge jump from -55 to $+55$ millivolts in a fraction of a second.

The strength of the synaptic potential is directly related to the number of ion channels opened when molecules of neurotransmitter released by the presynaptic membrane act on specialized postsynaptic membrane sites, and the density of the receptors sensitive to the neurotransmitter that are present at those sites. Depolarization is usually associated with a change in membrane permeability—in other words an opening of ion channels—permitting the influx of positively charged sodium and calcium ions. The synaptic potential fades quickly because the excess ions are quickly pumped out of the cell or otherwise neutralized.

Unlike action potentials, which are always the same strength, the strength (amplitude) of synaptic potentials is not fixed but is increased or decreased by a simple process of addition and subtraction. If synaptic potentials occur near each other, then their combined depolarizing effect is greater than if they are spread out over a large area of the postsynaptic membrane. Hyperpolarizing potentials tend to cancel out nearby depolarizing potentials. The neuron behaves something like an analog computer as it calculates the pluses and minuses of these synaptic potentials.

There is a fundamental relationship between synaptic potentials and the action potential. The greater the strength of the synaptic potentials registered by a neuron, the faster the neuron fires its action potential. Although the action potentials are all the same strength, their frequency or number of repetitions per second depends on the strength of the synaptic potentials. The stronger the net positive charge generated by the synaptic potentials, the greater the number of action potentials per second. In addition, the longer the excitatory synaptic potentials last, the longer the action potentials will keep firing. This variation in the frequency and duration of action potentials is a fundamental component of the synaptic code.

We can visualize how this type of coding works by comparing it to the way we sense heat. The potentials generated by receptors in the skin, like synaptic potentials, are usually graded potentials that can increase or decrease their response depending on the strength of the stimulus. The stronger the stimulus to the skin receptors, the stronger the graded potentials they generate. If we brush our hand on a hot stove, the skin receptors are strongly stimulated, generating a large graded potential that is recorded by the underlying nerve cells and results in a rapid volley of action potentials, like an alarm bell. Painful messages like this go directly to the spinal cord, where a reflex circuit is activated that jerks the hand away. This is all done in an instant, before we have a chance to consciously think about it.

Frequency coding is sophisticated and accurate. Often neurons fire action potentials spontaneously, without being stimulated. This rate of firing becomes a base level from which changes are measured. If the neuron receives a negative or inhibitory stimulus, then the level of firing will fall below this base. A subsequent positive stimulus will bring the rate of firing back to normal or even increase it. This system can be exceptionally sensitive to the subtlest changes.

It was once thought that the firing rate of action potentials was the essence of the nervous system's coding system. But the brain has proved much more complex than this. Aside from their link to frequency coding, the synaptic potentials also have an independent role in both coding and processing information. There are neurons deep within the brain that have no axons at all, or very short axons, and are incapable of firing an action potential. These neurons process information solely by integrating synaptic potentials. On the basis of these potentials alone they release their neurotransmitters and other chemicals.

The role of synaptic potentials in the neuron's tangled dendritic tree is also coming under closer scrutiny. Dendrites are not smooth branches but are covered with spines. The growth and retraction of dendrites and dendritic spines have an important role in learning and memory. They appear to be able to process a certain amount of information, even establish and break off synaptic connections, purely on the basis of synaptic potentials alone without the need for action potentials. This dramatically expands the power of the brain, since there are many more dendrites and dendritic spines than neurons. But there are even more puzzles. Neuroscientists have discovered that some dendrites are capable of generating mini-action potentials of their own that do not involve the whole neuron. The processing of information in the synaptic circuits is far more intricate than was once thought.

It is clear that the brain is different from a digital computer, the circuits of which are either on or off. The action potential has a digital dimension. It is either on or off and its strength is always the same. But it also has an analog dimension, because the number of action potentials fired and the duration that the firing continues codes for the strength and the duration of the stimulus. Synaptic potentials are purely analog. Their strength and duration completely depend on the strength and duration of the stimulus. With this combination of action potentials and synaptic potentials the brain can vary its responses continuously as its environment changes. If the brain is a computer, it is a kind of chemical computer with a mixture of digital and analog elements that resembles no computer ever designed by human beings. And, as we shall see, it engages in a massive amount of parallel processing, with its operations going on simultaneously rather than sequentially as in most digital computers.

Let us summarize our understanding of the synaptic code thus far by returning to our highly simplified example of a hot stove. Imagine a young child who has managed to climb up on a kitchen counter and is approaching a hot stove. He can see the coils of the burner glowing red. If he touches the burner, the pain receptors in the skin respond instantly and generate a strong graded potential onto the underlying nerves, which are made up of neurons. This causes the neurons to be strongly depolarized as ion channels open up and allow positively charged ions to flow into the cell. These positive charges reduce the negative electrical charge on the neuron membrane from -65 millivolts to well below -55 millivolts at the trigger zone of the neuron's axon. This opens up the voltage-gated sodium ion channels and sodium comes rushing in as an action potential is propagated down the axon. The great strength of the graded potential translates into the generation of many action potentials per second. This high frequency means that one action potential after another is causing the release of sacs of neurotransmitter at the terminal bulbs that stud the end of the axon. The result is a large amount of neurotransmitter release onto the dendrites of the next neuron, generating a large synaptic potential. This synaptic potential, in turn, generates a high frequency of action potentials, and this process continues until the message reaches the spinal cord.

In the spinal cord, the message takes two parallel pathways. The first goes to the reflex circuit that causes the child to rapidly snatch his hand away. The other goes to the brain itself for processing.

Although it is getting a little ahead of our story, let us look at what happens in the brain. The photons of light reflected off the stove and into the child's eyes have transmitted the picture of a glowing coil. At roughly the same time, the receptors on the fingers have transmitted a high frequency of action potentials that indicate a painful stimulus. The duration of these action potentials continues long after the hand has pulled away, because the skin was slightly burned. Neuroscience has begun to discover that in the brain these two sets of stimuli converge on a common group of target neurons, and these converging synapses release calcium ions into the target neurons. The calcium begins a biochemical cascade that activates genes in the neurons that establish a link between the image of the hot stove and the sensation of pain. As the child continues to feel his sore hand and thinks about it later, a long-term memory is established that will prevent him from making the same mistake again. Another piece has been added to the child's synaptic model of his environment.

The complexity of the universe has been sieved, and sieved again for billions of years until, on Earth, it has been distilled into the three marvelous pounds of matter that constitute a human brain. Matter and energy flowing through time have combined and recombined in accord with the quantum code producing, first, the genetic code and then the synaptic code—the operating system of the brain.

Nature tends to be conservative, using the same mechanisms over and over, finding new uses for old structures, and combining simple parts in complicated ways. We saw this in the evolution of the electrochemical synapse from simpler communication systems such as hormone signaling.

Remarkably, this most conservative of recycling programs has produced something quite new: consciousness. As we shall see shortly, by connecting billions of neurons using synapses, the brain is able to respond to stimuli through learning and remembering. This stored information is used to construct maps of its environment. In more complex brains these maps are interconnected to form models that enable the brain to predict and exert a measure of control over its environment. In the human being, this three-pound wonder is capable of creating a synaptic network that models the entire universe over the last 15 billion years and far into the future.

How does evolution make the leap from action potentials to consciousness? The first inkling of an answer came from the brain of a simple snail.

Chapter 6
Learning, Memory, Consciousness

A BIOLOGIST STUDYING THE NATURAL WORLD IS LIKE A CURIOUS CHILD in a fabulously elaborate toy shop. Not only is the shop full of enchanting toys; the toy shop itself is a giant toy. The fascinating toys are living things and the toy shop is the Earth, with its complex ecosystems. The inquisitive biologist, like a child, wants to understand how the toys work and assumes that they all operate on the same basic principles. Sensibly, the biologist studies the simplest, easiest to understand toys to learn the mechanisms underlying the most complex ones.

For this reason, neuroscientists often study the brains of simple animals, such as slugs and worms, to determine the mechanisms underlying more complex nervous systems, such as those of human beings. These modest creatures have relatively few neurons, which in many cases are unusually large and easily explored. This strategy only makes sense within the framework of evolution. Since all living things have descended from a common ancestor, we assume that many of the same biological mechanisms that were used in early forms of life have been inherited by the species that are living today.

Eric Kandel, a neuroscientist at Columbia University, has suggested that there is an alphabet of similar cellular processes that are activated in different kinds of learning and memory in all animals. From his office high above the Hudson River, he has assembled a world-renowned laboratory of neuroscientists dedicated to exploring this alphabet through the study of *Aplysia californica*, a marine snail about the size of a cucumber. It is through these studies that we have gotten our first detailed glimpse of how changes in behavior are reflected by changes in synapses.

Neuroscientists are ordinarily quite cautious about the implications of the rapidly evolving models that embody their scientific theories. Yet the flood of knowledge that has poured out of their laboratories over the past two decades has increased their confidence. Kandel put it this way:

> As science becomes more powerful it becomes more ambitious—it becomes bolder. In the early 1960s few molecular biologists worth their salt would publicly admit that their interests extended beyond bacteria and viruses. . . . Many molecular biologists now frankly admit that the ultimate object of their interest is not simply the system with which they work. . . . It is human biology. And some biological researchers are so bold as to see their ultimate interest as the function of the human mind. As science evolves, so does the nature of what is possible and of what is interesting for young people to explore. . . . As Darwin first impressed upon us, even the most unique aspects of human biology, such as mental activity, can be found in an elementary form in simpler animals.[1]

One of the surprises to come out of this kind of research is that animals such as snails or even the fruit fly, *Drosophila*, are capable of surprisingly sophisticated learning. They can, for instance, be taught to associate two different stimuli. Whereas human beings have 100 billion neurons, *Aplysia* has only 20,000 and these neurons are among the largest in the animal kingdom, making them particularly easy to study. Scientists have developed techniques that allow them to eavesdrop on neurons as they communicate through their synapses. Tiny micropipettes can puncture an individual nerve cell and record the pattern of action potentials. Even more amazing are techniques that allow the scientist to monitor individual ion channels in the cell membrane.

THE BOREDOM REFLEX

Kandel has focused particular attention on several basic forms of learning, beginning with habituation and sensitization. Habituation is the decline in a behavioral response to a stimulus that was once noticeable. This is one of the most common forms of behavioral learning among all species, including humans. When we see or otherwise experience something over and over again, and it is of no pressing importance, we often tune it out. Habituation is basically a form of boredom. Sensitization is just the opposite: an increased sensitivity to stimuli.

If you drive to work every day, you have probably become habituated to the routine. You know the route and the traffic lights well and your mind is apt to be operating on autopilot while you drive. When you get to work you probably could not remember the details of the trip even if you tried. But on a rainy morning when someone pulls out of a side street and narrowly misses slamming into you, your level of awareness increases dramatically. Suddenly every detail becomes important and you watch each intersection with wary attention. You have become sensitized.

The evolutionary advantages of habituation and sensitization are obvious. Habituation allows an organism to reduce the attention it pays to those elements in its environment that hold no compelling interest and pose no immediate threat. Sensitization forces an organism to pay attention to impending danger.

Kandel and his colleagues have offered the first explanation of habituation and sensitization at the level of neurons and synapses. Through their work we can begin to see the synaptic code at work.

Aplysia has three innate defensive responses that researchers probe. They center on its tail, its gill, and its siphon, which is a small spout above the gill used to expel seawater. Each of these is withdrawn if touched. In the *Aplysia* studies, the snail's spout is squirted with a stream of water. The snail immediately withdraws its spout and gill. *Aplysia* associates the stream of water with a potential threat. Yet after many stimulations and with no danger ever materializing, the snail becomes habituated and fails to withdraw its gill at all.

In studying the snail's nervous system, Kandel and his colleagues found that when the sensory neurons in the spout are first exposed to the squirt of water they send a strong electrical signal, in the form of a synaptic potential, to the interneurons connecting them to the motor neurons that control the muscles in the gill. Interneurons are the neurons found in between input neurons—such as the sensory neurons that detect activity through touch, vision, and so forth—and output neurons. Motor neurons are output neurons because they control the muscles' response to stimuli registered by the sensory neurons. The strong synaptic potential signaled to the motor neurons by the sensory neurons via the interneurons causes the motor neurons to fire a rapid train of action potentials to the muscles, which rapidly withdraw the gill.[2]

After repeated squirts to the siphon, however, the synaptic potentials generated by the sensory neurons grow smaller and smaller, until they decline below the threshold required to trigger an action potential in the motor axon. The motor axon no longer fires a string of action potentials and the gill is not withdrawn. Kandel found that the calcium ion channels in the synaptic terminals of the sensory neurons had become partially inactivated. One of the important functions of calcium ions in the synaptic terminal is to promote the chemical reactions necessary for the release of sacs of neurotransmitter. Calcium enables the sacs to fuse with the presynaptic membrane and release their neurotransmitter into the synaptic cleft. Since the ion channels that normally admit calcium into the terminal were inactivated, little calcium was entering the terminal and thus few sacs of neurotransmitter were being released. This crippled the ability of the sensory neurons to communicate with the motor neurons. The sensory neurons still registered the squirt, but their ability to communicate with the motor neurons by releasing neurotransmitter to produce a synaptic potential was severely limited. (See Figure 6.1.)

Kandel noted both short-term and long-term changes in *Aplysia*'s behavior. A single training session would habituate *Aplysia* for several minutes. Four training sessions of only ten stimuli each were sufficient to habituate the snail for up to three weeks.

The precise mechanism by which the calcium channels are inactivated is still under study. But habituation is an important example of the depression of a synaptic circuit, in this case the reflex circuit for gill withdrawal. The synaptic terminal is inhibited from

Elements of Learning and Memory (1)

Presynaptic Habituation

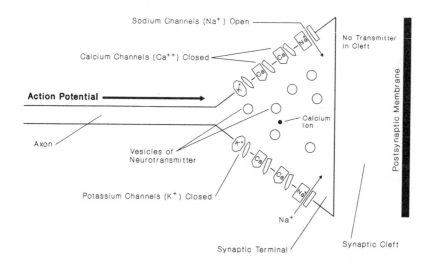

Figure 6.1. During habituation at a presynaptic synaptic terminal, an action potential continuously stimulates the terminal until its supply of calcium ions is used up. Since the calcium is essential for releasing neurotransmitter, the terminal's release of neurotransmitter falls off sharply.

communicating with the postsynaptic neuron through changes in ion channels that result in a reduced output of neurotransmitter.

Kandel and his colleagues also performed experiments to sensitize *Aplysia* using mild electrical shocks. (See Figure 6.2.) In these experiments they discovered a more complex synaptic circuit involving facilitating interneurons, which make their synaptic connections onto the synaptic terminal that connects the sensory neurons in the siphon area with the motor neurons that control the gill-withdrawal muscles. When the tail of *Aplysia* is shocked, the interneurons from the tail begin releasing the neurotransmitter serotonin onto the synaptic terminals of the sensory neurons. The serotonin along with other neurotransmitters as well, through an elaborate biochemical process, has the effect of releasing two important second messengers in the synaptic terminals: cyclic AMP (cAMP) and protein kinase C. Among other things, these second

Elements of Learning and Memory (2)

Presynaptic Facilitation

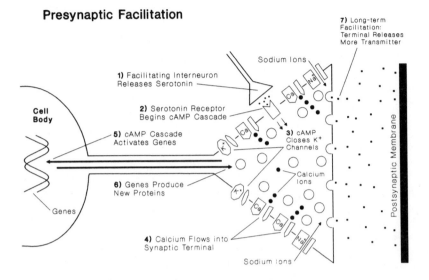

Figure 6.2. The release of serotonin by a facilitating interneuron on a presynaptic terminal causes a cAMP biochemical cascade that closes the terminal's potassium channels. By preventing repolarization of the membrane, this prolongs the action potential and opens voltage-sensitive calcium channels. This large pulse of calcium signals the genes in the cell body to produce new proteins, thus permanently enhancing the synaptic connection.

messengers inactivate an important type of potassium (K^+) ion channel responsible for getting the cell membrane back to its normal electrical charge after an action potential. Without these channels, the presynaptic membrane of the sensory neuron is slower to recover and the action potential lasts longer. A longer action potential means that voltage-gated calcium channels stay open longer, allowing more calcium ions to flow into the synaptic terminal. Since calcium is responsible for releasing sacs of neurotransmitter, the increased flow of calcium stimulates the sensory neuron's synaptic terminal to release more neurotransmitter than usual onto the motor neuron controlling gill withdrawal. This prompts the motor neuron to briskly withdraw the gill. As long as the potassium channels are inactivated, any action potential fired by a sensory neuron is prolonged and amplified—thus, the snail has been sensitized.

Remember that an action potential is caused by a chain reaction of inflowing sodium ions (Na^+) along the axon. This flow makes the interior of the axon much more positive than its normal resting state of roughly -65 millivolts. To restore the axon to its negative resting state, potassium ions (K^+) stream out of the axon through voltage-gated channels that open just after the sodium ions have flowed in. This subtraction of positive charges makes the axon's charge negative again. But when the synaptic terminals are sensitized by serotonin, some of these potassium channels are shut off so that the axon is slower to return to its negative state. This prolongs the action potential, which normally lasts for less than a thousandth of a second.

Within the neuron there is a much higher concentration of potassium ions than there is outside the neuron. Therefore when the potassium channels open, potassium ions rush out of the cell. At the same time, there is a much higher concentration of sodium, calcium, and chloride ions outside of the neuron than within the neuron. This is why sodium ions zip into the axon when sodium channels open during the action potential. But calcium ions are also controlled by voltage-gated channels that are opened during the action potential. Prolonging the action potential means more calcium ions also flow into the cell, releasing more neurotransmitter.

There is another important effect of the cyclic AMP on the synaptic terminal. This second messenger activates another protein kinase: protein kinase A. Protein kinases are enzymes that have wide-ranging effects throughout the nervous system. Protein kinase C and protein kinase A are thought to mobilize additional sacs of neurotransmitter along the active zones of the presynaptic membrane, where they can be released by the action of calcium ions. Protein kinase A is also responsible for the process that leads to the inactivation of the potassium channels.

In short, after shocking *Aplysia*'s tail repeatedly, the sensitized animal swiftly withdraws its gill whenever its tail is touched thereafter. Even a slight touch that ordinarily would elicit little or no response causes the gill to withdraw. *Aplysia* is responding defensively to a hostile environment. The facilitating interneurons have used serotonin as a kind of volume control, making the sensory receptors much more sensitive to being touched.

Kandel's research concluded that habituation is caused by the decline in the release of neurotransmitter in the presynaptic terminal while sensitization is caused by an increase in transmitter release.

THE MEMORY GENES

Kandel has amassed evidence for another important conclusion: the long-term sensitization of *Aplysia* requires the activation of the genes within the nucleus of the neuron. (See Figure 6.2.) A single session of shocking *Aplysia*'s tails results in sensitization lasting a few minutes. Four or more sessions sensitize the animal from a day to several weeks. Kandel's group has discovered that the application of chemicals that block the genetic synthesis of proteins prevents long-term sensitization from taking place. *Aplysia* is still sensitized for short periods of time but seems to quickly forget its fear and return to normal.

Kandel argues that in long-term sensitization (also referred to as long-term facilitation), protein kinase A acts as a messenger to the genes. By turning on certain genes, it begins a sequence of protein transcription via messenger RNA that leads to two specific results. First, more protein kinase A is activated, which means that the potassium channels are shut down for a longer period of time. Second, another set of proteins is produced that stimulates the neuron to establish more synapses with the sensory neurons. Kandel has found that snails undergoing many sensitization training sessions have twice as many synapses onto sensory neurons as untrained snails, and these synapses produce more neurotransmitter than normal.

Just the opposite process was found in long-term habituation. There the number of synaptic connections with the sensory neurons shrank by one-third and the remaining synapses became less active.

What is *Aplysia* telling us about learning and memory? One important lesson is that the brain remembers because its synapses remember. The way an electrochemical synapse responds to an action potential depends on the history of its previous responses. If the calcium channels in the synaptic terminal have been closed, then the synapse has been habituated and will respond weakly to the next action potential. If the synaptic terminal's potassium channels have been closed, however, it has been sensitized and will respond strongly to the next action potential. The great evolutionary advance of electrochemical synapses—those that transmit their messages across the synaptic cleft using neurotransmitters—over purely electrical synapses is their ability to record the changing interaction between the brain and its environment through this biochemical memory.

Kandel's research provides an astonishing link between the genetic and synaptic codes and outlines a theory of learning and memory that can be understood down to the molecular level—that is, the level of the quantum code. If Kandel is right, short-term memory is produced by the strengthening or weakening of synaptic connections. Short-term memory is consolidated into long-term memory through the activation of the genes. This genetic activity can change the number of synaptic connections among the relevant neurons.

If we think of an event as producing a particular pattern of synaptic connections in the brain (a memory), then activating the neuron's genes produces a type of permanent or semi-permanent glue that makes these connections stick. This is long-term memory. Without the genetic glue the much weaker glue of short-term memory quickly fades away and with it the memory.

To illustrate his approach to memory, Kandel uses the example of a boxer who has been knocked out in the fifth round. Often the boxer will remember nothing at all about the fight (short-term amnesia often accompanies head injuries). Although he experienced everything that happened up to the final blow, the boxer's knowledge was stored in short-term memory. The blow to the head disrupts memory processes and may short-circuit the switching on of the genes necessary to consolidate the boxer's memories into long-term synaptic connections. The memories are lost.[3]

If this revolutionary theory put forward by Kandel and many others in the neuroscience community is correct—and a rapidly growing body of evidence indicates that, at least in outline, it is—then all our learning and all our long-term memories, the very essence of our individuality, are etched into our brain by turning on genes that consolidate short-term changes in the strengths of connections among synapses into long-term synaptic networks.

Research by the Kandel group has also provided insights into how the brain develops its ability to predict regularities in its environment. This comes from the study of classical conditioning, the discipline that the Russian physiologist Ivan Petrovich Pavlov made famous. Pavlov, who won the Nobel Prize for Physiology or Medicine in 1904, found that he could develop a conditioned reflex in dogs, making them salivate at the sound of a bell just as if they were about to be fed. He did this by ringing the bell just before the dogs were fed. After many training sessions, the dogs began to associate the bell with food and would salivate whenever it rang. But in order to train the dogs, the bell had to ring *before* they were fed. If it rang afterward, the dogs would make no association between the bell and the food.

Pavlov and others showed that in most species the conditioned stimulus (the bell) must precede the reward or punishment by a critical interval that could be as short as five-tenths of a second. If the reward occurred outside this interval, the association between the conditioned stimulus and the response would not be made. Psychologists had theorized that the reward (or punishment) following the bell or other stimulus reinforced the association between the bell and the food. But these were just words and no one had any idea what this meant at the molecular level of the brain or why the timing was so important, that is until *Aplysia*.

The snail was conditioned to associate a tap on its mantle shelf—a structure near the siphon that normally elicits only a slight withdrawal of the gill—with a subsequent shock to its tail. After training, any touch on the mantle shelf is followed by a rapid withdrawal of the gill, even though no shock is forthcoming.

Studies of the snail's neurons began to piece together a molecular sequence of events that may explain at least some kinds of conditioning. According to Kandel, conditioning resembles the sensitization process, but with some important differences. When the conditioned stimulus (tapping on the mantle shelf) is applied, the sensory neurons originating at the mantle shelf fire a relatively weak set of action potentials that travels from the sensory neuron to its synaptic connection with the motor neuron, which controls the gill muscles. The action potentials are sufficient, however, to open the voltage-gated calcium channels in the synaptic terminal, allowing a modest number of calcium ions to enter the terminal. Some of the ions bind to a versatile protein named calmodulin. This, in turn, causes the calmodulin to bind to an enzyme called adenylyl cyclase, which makes cyclic AMP when it is released into the interior of the synaptic terminal. When calmodulin is added to adenylyl cyclase, it becomes much more efficient at making cyclic AMP. But the adenylyl cyclase has not yet been released. It is attached to a serotonin receptor that is embedded in the terminal membrane.

Just after the calmodulin has attached itself to the adenylyl cyclase, the snail gets a shock to its tail. This generates an intense string of action potentials that triggers a facilitating interneuron to release serotonin onto the mantle shelf's synaptic terminal. The serotonin releases the adenylyl cyclase-calmodulin combination into the synaptic terminal, where it produces large quantities of cyclic AMP. (The arrangement is the same as the one shown in Figure 6.2. In this case, the main synaptic terminal represents the signal from the mantle shelf and the facilitating interneuron represents the signal from the tail.)

As with sensitization, the cyclic AMP in the mantle shelf terminal sensitizes sensory neurons leading from the mantle shelf and amplifies any subsequent action potentials. Thus when the mantle shelf is tapped again, the action potentials generated are amplified at the sensitized synaptic terminals and much more neurotransmitter is released onto the motor neurons. Instead of withdrawing slightly, the stimulated motor neuron withdraws the gill rapidly. If the conditioning continues long enough, the cyclic AMP will stimulate genetic changes that result in the long-term sensitization of the terminals and the stabilization of the conditioned learning. Whenever the mantle shelf is tapped lightly, the gill will withdraw rapidly.

Beneath this dizzying series of biochemical cascades lies a simple mechanism. The release of calcium ions by the tap on the mantle shelf primes the adenylyl cyclase for a miniature explosion of cyclic AMP production. But the explosion only takes place if the adenylyl cyclase is released from its receptor by the neurotransmitter serotonin. And that occurs only if the tail is shocked, firing a series of serotonin-producing action potentials.

The adenylyl cyclase stays primed for just a short time. The calmodulin primer quickly disperses, leaving the adenylyl cyclase in its normal state, which cannot produce enough cyclic AMP to sensitize the synaptic terminal.

The logic of conditioned learning starts to become clear. The tail shock must quickly follow the mantle tap to activate the primed adenylyl cyclase. If the tail shock follows too slowly, then the enzyme will no longer be primed and the mantle shelf terminal will not be sensitized; no conditioned learning will take place. Similarly, if the tail shock comes before the mantle tap, then the adenylyl cyclase will not have been primed and there will be no association between the tap and the shock.

How would this work with one of Pavlov's dogs? When the bell rings, the neurons in the dog's ears detect it and fire a set of action potentials that spread through the brain. A few of these action potentials end up at synaptic terminals that synapse onto the motor neurons controlling the dog's salivating reflex. These action potentials allow a small amount of calcium to enter the terminals, releasing a modest quantity of neurotransmitter onto the motor neurons. But this is far too little to activate the reflex. Until now, there is no reason for the dog to salivate at the sound of a bell. But the calcium ions released by the bell action potentials have primed enzymes in the synaptic terminals to produce significant amounts of cyclic AMP, which can, like a volume control, turn up the amount of neurotransmitter released by the terminals. If there is no immediate additional stimulus, then this amounts to nothing. But if the dog is presented with food just after the bell sounds, then the sight and smell of food sets off another series of action potentials that releases serotonin onto the primed bell terminals, resulting in an orgy of cyclic AMP production. If the sequence of bell ringing and feeding happens often enough, the synaptic terminals signaled by the bell are sensitized. Eventually the sensitization becomes so great that whenever a bell rings the sensitized terminals release enough neurotransmitter to activate the salivating reflex whether the dog is being fed or not.

No one is sure whether this precise sequence actually occurs in dogs or other animals aside from *Aplysia*. Yet Kandel and others are prepared to argue that the sensitization process highlights a general pattern that does occur in all conditioning, and probably in all associative learning. The pattern is this: an initial signal primes certain synaptic connections to either increase or decrease the strength of their connections. If a second signal is then sent within the critical interval when the connections are primed, a series of molecular reactions takes place that consolidates the new strength of the synaptic connections. If these two signals continue to occur time after time in the same order, then further biochemical reactions take place that turn on the genes in the nuclei of the respective neurons and consolidate the learned response into a long-term memory.

Remember this synaptic priming mechanism. It will play an

important part in our discussion of the steps that the brain goes through in creating the elaborate synaptic networks that form the maps and models that produce consciousness.

Conditioned learning represents a basic evolutionary strategy for associating cause and effect. What Kandel has found is a synaptic mechanism capable of sorting through the millions of stimuli that impinge on the brain and linking those that reliably and repeatedly follow each other. One can easily imagine how critical this strategy is for survival. A dog in the wild rather than in a laboratory might chance upon a water hole at which game were especially plentiful and easy to catch. The sight of the water hole would quickly be followed by a meal. If the water hole continued to be a reliable source of food, its image would develop a long-term association with the satisfaction of the dog's hunger. We can picture the hungry dog salivating at the sight of the water hole, associating it with the meal to come. More importantly, this deeply-rooted memory would allow the dog to predict a regularity in its environment that would contribute to its survival.

MORE OF THE ALPHABET

Kandel's research on *Aplysia* has uncovered a portion of the cellular alphabet that is used by the brain to forge learning and memory. This alphabet includes closing potassium channels, turning up the production of neurotransmitters, triggering second messengers through the action of serotonin on protein receptors, and the initiation of the cyclic AMP cascade involving calmodulin, adenylyl cyclase, protein kinase C, and protein kinase A. All these mechanisms are aimed at amplifying the effect of the action potential at the synaptic terminals. And note the central part played by calcium ions in this process. Calcium turns up over and over again in the most important mechanisms of learning and memory.

Kandel is the first to acknowledge that there are other mechanisms as well. His studies have focused on changes at the synaptic terminals. All these mechanisms are presynaptic. They involve only the signaling half of the synapse. There is a major debate going on in neuroscience today about whether the presynaptic mechanisms outlined by Kandel are most important in learning and memory, or whether additional mechanisms that operate at the receiving or postsynaptic side of the synapse are more critical.

Recall that the synapse consists of two parts: a signaling side that is referred to as presynaptic and a receiving side that is called postsynaptic. The synaptic terminal is on the presynaptic side and is part of the signaling neuron. The postsynaptic membrane that detects the signal is part of the receiving neuron. The signaling neuron uses the synaptic terminals at the end of its axon to transmit messages to the postsynaptic membrane that is located on the target neuron. This postsynaptic site is usually located in the branching dendrites of the target neuron, which act as its antennae. Dendrites are often covered with thousands of tiny spines, which are the focus of many synaptic connections. Many neuroscientists believe the complex chemistry within the spines plays a crucial role in thought and behavior. Synapses can also be made with the cell body. The two halves of the synapse are separated by a tiny gap: the synaptic cleft. (Refer to Figure 5.2.) The action potential from the signaling neuron travels to the synaptic terminal, which releases neurotransmitter across the synaptic cleft. These neurotransmitter molecules are detected by protein receptors embedded in the postsynaptic membrane.

Just as receptors appear to release second messengers in *Aplysia*'s synaptic terminals, receptors on the postsynaptic side can release second messengers into the target neuron that change its behavior, even turning its genes on and off. Receptors can also open and close gates and channels in the postsynaptic membrane that are permeable to ions such as sodium, potassium, calcium, and chloride. The flow of these ions into and out of the postsynaptic membrane changes the electrical charge of the target neuron. The neuron continually integrates all the positive and negative electrical charges generated by all the synaptic messages it is receiving. A typical neuron is on the receiving side of thousands of synapses and may be recording messages in its dendrites and on its cell body from one thousand other neurons. The neuron normally integrates these signals at the trigger zone—that is, the portion of the neuron's membrane at which its axon joins the cell body. If the composite electrical charge at the trigger zone becomes sufficiently positive, then the target neuron becomes a signaling neuron. It fires an action potential of its own, which rolls down the axon beginning at the trigger zone and ending at the synaptic terminals at the tips of its branches. This action potential sends messages to all the neurons with which the axon has established synaptic connections.

One important study of associative memory was conducted at the National Institutes of Health using both rabbits and *Hermissenda crassicornis*, a second kind of marine snail. Normally, whenever the snail senses ocean turbulence, it anchors itself to a hard surface. The snail was trained to do this solely in response to a flash of light. Similarly, rabbits naturally blink when they feel a puff of air in their eye, and they were trained to associate this natural response with an auditory tone.

When the neurons of the snails and the rabbits were analyzed, researchers found no sign of a change in the amount of neurotransmitter released by the synaptic terminals. Instead they found an important change in the postsynaptic membrane: the potassium ion flow was reduced—the same mechanism that Kandel had found in the presynaptic membrane. Reducing the potassium flow had the same effect in the postsynaptic neuron as it had in the synaptic terminal. It increased the duration of the action potential fired by the postsynaptic neuron by slowing the recovery to its resting state of −65 millivolts. Additionally, the researchers found that after long-term training there were fewer dendrites connected to the synaptic terminals involved in the conditioned learning than there had been previously. They interpreted this as a sign that the synaptic connections were now focused on the conditioned learning and had eliminated unnecessary dendrites.[4]

Now we have two apparently independent mechanisms for synaptic learning, one presynaptic and the other postsynaptic. Kandel's presynaptic mechanism is characterized by increased sensitivity of the synaptic terminal, a greater release of neurotransmitter, and a change in the number of synaptic terminals after long-term training, which is apparently the result of gene activation. In contrast, the *Hermissenda* showed increased sensitivity of the postsynaptic neuron and a change in the number of dendrites. But the situation is even more complex because neuroscientists have uncovered the NMDA receptor, another postsynaptic switch that operates throughout the brain, but particularly in two vital structures: the neocortex and the hippocampus. With the NMDA receptor we are beginning to approach not only the heart of learning and memory but the secret of consciousness itself.

There are many complex structures in the human brain but none is as impressive as the neocortex, which is the heavily wrinkled outer layer of the brain. It is disproportionately large in human beings compared to other animals. Neocortex simply means "new" cortex. The old cortex that we inherited from earlier mammals has been pushed inside the neocortex to form the limbic system, which has many important functions including memory-formation and emotion. The hippocampus is part of the limbic system.

The large neocortex epitomizes a basic principle of evolutionary design. Between the neurons that detect information from the senses and the neurons that order the muscles and other organs to respond, there is an enormous intermediate network of neurons that elaborately processes incoming information and spontaneously generates signals of its own. It is in this network that information is mapped and modeled. The human neocortex represents the extreme expansion of intermediate processing. If brains consisted entirely of input neurons connected to output neurons, there would be no thought, only reflexes. It was the evolutionary innovation of a substantial intermediate network of neurons that led to learning, memory, and consciousness.

The cortex is divided into two cerebral hemispheres, left and right. One of the most intense research programs in recent years has been to document the different functions performed by each of the hemispheres. If the cortex could be removed from the brain and spread out flat, its surface area would be about 350 square inches. It fits into the skull by being deeply folded. This allows the maximum contact between the neurons in the cortex and all parts of the brain. Each hemisphere of the brain is divided into four lobes. (See Figure 6.3.) The primary visual cortex, where the signals from the eyes are relayed, is at the very back of the brain in the occipital lobe. The auditory cortex is at the bottom front of the temporal lobe. A pronounced crevice in the hemisphere, the Sylvian fissure, runs along the top of the temporal lobe. Many of the areas of the cortex associated with language are located along that fissure. A strip of the cortex running from ear to ear contains a map of the body that is used in receiving sensations and moving muscles. The map is distorted by the relative use and sensitivity of the body part. The face, for example, takes up much more space in the somatosensory map than does the back. These maps can be modified by experience.

The hemispheres of the brain are connected by a bundle of millions of nerve fibers called the corpus callosum that is about four inches long and less than half an inch thick. Individuals who have

Major Divisions of the Cerebral Cortex

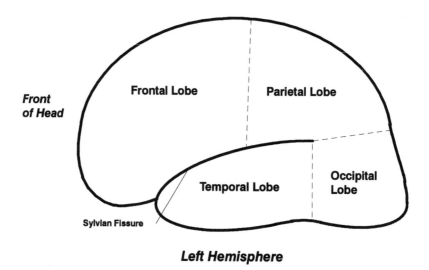

Figure 6.3. The left cerebral hemisphere is shown with the division into four lobes. The right hemisphere is also divided into four lobes, reflecting a very rough division of labor among the sections of the hemispheres.

had their corpus callosum cut for medical reasons (the procedure is a treatment for severe epilepsy) have effectively had their hemispheres disconnected. This normally does not present a problem because each half of the brain shares the same information through the senses. But careful studies that isolate the hemispheres from each other have shown some striking differences between the two. In most people, the left hemisphere has the primary language functions and only this hemisphere can speak fluently. The right hemisphere's language ability is rudimentary, but it seems to be better at recognizing the emotional overtones of speech. There are a whole array of differences between the hemispheres that have been documented, although the precise pattern of these differences varies from person to person. Some researchers have concluded that consciousness is not unitary. But most believe that the hemispheres have evolved to work together and complement each other.

Mathematically, the brain is a dynamical system, the interacting parts of which continuously evolve over time. The brain never rests even when it is asleep. It always registers a wide variety of spontaneous electrical activity, called spontaneous potential. The brain's response to being stimulated by the environment is termed evoked potential.

The brain harnesses spontaneous fluctuations in many ways. A steady background of fluctuations sets a threshold that allows a neuron to measure events that either exceed the threshold or fall below it. This provides a subtle and sensitive method of measurement. I would argue that the fluctuations are also a source of random variations in the thought process.

The brain's spontaneous nature is not always emphasized among those who prize determinism and predictability. Yet we can eavesdrop on an important aspect of it by simply paying attention to our own stream of consciousness, monitoring the brain as it makes an endless series of unpredictable associations. These variations in thought are grist for the evolution of ideas.

ASSOCIATING IDEAS

Out of the streams of internal thoughts and external stimuli the brain must make associations vital to its survival. The NMDA receptor seems to be perfectly suited to act as a switch that turns on the neuron's capacity to make connections with other neurons as the brain builds its models of the world. The receptor does this by allowing pulses of calcium ions from outside the neuron to enter the cell. It acts as a kind of trigger for many complex chemical processes within the neuron. Although much remains to be learned about brain receptors, it seems clear that the NMDA receptor is a fundamental part of the emerging synaptic code.

The NMDA receptor takes its name from the chemical (N-methyl D-aspartate) that was first used to identify it. It is a protein structure embedded in the membranes of many of the brain's neurons. The receptor has a mechanism a bit like a microscopic channel that is sensitive to the neurotransmitter glutamate. When the receptor detects glutamate it tries to open its channel to allow calcium ions to flow into the neuron. But there is a catch. Usually the NMDA receptor's channel is blocked by positively charged magnesium ions (referred to as Mg^{2+} or Mg^{++}), which are attracted by the negative charge of the inside of the neuron. If synaptic terminals stimulate the neuron's membrane strongly enough, then the voltage of the membrane becomes more positively charged, temporarily repelling the magnesium ions. They pop out of the NMDA receptor's channel and if the receptor is then stimulated by glutamate, the channel is free to open and calcium ions can flow into the neuron. This begins a biochemical cascade that establishes stronger connections with the signaling synapses. (See Figure 6.4.) Sodium ions can also flow into the neuron through the NMDA receptor channel and potassium ions can flow out, but the channel is about ten times more permeable to calcium than to sodium. The NMDA receptor has been linked to the formation of changes in the synapses that are implicated in learning and memory.

The NMDA Receptor

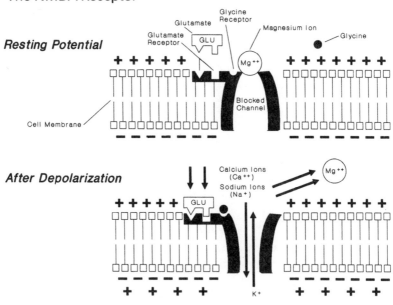

Figure 6.4. Perhaps the most important of all the brain's receptors, this receptor plays a fundamental role in the synaptic code. It is unique in being sensitive to both voltage changes and a neurotransmitter, glutamate. The neurochemical glycine acts as a volume switch, making the NMDA receptor more sensitive. At resting potential, its channel is blocked by magnesium ions. After the surrounding membrane is depolarized, the magnesium blockade temporarily lifts and the channel can be opened by glutamate, allowing calcium ions and sodium ions to flow into the cell and potassium ions (K^+) to flow out. The interior of the neuron receives a strong pulse of calcium because the inflowing calcium ions outnumber the incoming sodium ions by about ten to one.

The beauty of this complex process is that alone among the many different kinds of receptors that have so far been identified in the brain, the NMDA receptor requires both an electrical and chemical signal for its channel to open. Thus the NMDA receptor will only be activated when there are intense and highly correlated patterns of signaling going on between neurons. These are exactly the kinds of correlations that are used to build the associations out of which learning, memory, and ultimately consciousness emerge. The NMDA receptor naturally acts to associate excitatory signals arriving at the same time at the same postsynaptic membrane.

Neuroscientists call the process by which the NMDA receptor associates incoming signals "long-term potentiation." Experiments with rats have shown that long-term potentiation is involved in certain kinds of memory. Rats treated with chemicals that block the activity of the NMDA receptor cannot perform the memory phase of certain kinds of maze tests.

Although there is much we are still learning about the detailed workings of the NMDA receptor—the gene that produces it has only recently been cloned—let us take a simplified and schematic example of how the receptor might do its job of making an association. Assume for a moment that the postsynaptic neuron on which the NMDA receptor is located has come to represent the word "snow" in the brain—just the sound of the word, not its meaning. In reality, of course, many neurons and many NMDA receptors would be involved in a complex language association such as this. The incoming synaptic terminals symbolically represent the qualities wet, white, and cold. The NMDA receptor is bunched with other related glutamate receptors known as quisqualate (Q) and kainate (K) receptors. When the information channels labeled "white," "wet," and "cold" are stimulated by external stimuli (for example, feeling wet or seeing white), the incoming terminals fire action potentials. To remove the magnesium blockage, at least two of the terminals must fire simultaneously.

If a very young child has been told it is snowing and has then been taken out into his first snow, the child's strongest reactions will probably be to the whiteness and the cold. The neurons associated with seeing whiteness and feeling cold will be stimulated at the same time and fire quite strongly. The child may also feel the dampness of the snow, but probably not with the same intensity as he sees the white and feels the cold. The receptor associated with the sensation of dampness will probably be firing but not as strongly or as regularly as the other two. (See Figure 6.5.)

The synchronized and sustained firing of the white and cold terminals activates the Q and K glutamate receptors, opening their sodium ion channels and adding a positive charge to the membrane sufficient to repel the positively charged magnesium ion from the NMDA receptor channel. Now glutamate, which is also being released by the white and cold terminals, is able to open the NMDA receptor's calcium ion channel, which is no longer blocked by magnesium ions, allowing a pulse of calcium ions to enter the cell.

Associative Memory and NMDA

Stage One: Exceeding the Threshold

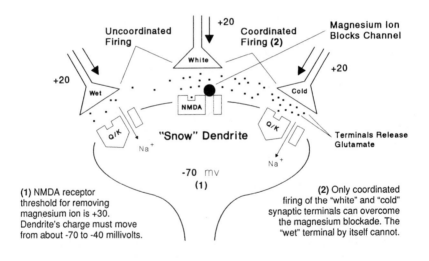

Figure 6.5. An NMDA receptor couples with two Q/K glutamate receptors. The two Q/K receptors actually represent groups of quisqualate and kainate receptors. The terminals representing "white" and "cold" are synchronized and their release of glutamate is sufficient to remove the magnesium blockade from the NMDA receptor calcium channel. The NMDA receptor must be depolarized from -70 millivolts to at least -40 millivolts. The combined effect of the white and cold terminals is to depolarize the membrane by 40 millivolts. The "wet" terminal cannot depolarize the membrane sufficiently by itself, and it is not synchronized with the others.

As indicated in Figure 6.6, this flow of calcium ions triggers a series of biochemical cascades involving protein kinase C and calmodulin that activate the postsynaptic cell's genetic machinery, establishing stronger synaptic connections between the snow neuron and the white and cold synaptic terminals, probably through the production of new membrane proteins. Next time the white and cold terminals signal the snow neuron, their signals will be received much more readily. The meaning of the word "snow" is being built in the child's mind through a process of association.

The NMDA receptors on postsynaptic membranes are ideally suited to associate converging inputs to a membrane. In this way, the sound of a word like snow could be associated with meanings

Associative Memory and NMDA

Stage Two: The Calcium Pulse and Beyond

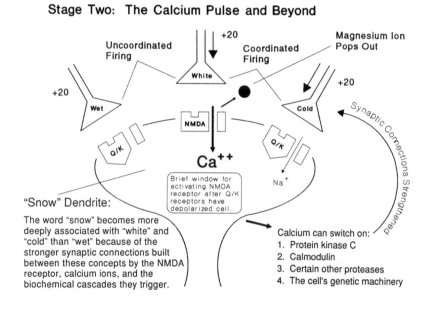

Figure 6.6. Calcium inflow from the NMDA receptor channel triggers a postsynaptic biochemical cascade that turns on the cell's genetic machinery and strengthens the membrane's synaptic connections with the "white" and "cold" terminals—probably through the production of additional proteins. This builds an association between the word "snow" and the concepts of white and cold. This is a highly simplified illustration. In reality, this process probably requires many neurons with complicated interconnections.

like cold and white. The postsynaptic mechanism operates by increasing the neurons' sensitivity to neurotransmitters. The NMDA receptor has caused so much excitement in the neuroscience community because it is so pervasive in so many crucial areas of the brain, and because it seems fundamental in establishing much of the essential wiring in the nervous system during gestation and after birth.

For example, animal experiments have shown that artificially blocking the NMDA receptors' action in a young animal will keep the animal's visual system from wiring itself properly. Most mammals, including humans, are born with visual systems that must be "tuned" by activity during the first few days and weeks of life. Visual fields must be sharpened by use during a critical period, or vision never becomes fully functional.

Neuroscientists believe that NMDA receptors are unusually active during this critical period and are crucial to ensuring that the correct nerve endings converge on the correct neurons in the visual system. These findings raise the intriguing possibility that learning in adults—neuroscientists call the ability to learn "plasticity"—is an extension of the developmental process by which other systems in the brain are wired.[5]

Ronald E. Kalil, a neuroscientist at the University of Wisconsin, summarized the attractiveness of this idea:

> An added advantage of the model is that it can account for protracted plasticity in other parts of the brain. All that would be required is that neurons be genetically programmed to produce NMDA receptors or functionally related molecules indefinitely instead of halting production at some specified time. Thus, variation on a single biochemical theme could account for relatively brief periods of activity-dependent plasticity, such as is found in the developing visual cortex, as well as for the apparently life-long plasticity found in other parts of the brain, such as the hippocampus.[6]

We are left with the question of which are most important to learning and memory: the presynaptic mechanisms outlined by Eric Kandel or the postsynaptic mechanisms exemplified by the NMDA receptor? Kandel proposes a grand synthesis. He acknowledges that the NMDA receptor must initiate long-term potentiation in areas of the brain such as the hippocampus, but he cites evidence that the stabilization of long-term potentiation is characterized by an increased flow of the neurotransmitter glutamate from the synaptic terminal. He therefore proposes that long-term potentiation first requires the activation of NMDA receptors, but the maintenance of this state requires that the postsynaptic membrane send a reverse or retrograde signal back to the synaptic terminal, perhaps in the form of a flow of calcium ions. This retrograde signal would begin a presynaptic biochemical cascade that increases the output of glutamate by the synaptic terminal.

Kandel and others are searching for definitive evidence that would prove the existence of a retrograde messenger. Recently they turned up an intriguing candidate: the gas, nitric oxide. Over the last few years, biologists have been astounded to find that molecules of this gas are produced by cells in many parts of the body and are used to send messages to other cells. When generated by one cell, nitric oxide molecules rapidly diffuse through the membranes of nearby cells into the interior, where they can stimulate chemical reactions.

Recently neuroscientists have discovered that neurons, too, can produce nitric oxide. The calcium influx stimulated by the activation of NMDA receptors seems to switch on the production of the gas in the postsynaptic neuron, which may then diffuse back to the presynaptic neuron in a feedback loop that could strengthen the synaptic connection. Some researchers report that long-term potentiation can be blocked by agents that suppress the production of nitric oxide.[7]

Whatever the mechanism that is ultimately found to wire synapses together, it is becoming clear that the brain has an explicit circuit for processing conscious memories and that the circuit centers on the hippocampus.

THE STORY OF H. M.

In the fall of 1991, two neuroscientists—Larry R. Squire and Stuart Zola-Morgan—published a path-breaking paper in the journal *Science* that outlined neuroscience's new understanding of conscious memory. The research that led to this paper began with a report in 1957 about one of the most famous amnesiacs who ever lived: a man known in the medical literature only as H. M.[8]

Patient H. M. suffered from severe epilepsy and in the 1950s doctors frequently treated such cases by removing a portion of the brain. In this case H. M.'s doctors quickly realized that in removing his hippocampus and some surrounding tissue, they had removed too much. After the operation, H. M. lost the ability to store long-term memories. His short-term memory is unimpaired and he can remember a telephone number or recall the contents of a newspaper article for a few minutes. But in twenty minutes or so he will have no memory of ever having memorized the number or reading the paper. He is now in his mid-sixties and living in a nursing home. One of his chief pastimes is crossword puzzles, because he can make progress by referring to what he has written even though he has no memory of ever having started the puzzle.

H. M. made neuroscientists realize that memory is not a unitary phenomenon. We can distinguish not only between short-term and long-term memory, but also between what is called procedural and declarative memory. Procedural memory is sometimes called know-how, in other words knowing how to do things. It is our accumulated habits and skills: riding a bicycle or playing the piano. This kind of learning is at least partly unconscious and is not governed by the hippocampus. H. M.'s ability to learn and remember a skill such as mirror reading (learning to read something that is upside down and backward) is unaffected. He can use the skill though he cannot remember learning it.

Declarative memory is referred to as "know what," in other words what we know. It is conscious knowledge of ourselves, our friends and acquaintances, and our experiences that we can retrieve and repeat to others. This is the kind of memory that H. M. no longer has the ability to store long-term. In the early 1980s neuroscientists were able to reproduce in monkeys the kind of brain damage suffered by H. M. They began an intensive study of exactly what areas of the brain were involved and how the system worked.

Squire and Zola-Morgan report that the areas of the brain involved include the hippocampus and three nearby areas of the cortex: the entorhinal cortex, perirhinal cortex, and parahippocampal cortex. Images in the brain seem to be stored as a whole, but they are not stored in the same place. If I meet someone, I remember his face, the sound of his voice, and perhaps the firmness of his handshake. Each of the perceptions appears to be stored in separate areas that specialize in mapping visual, auditory, and somatic information. Within these areas, the perception may be broken down even further. Yet a hallmark of human memory is that we remember things as a whole. We do not memorize a face feature by feature, but as an entire image. That is why a sketch that contains only a few lines can bring back an entire image.

Squire and Zola-Morgan propose that the hippocampal system is responsible for retaining an index that contains all the pieces of the memory that are scattered throughout the neocortex. This storage in the hippocampus area is not permanent, but only continues until the memory either is forgotten through lack of reinforcement or enters long-term storage and is shifted completely to the neocortex, where it is knitted together by some not yet understood process. By moving older memories to other parts of the brain, the hippocampal system retains the capacity to continue storing the location of new memories.

What molecular mechanism does the hippocampal area use to keep track of these scattered memories? Squire and Zola-Morgan suggest that long-term potentiation, which as we have seen intimately involves the NMDA receptor, "would be an appropriate mechanism for this specialized role of the hippocampus in rapidly forming conjunctions between unrelated events."

The brain seems to have a number of memory systems that work in parallel. One of the most interesting is emotional memory. Whereas conscious memory is centered on the hippocampus, emotional memory seems to be coordinated by a small structure near the hippocampus called the amygdala. Certain sensory pathways lead directly to amygdala, bypassing the hippocampus and neocortex. This may be why an event can trigger a strong emotional reaction before one is able to rationally analyze it. This parallel system for registering associations of pleasure and pain appears to be intimately involved with conscious memory, however. Emotions can provide the presynaptic and postsynaptic priming necessary to establish the synaptic connections for learning and memory. In *Aplysia*, the prodding that accompanies the squirt of water can be thought of as associating an unpleasant emotion with an event. Remember our example of the assassination of President Kennedy and the *Challenger* disaster? Undoubtedly the emotions of pain and shock that accompanied the information about the events provided ample priming to establish lifelong memories. From an evolutionary point of view, events that cause us extreme pleasure or pain represent important data for survival and adaptation. Thus they are remembered with exceptional clarity.

Now that we have begun to understand conscious memory, are we closer to understanding consciousness itself? Many neuroscientists have come to believe that consciousness, like memory, is the result of sophisticated connections between widely scattered areas of the brain that specialize in distinct operations. It is these connections that generate the dynamic model that we experience as consciousness. If some of these connected elements are damaged or destroyed by a stroke or accident, our consciousness does not necessarily terminate, though we may lose certain aspects that we normally take for granted, such as the ability to recognize faces.

As Eric Kandel concludes:

> The functions localized to discrete regions in the brain are not complex faculties of mind, but *elementary operations*. More elaborate faculties are constructed from the serial and parallel (distributed) interconnections of several brain regions. As a result, damage to a single area need not lead to the disappearance of a specific mental function. . . . The most astonishing example of the divisible nature of mental processes is the finding that our very sense of ourselves as a *self*—a coherent being—is achieved by connecting neurally, a family of distinct operations carried out independently in the two cerebral hemispheres.[9]

One of the most striking conclusions that neuroscientists have come to is the one Kandel highlights: there is no single seat of consciousness in the brain. Many in the artificial intelligence community, which models the mind on computers, have reached the same conclusion. For decades researchers believed they would discover a single center in the brain that is responsible for consciousness. But no such area has ever been identified. Instead, researchers have found that consciousness can be selectively impaired, depending on which portions of the brain are damaged. H. M., for example, is fully conscious though his ability to form long-term memories has been destroyed.

Out of this research have come a number of theories that attempt to construct consciousness out of the complex interconnection among specialized areas of the brain. Neuroscientist Gerald Edelman, a Nobel laureate, has written several books proposing a fascinating model that he calls neural Darwinism or the theory of neuronal group selection. He suggests that groups of neurons form explicit units and compete with each other in a kind of ongoing Darwinian struggle to perform different specialized tasks. Consciousness, he believes, emerges from the dynamic connections between these groups.

Jean-Pierre Changeux, a French neuroscientist, has put forward similar ideas that center around units he calls neuronal assemblies.

Antonio Damasio, a neurologist at the University of Iowa, has proposed that the distributed centers of the brain are linked by convergence zones. This is a bit like the example of the NMDA receptor illustrated in Figure 6.5. When we think of a word like "snow," Damasio suggests, the scattered concepts and associations that make up the word (white, cold) are integrated at a convergence zone into a unified idea. There are many convergence zones in the brain performing many different functions. Convergence zones, I would argue, are areas at which synaptic models are formed by integrating the brain's widely scattered synaptic maps.

Each of these models seeks to resolve what is known as the binding problem: how does the brain generate a unified sense of perception and awareness from a scattered collection of specialized neural centers? Francis Crick and others suggest another solution: perception and consciousness may be produced by the rhythms of the brain. Neurons from different parts of the brain that are involved in a single perception could tune themselves to the same frequency in a process called phase locking. This tuning would take place through the coordinated firing of the neurons through their synapses, a process that might facilitate the integration of perception. Here again, the NMDA receptor could be deeply involved since research has shown that these receptors may serve as pacemaker cells for certain brain rhythms.

The binding problem has not yet been solved. But many neuroscientists believe that tremendous progress will be made over the next decade.

One of the principal ways that our consciousness is bound together is through language. In the next chapter we will explore the roots of our ability to exchange living thoughts.

Chapter 7

Skin of a Living Thought

THE SHOCK OF SEEING ADVANCED ALZHEIMER'S DISEASE FOR THE FIRST
time is something you never forget.

When I was an undergraduate at Harvard, my roommate and
I received a grant from the Institute of Politics of the Kennedy
School of Government to study the pharmaceutical industry. It was
in the 1970s and a wave of prescription drugs designed to treat
psychiatric illnesses dominated the market. Librium and Valium
were widely prescribed for depression, and powerful antipsychotic
drugs such as Thorazine were beginning to empty the mental hos-
pitals of schizophrenics, many of whom were once more able to
function in society, at least temporarily. Yet there were problems of
overprescription, side effects, and cost, particularly for the elderly,
and there was a lack of outpatient care for those who had been
formerly institutionalized.

One morning we appeared on a television talk show in Boston
with a doctor friend of ours to discuss our research. After the show,
a local psychiatrist called and invited us to visit him at his clinic. A
few days later, we took the subway over to see him.

As we waited outside his office, a woman was sitting in a

wheelchair in the hall, tightly clutching a blanket. She was about seventy-five, thin, with sunken cheeks and wispy gray hair. But what struck me were her eyes. They were utterly vacant. Then she opened her mouth and uttered the most pitiful cry. "Mama, mama," she wailed over and over in an unearthly voice.

At that time most doctors did not realize how widespread Alzheimer's was becoming. Many thought "dementia" was a natural part of old age. We now know that Alzheimer's is a disease that attacks the brain, clogging the cerebral cortex, hippocampus, and nearby areas with huge numbers of plaques consisting of misshapen tangles of axons, dendrites, and a substance called amyloid beta-protein, which may be responsible for the illness. As the plaques build up, the symptoms gradually become devastating and ultimately prove fatal. According to *Principles of Neural Science*:

> Early manifestations include forgetfulness, untidiness, transient confusion, periods of restlessness and lethargy, and errors in judgment. The storage of new memory becomes impaired, but memory previously stored is less severely affected or for a time not affected at all. Patients eventually lose interest in their surroundings and become confined to wheelchair or bed. The course of the illness is highly variable. The final stages of the disease, marked by mental emptiness and loss of control of all body functions, may not occur until 5–10 years after onset.[1]

Alzheimer's disease robs its millions of victims of memory, language, and rational consciousness. Yet there is hope that the disease will one day be cured through genetic engineering. Many researchers believe that Alzheimer's is caused by a malfunction in the gene that produces the amyloid beta-proteins. If we can identify how the gene malfunctions, we may be able to prevent it from going awry or replace it.

Alzheimer's disease may represent a failure of the immune system to protect the vulnerable circuits of the brain from attack by the amyloid beta-proteins. Like the synaptic code, the immune system is capable of learning and remembering. It both learns what foreign organisms should be destroyed (through an intricate process of variation and selection) and remembers what it has learned— which is why we only need to be vaccinated once or twice against many diseases in order to have lifelong protection.

TRANSCENDING THE GENES

Individual immune systems, like human minds, are fallible. Yet the successes achieved by an immune system during a lifetime of fighting disease are locked away within the individual organism and cannot be directly communicated to other organisms. If the immune system of a person has found a way to counter an attack of the amyloid beta-proteins, it cannot inform other immune systems of what it has learned. The only communication is genetic—when the genes that code for the immune system are passed on to the individual's offspring. In the long run, those people with better resistance to Alzheimer's disease may have an evolutionary advantage over those who are more susceptible to the disease.

In contrast, the synaptic code has evolved the ability to transfer its learning independently of the genetic code, through direct communication with other synaptic systems (brains) using language. The synaptic code reproduces its knowledge independently and must be viewed as a separate code, although it evolved from the genetic and quantum codes and conforms to their rules. It is through the synaptic code that we exchange information about Alzheimer's disease and search for a cure, something that might take the immune system thousands of years.

There is a tremendous economy of communication for a human being to be able to say the word "snow," which would just be a meaningless sound to any other animal, and have the brain of another human activate a wide variety of shared associations that have been synaptically linked to that word. The power of words allows individuals to create many different levels of symbols, from basic associations of words with sensory perceptions (snow) to more abstract associations (snow is one kind of weather). Even higher levels of abstraction are reached when minds create scientific models (weather is produced by the differential heating and cooling of the earth's atmosphere, land masses, and oceans by the sun's radiation).

When the U.S. Supreme Court Justice Oliver Wendell Holmes, Jr., wrote that a word "is not a crystal, transparent and unchanged; it is the skin of a living thought and may vary greatly in color and content according to the circumstances and the time in which it is used,"[2] he captured two of the most important qualities of language. Words allow us to clothe living thoughts in sound so that we can harness the power of our brains not only to communicate and manipulate, but to engage in discussion that allows our thoughts to evolve rapidly. Words can also have different associations depending on the context, which gives them great flexibility as a tool of communication.

Learning a language has been compared to the well-studied process of learning to play chess. Both chess and language depend heavily on memory, and in both the memories seem to be organized into an array of specific maps. Psychologists sometimes call these maps "chunks." The difference between a chess master and an amateur is that the master has organized the board and the subsets of chess pieces into thousands of maps that he can recall almost instantly. These maps can be compared to words in a language. Any legitimate configuration of chess pieces is thus seen by a chess master as a meaningful sentence, and he can easily remember it. Yet if a master is shown a random board setting, he has as much trouble remembering it as an amateur does because it is meaningless and cannot be associated with his set of maps.[3]

To illustrate how synaptic mapping works at the simplest level, close your eyes and write something on a piece of paper. Notice how you can "see" the words in your mind as you write them. Your mind contains a map of letters of the alphabet, and as you blindly write on the paper, the shape of the letters is also written in your mind. You can also experience this map if, with your eyes closed, you use your finger to trace the words on a tabletop.

The enormous amount of research documenting the brain's profound mapping and modeling ability continues to pile up. In one famous study, subjects were asked to imagine rotating three-dimensional objects in space. Not only did they appear to use internal models to perform the rotations, the time the imaginary rotations took to perform were similar to the time it would take to deliberately rotate a real object. You can try this experiment yourself. After reading these instructions, close this book for a moment and hold it so that the cover is facing you. Now close your eyes and imagine rotating the book so that its spine is facing you. Try to mentally read what is on the spine. Do this several times and then open your eyes and actually perform this maneuver. Notice how your imagined rotation probably tracked the actual rotation, even taking about the same amount of time. It seems clear that the brain contains maps of the visual space and interconnects those maps to build a model in which imaginary objects can be realistically moved around.[4]

In the 1950s, at the height of the influence of behaviorists in the United States, any notion of internal models was rejected and all thought and behavior was believed to be reducible to stimulus and response. Noam Chomsky, the celebrated linguist, caused a sensation when he insisted that language was not possible without internal representations and innate mechanisms. Although the specific mechanisms that Chomsky suggested have not yet been proved, he performed a valuable service in widening the horizons of those seeking to explain the mind.

MAPPING WITH PRECISION

How does the brain manufacture such precise maps and interconnect them into models? Recent research points to a pivotal role for the NMDA receptor. Studies of the visual systems of cats have shown that the cats must use their eyes normally during a critical two-month period after birth or the wiring of their visual system, which consists of synapses from the retina mapping themselves onto other parts of the brain, including the cortex, will not form properly. The initial axons from the retina to the rest of the brain seems to form under the influence of chemical signals without the need for NMDA receptors. But this wiring is relatively haphazard. The fine-tuning of the wiring, which produces the precise maps necessary for vision, seems to be under the control of the NMDA receptors. If a cat's eyes are treated with a substance that blocks the action of NMDA receptors, then the proper maps do not form.

It is easy to see why the NMDA receptor is so well suited to forming maps and models. The receptor must be stimulated with a particularly large electrical charge to remove the magnesium ions blocking its calcium channel and allow the neurotransmitter glutamate to open that channel. This means that it only responds to correlated patterns of particularly strong and sustained stimulation.

Axons coming from adjacent areas of the eye normally fire when detecting the same kind of stimuli. Thus they emit action potentials at roughly the same time. These simultaneous action potentials are probably sufficient to trigger NMDA receptors on the target cell to open their calcium channels and strengthen synaptic connections with the axons. Two axons not adjacent to each other will not fire simultaneously and will not exceed the receptor's threshold. The NMDA receptor can thus produce maps in which the point-to-point wiring in the brain precisely reflects the topography of the retina.

In my view, this is an example of a vital three-part role that NMDA receptors and a few other mechanisms (including the cAMP cascade) play in wiring the brain. First, they make associations among synapses. Second, they map those associations. Finally, they interconnect those maps into functional models. The ultimate creations of synaptic maps are synaptic models. It is these models that I believe are at the foundation of thought.

Very young children are born with an innate ability to learn a natural language by simply being around people who speak it. This seems to be the result of a critical period in the child's development that lasts through the early years of life. During this period there is an overproduction of both neurons and synaptic connections. There is also the production of a wealth of NMDA receptors to sort out the proper linguistic wiring. This luxuriant production of neurons, synapses, and receptors is under genetic control, but the actual language learned depends on what language happens to be spoken around the child. Studies have shown that infants can discriminate among every sound a human being can make. As they get older, however, they lose the ability to discriminate between sounds that are not used in their native language. Japanese babies, for example, can distinguish between the "l" sound and the "r" sound. But most Japanese adults cannot, because their language makes no distinction between the two.

The overproduction of neurons and synapses in the early years is accompanied by the drastic pruning of these structures as the basic wiring of the brain emerges through an intense competition among neurons seeking to make synaptic connections. This pruning is one of the most important episodes of unified selection that goes on in the brain. Large areas of the developing cortex become association areas, so named because they connect separate areas of the cortex, including areas in the opposite hemispheres.

For cats, the production of NMDA receptors in the visual system ceases at the end of the critical period and the visual system's wiring cannot change any further. There is no need to have a visual system that constantly rewires itself. This is true of the human visual system, too. Yet the production of NMDA receptors does not stop but only declines in the linguistic system of a human. We can still learn new languages but the task is much more difficult. The continued supply of NMDA receptors allows us to learn and remember new experiences. This ability provides the flexibility to continue adapting to the environment.

Once associative language networks are set up in the brain using the NMDA receptor and other mechanisms, how does the brain process language? Years of study by neuroscientists of the effects of stroke and other brain damage on the language abilities of patients has given us a rough idea of the brain's circuitry. Figure 7.1 shows a schematic representation of what the brain is doing when it is asked to recognize a spoken word and then repeat the word (I say

Hearing and Then Speaking a Word

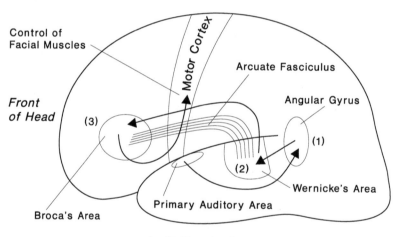

Left Hemisphere

Figure 7.1. When the brain hears a word, the signal is translated by the primary auditory area and related areas into a recognizable sound, then is successively transferred to the angular gyrus (1) and Wernicke's area (2). These are association areas of the cortex in which the sound is associated with a specific word and its meaning. Next, the information is transferred to Broca's area (3) through a bundle of nerve fibers called the arcuate fasciculus, where the appropriate motor program for saying the word is selected. Finally, commands are sent to the motor cortex, which instructs the facial muscles to say the word.

"snow" and you repeat "snow"). This model was first suggested by the German neuroscientist Carl Wernicke in the 1870s and was refined in recent years by Norman Geschwind of Harvard. Wernicke had been intrigued by the pioneering studies in the 1860s undertaken by Paul Broca in France. Broca showed that damage to a particular portion of the cerebral cortex, usually in the left cerebral hemisphere, causes speech disorders, or aphasias. Two of the most important areas in the brain's language circuit have since been named after Broca and Wernicke.[5]

Broca's area is located near the motor cortex, which contains an abstract map of the body in a strip across the top of the head. This map is used by the cerebral cortex to activate the body's muscles. Broca's area is attached to that part of the map that activates the muscles in the face and jaw. Wernicke's area is located in the pathway of signals from the primary auditory area, which receives information from the ears. Wernicke's area and Broca's area are linked by a bundle of nerve fibers called the arcuate fasciculus.

Wernicke's area affects comprehension; Broca's area affects the coordination and control of the muscles that are used in vocalizing a word. This simple model explains many of the speech disorders that are produced by brain damage. Normally when the brain hears a sound, the auditory system transfers the information to the primary auditory area, which then transmits it to Wernicke's area. It is in Wernicke's area that the sound is associated with a word. That information is passed on to Broca's area, which signals the motor cortex to begin the appropriate movement of the muscles that will allow the mouth and vocal cord to repeat the word.

If Wernicke's area is damaged, a person often cannot recognize as words the sounds he hears. The association between sound and meaning has been broken. The word is just gibberish with no associations linked to it. If Broca's area only is damaged, the patient may well continue to understand perfectly what is being spoken. But the motor program that controls vocalization is not being activated properly, and the patient has difficulty repeating the word. If the arcuate fasciculus only is damaged, then Wernicke's area is unable to communicate with Broca's area. Often the patient understands what is being said but when asked to repeat the phrase, utters a string of perfectly articulated but totally inappropriate words. Wernicke's area is not able to signal Broca's area to select the correct words, so the brain just seems to guess. This kind of nonsense speaking is also seen when Wernicke's area is damaged, but it is accompanied by lack of comprehension of what was said.

Next examine Figure 7.2, which describes a model of seeing and then repeating a word. New studies using positron emission tomography (PET scans) show which brain areas are active while the brain is performing this task by measuring the relative blood flow to different areas of the brain. The studies reveal that information goes directly from the primary visual area to the angular gyrus, an area of the brain that seems to be responsible for recognizing the shape of words. Damage to the angular gyrus can lead to an aphasia called word blindness, in which a person cannot recognize written words, though he can speak and recognize spoken words. The angular gyrus

Seeing and Then Speaking a Word

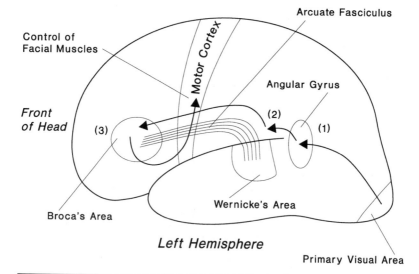

Figure 7.2. Recent studies indicate that the act of seeing and repeating a word has a different neural pathway than hearing and repeating a word (see Figure 7.1). Information from the eyes is transferred to the primary visual area at the back of the head. It is then transferred to the angular gyrus (1), where it begins the process of being associated with sounds that can be spoken. The processed information bypasses Wernicke's area and is transferred, via the arcuate fasciculus (2), directly to Broca's area (3), where the motor cortex is instructed to speak the word. Both this figure and Figure 7.1 show only simplified versions of complex processes.

is another of the specialized areas of the brain. Unlike the pathway in hearing a word, the angular gyrus does not appear to transmit the visual information to Wernicke's area for association with meaning. Instead the information bypasses Wernicke's area altogether and goes to the arcuate fasciculus for transfer to Broca's area.

The association with meaning is performed somewhere other than Wernicke's area, apparently in visual association areas in front of the primary visual area. PET scans show, in fact, that the neural pathways for processing language are far more complicated than these sketches. They involve not only the cortex but deeper layers of the brain. Different classes of words seem to be processed differently; nonsense words are processed differently from standard words. There is parallel processing (computation that goes on simultaneously in many different areas) as well as serial processing (processing information one step at a time).

Parallel processing of information along multiple pathways simultaneously is a vital strategy that the brain uses not only in perceiving and thinking, but in responding to injury. As Eric Kandel points out, only elementary operations, not complex abilities, seem to be localized. Complex abilities such as language are produced by the interconnection of many different elementary operations (neural pathways) in parallel. If complex abilities were produced by serial operations, like links in a chain, then the destruction of one link would cripple the ability, just as the failure of one component in a serial computer shuts down the entire machine. But this rarely happens in the brain because many pathways operate in parallel. If one pathway is disrupted, then the other pathways continue to function and can sometimes compensate for the damage.

This explains the brain's ability to recognize patterns from very little or poor-quality information. A cartoonist uses this ability to draw cartoon figures with a minimum of lines.

On the other hand, the brain tends to be slow and inaccurate at performing large numbers of serial computations, such as those required by mathematics. Serial computers, in contrast, excel at such computations but do badly at pattern recognition. Within the parallel pathways, however, there probably are serial operations. And different abilities built on parallel processing may combine in a serial fashion to generate certain higher brain functions. There may be a synthesis of serial and parallel processing (although the foundation of all operations is probably parallel processing).

Making maps and interconnecting them into models that can transform raw data into meaningful information is clearly the brain's most important function. The picture that your eyes are producing of this book is the result of the interconnection of at least eighteen to twenty-four different visual maps in the brain. These maps, in turn, are connected with maps that link the visual information recorded by your eyes, such as the shape of the words, to maps that give the associated meanings.

Diagrams of the brain always oversimplify its staggering complexity. The brain does not have a neat, logical, compartmentalized organization. As I have pointed out, it is messy, redundant, and variable, reflecting the messy, variable world with which it must cope. It is a nonlinear organ for a nonlinear world. Different brains develop different strategies for processing information. Although virtually all right-handed people and the majority of left-handers have their primary speech centers in their left cerebral hemisphere, some people have them on the right.

When the brain is damaged, lost functions are often at least partially restored after a period of time. Children tend to be much more resilient than adults, probably reflecting the greater activity of their NMDA receptors, which help rewire the brain.

The brain's two hemispheres do have a certain number of specialized functions. A region of the brain called the planum temporale, which is hidden within the folds of the Sylvian fissure (see Figure 6.3), is larger on the left side in most people. The planum is associated with the language centers. This asymmetry can be seen even in the fetus. For most of us, the left hemisphere seems to be genetically programmed to specialize in the production of certain kinds of speech.

Yet it is a popular misconception, rejected by most neuroscientists, to assume that there are radical differences in left-brain, right-brain thinking that can be exploited to improve creativity or critical thinking. The hemispheres of the brain are somewhat redundant and have evolved to work together. Language is designed to be produced and interpreted by both hemispheres. Someone with damage to the right hemisphere may seem on the surface to continue to speak and understand normally. But the emotional centers of the right brain may be impaired, preventing the brain-damaged person from understanding the emotional overtones of what another speaker is saying.

THE CONTEXT OF THOUGHT

Far more important than the differences in the hemispheres is the basic point that synaptic connections are associated by NMDA receptors, cAMP cascades, and other means to form models of the inner and outer environment. One of the most important conclusions of this book is that learning is modeling and consciousness is modeling at its highest level of abstraction. Through consciousness, we not only model the environment but know that we are modeling it. Models can be nested within models and all of them can be used to alter behavior. The more effectively a model is learned, the more it is related to other models that already exist in the brain to form a larger picture of reality that can be used to predict the future and manipulate the future potentialities.

We remember associative maps, not isolated facts. The only exception is short-term memory, which allows us to remember a telephone number or other item for a few minutes. Long-term memory consists of maps and models built through association—the language map, the body map, the causality map, the logic map, the map of acquaintances, and so forth—not of unconnected facts. These maps in turn are interrelated. When we remember something we do not just record it as a computer would; we must place it in a location on a map or maps. We do not simply remember things; we map things. To move a fact from short-term to long-term memory, we must make the associations necessary to map it, such as linking it to our family or our business. Placing a fact or concept in a map is placing it in a category. Our memory is therefore not like the disassociated memory registers of a computer.

The best evidence that the natural operating system of thought, unlike a computer, is associative rather than logical is the fact that the brain is relatively inaccurate and slow in performing logical functions. Yet it is wonderfully swift at making complex associations, such as recognizing a face from just a few features—something that no computer has been able to master.

One of the major implications of the associative nature of the brain's operation is that the mind does not create context-free interactions with the world. Through associations, the synaptic code always creates contexts for information. A vital part of unified selection is the process of shaping and sorting contexts. Just as a living organism is shaped by the niche in which it lives, an idea takes on meaning from the context in which it exists. Every word and idea has meaning within a given context, and this meaning shifts as the context shifts. The interpretation of the same written words through history changes with the context of the times. To an Elizabethan audience, *Hamlet* might be a poetic play of supernatural revenge, while to a twentieth-century audience, it might be a study in Freudian psychology. Language is supremely contextual. The meaning of any sentence is embedded in the entire network of assumptions of the language. Meaning and context are inseparable. As the language evolves, meaning evolves.

Our sensory perceptions are embedded in contexts, and part of the marvel of the brain is its ability to keep up with shifting context. The sensations of temperature, light, sound, and touch, for example, depend on the context. The temperature of bath water may at first feel uncomfortably warm, but as our body adapts to it we cease to notice.

Consciousness is the epitome of context creation. It devises contexts for not only the patterns we perceive but for our own role as perceivers and actors in the world. A society tries to create a shared context among its citizens. In one context, someone may be a freedom fighter; in another, a terrorist. Influencing context is the essence of the power of opinion makers.

Human beings are not unique in their evolution of consciousness. It appears that chimpanzees and certain other primates share our sense of consciousness to some extent. While most animals do not recognize themselves in mirrors, studies have shown that chimpanzees do. In one study, chimpanzees were given access to a full-length mirror for ten days. At first they threatened and screamed at it, just as they would another chimpanzee. Within two or three days, however, their responses changed and they began to exhibit self-directed behavior. They used the mirror to groom themselves and inspect parts of their bodies that they could not otherwise see. On the eleventh day, the chimps were anesthetized and marked with harmless red spots on their faces. When they were again given access to a mirror, the chimps indicated a strong interest in the spots, which they could not otherwise see. Other chimps that had not been introduced to the mirror before being marked with the spots, showed no interest in them.

Chimpanzees and other primates have already shown an ability to learn in many ways, including the use of human sign language.

This is one more indication that their synaptic organization has many similarities with our own.

In the evolution of ideas, the fundamental unit is the individual mind. Every mind has available to it a pool of ideas, or a concept pool, contained within its memory and in its immediate environment. This is the equivalent of the organism's gene pool and is the source of synaptic variability and adaptability. Within the society as a whole, there is normally a more extensive pool of ideas that includes books, journals, and all other written and otherwise archived records. The pool also theoretically includes the contents of the minds of every member of society. Not all these ideas or idea fragments are equally accessible, of course.

Each mind selects from among the pool of available ideas. This selection may simply involve the sorting of ideas, or it may involve shaping ideas into new forms. The final idea can be reproduced in the minds of others through communication. Ideas can be put to use to organize other ideas, shape behavior, or shape forms of matter. With respect to its technology, laws, and educational system, a society uses a fundamental set of ideas to do all three.

For an idea to survive in a given brain, it must be consolidated from short-term to long-term memory. This involves specific associative processes affecting the number of synaptic connections between neurons, the strength of those connections, the amount of neurotransmitter vesicles in the presynaptic membrane, and the sensitivity of the postsynaptic membrane. We can observe the evolution of thought and behavior in a simple organism such as *Aplysia*. When it is sensitized, the number of neurotransmitter vesicles in the presynaptic membrane increases. This is tangible evidence of the existence of a thought or behavior. For *Aplysia*, the unspoken idea is, roughly, "I am threatened and must protect myself by withdrawing my gill." As *Aplysia* continues to respond to the environment, we can measure how the behavior changes. The behavior may be reinforced by the establishment of new permanent synaptic connections. If there is no reinforcement and the number of vesicles returns to normal, however, then the behavior "dies," just as an idea fails to survive in a human brain if it is forgotten.

As we saw in the earlier example of the amnesiac boxer, who was knocked out and lost his memories of the fight, forgetting may involve a disruption in the cellular processes that consolidate short-term memory into long-term memory. The synaptic connections that represent the memory are not preserved. This is most likely what happens when we memorize an unfamiliar telephone number just long enough to make a phone call. The short-term synaptic connections quickly dissipate. Yet this is only one of what are undoubtedly several different mechanisms of forgetting. Most of these mechanisms are not yet understood. For example, a memory can be successfully stored in long-term memory; nevertheless, it will fade over time. Our forgetfulness may be only partial since, as we have discussed, a memory is normally broken into pieces and stored in different parts of the brain. We may remember someone's face but not his or her name. It may well be that all forms of forgetfulness are linked to the relative strength of the synaptic connections that represent the memory and, in addition, the strength of the connection between this synaptic network and the portions of the brain that generate consciousness. If any of these connections are weak, then the probability that we will forget increases.

How did language originate? There are as many theories as there are experts. One intriguing idea compares synaptic maps in the brain to genes in the chromosomes. One way genes are thought to evolve is by unintentional duplication. The offspring of an organism may, by chance, sometimes have an extra copy of a useful gene. If this copy does no harm, then it may be preserved in the descendants. Over the generations, this extra gene develops a new function that may prove useful in adapting to the environment. The gene then spreads throughout the gene pool.

Similar ideas have been put forward about maps in the brain. Some individuals may be born with duplicate areas for mapping vision or hearing or some other function. This would require a slightly larger cortex. Since these duplicate areas are not needed, they can develop other specialties that may be useful. This is one way language might have developed. Duplicate brain areas by chance developed specializations in communication, and these skills were so valuable that the gene for this enlarged cortex spread throughout the human gene pool.

Language, and consciousness itself, may have developed as specializations in areas duplicating other sensory processing maps, such as vision or hearing. From one perspective, language itself is a kind of sense. Many animals mark their territory with scents. They recognize friend and foe by their scent. Human beings have a relatively poor sense of smell. But we have developed the compensating ability to mark our world with words. Language and consciousness are, in a way, the senses through which we see the world.

There is evidence, though still highly controversial, that language was an innovation that may have evolved in a small group of humans and then spread as that group spread throughout the world perhaps 100,000 years ago. Genetic studies indicate that the original population of *Homo sapiens* may have migrated out of southern Africa. A number of linguists contend that all human languages evolved from a single proto-language that may have originated with this same group. Some linguistic studies have pointed to southern Africa as the origin of this proto-language.

Cracking the synaptic code will give us the use of the tools nature created through billions of years of evolution for manipulating the maps and models created by the mind. If we use these tools wisely, we can eliminate mental illness and develop the abilities of the brain to their fullest capacity. We will enter an era of synaptic engineering, just as deciphering the genetic code has led to an era of genetic engineering.

PART FOUR

Cosmic Synthesis

It looks strange and it looks strange and it looks very strange; and then suddenly it doesn't look strange at all and you can't understand what made it look strange in the first place.

—GERTRUDE STEIN

C h a p t e r   8

Time Frames

WHAT IS THE NATURE OF TIME? AFTER SURVEYING THE THREE CODES, we are left with that basic question as we try to fathom the mystery of evolution. Time, it would seem, is a measure of change, yet change is a measure of time. How can we transcend these complexities?

Quantum mechanics provides a way. Remember that the fundamental tenet of quantum mechanics is that matter cannot be infinitely divided. There are basic units of matter, such as the electron and quark, that appear to be indivisible.

I would argue that time in the quantum universe also cannot be infinitely divided. There is a basic unit of time and it has been calculated using the fundamental constants of physics: Planck's constant, the constant of gravitation, and the speed of light. The result is what is called Planck time, which has a value of about 10^{-43} second. Let us call the duration of the Planck time a Planck instant. There are 10^{43} Planck instants in one second, in other words ten million trillion trillion trillion.

That may seem like a ridiculously large number, but physicists are used to breaking up time into incredibly small units. Molecules, for example, constantly vibrate. The bonds between atoms that form molecules vibrate about a trillion times a second. Atomic clocks that are used as the world's standard time pieces measure billions of atomic vibrations per second to keep track of the time. When you see a picture of an atom taken by a scanning tunneling electron microscope, remember that the atom you observe is not an ordinary object with an exact position and momentum. The atom must obey the uncertainty principle, therefore all a photograph can show is its approximate position, like the blurred picture of a fast-moving car.

What, then, is the significance of the Planck instant? I contend that this is the basic time frame of reality—that the entire universe collapses from multiple potentialities to a single actuality at every Planck instant, or 10^{43} times per second. No wonder reality seems so continuous and smooth to us. This rate of collapse is utterly undetectable. Commercial films give us the illusion of continuous motion and they are projected at a mere twenty-four frames per second.

My interpretation of quantum mechanics is controversial, of course. Yet all other interpretations are controversial as well. In the decades since the development of quantum mechanics, the meaning of the theory is still a matter of debate. The most widespread interpretation of quantum theory is the Copenhagen interpretation championed by Niels Bohr, which incorporates his principle of complementarity. This interpretation stresses that quantum reality only emerges when a measuring device interacts with a quantum phenomenon and collapses the wave function. I expand this interpretation by defining the measuring device as the universe as a whole. In other words, the structure of the universe as a whole at any given moment in the present, determines the probabilities for the structure of the universe as it will exist at the next moment through the collapse of the wave function.

Another more radical interpretation of quantum mechanics was developed in the 1950s by physicist Hugh Everett while at Princeton University. This is called the many worlds interpretation and seeks to dispense with the collapse of the wave function altogether. Everett argued that whenever a quantum measurement is made, the universe splits into many universes. Each of the new universes contains one possible result of the quantum measurement. Thus in the example of Schrödinger's cat—where there were two possibilities, one with the cat living and the other with the cat dying—rather than have these two potentialities collapse into one, the universe would split into two universes. The first universe would have a living cat and the second would have a dead cat. Although this interpretation is mathematically consistent, it requires the universe to constantly split into countless other universes as quantum measurements are made. Our consciousness somehow splits, too, so that we are only aware of one universe at a time. I find this interpretation unsatisfactory because it proposes no mechanism for understanding why we only perceive one universe at a time. What Everett believes are other concrete universes, I contend are simply future potentialities that cease to exist when the universe as a whole collapses into the present, from quantum moment to quantum moment.

This collapse of the wave function of the universe began with the big bang. At that point the universe began moving from potentiality to the actuality of evolving space, time, and matter. I call the continuing collapse of the wave function at every Planck instant the thermodynamic pulse. It was set in motion, like a massive shock wave, by the big bang itself. The change obeys the second law of thermodynamics because the state of the entire universe moves toward greater and greater disorder. The history of the entire cosmos can be characterized as the rippling of the thermodynamic pulse, as the universe collapses into existence one Planck instant after another. This constant collapse is the engine of unified selection and the evolution of the universe. (See Figure 8.1.)

As part of this evolution, the four fundamental forces of gravity, electromagnetism, the strong force, and the weak force split apart as time progressed. To reunite them would require the stupendous temperatures that could only be produced in a particle accelerator whose length would be measured in light years. [1]

For unified selection, the most important symmetry broken in the expansion and cooling of the macroscopic universe is the symmetry of time. In the microscopic world of atoms and subatomic particles, time is symmetric. There is no past or future, only a constant reshuffling of particles and forces according to the rules of the quantum code. If the probability waves that can manifest themselves as atomic particles are thought of as billiard balls on a frictionless billiard table, they simply roll around striking each other endlessly. With few exceptions, time has no direction at this level. If a film of these billiard balls rolling around were shown backward, we would not be able to tell the difference. Time is reversible and

The Thermodynamic Pulse

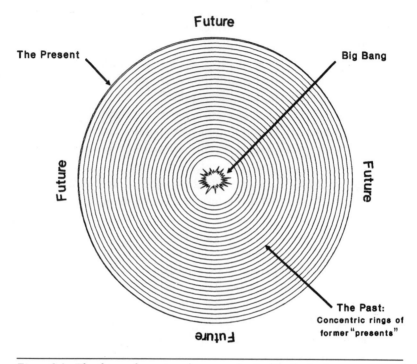

Figure 8.1. The thermodynamic pulse was unleashed by the broken symmetry of the big bang. It collapses future potentialities into the actuality of the present. The outer edge of the circle in the illustration represents the wave front of the collapsing present. The inner circles represent former presents that now constitute the past. Beyond the edge of the circle representing the present is the future with its infinite potentialities.

symmetrical. There is no preferred direction. The past and the future all look the same.

In the microworld, nuclear reactions that can take place in one direction can take place in the other direction as well. A nucleus of the radioactive element uranium^{238} can emit an alpha particle (a bundle of two protons and two neutrons) and transform itself into another element, thorium^{234}. But the reverse can also occur. An alpha particle can strike thorium^{234} and create an atom of uranium^{238}. In the macroworld, this is a bit like having equal probabilities that a dropped glass will shatter on the floor, and that shards of glass on the floor will suddenly form themselves into a glass and pop back into your hand.

As countless trillions of atomic and subatomic particles were created and the universe expanded from the microscopic to the macroscopic scale—from the scale of electrons and protons to the scale of stars, planets, life, and thought—time underwent a profound transformation; it gained an arrow, a direction. The future became distinguishable from the past. If we watch a film of a normal-size billiard table and see the ricocheting balls suddenly forming a neat triangle in the middle of the table with the cue ball bouncing off the point of the triangle, we know the film is running backward. Such an occurrence is so improbable that it is out of the question.

The direction of time is closely bound up with the concepts of order and disorder: the concepts of thermodynamics. The first law of thermodynamics states the familiar principle that energy cannot be created or destroyed, it can only be transformed. The total amount of energy in the universe is constant. There is no way to create any more of it. Energy can only change from one form to another. (Remember, matter is a form of bound energy.) In any given reaction, the total amount of energy that was there at the beginning is there at the end. Only the forms of energy change. When a stick of dynamite (the invention that made the philanthropist Alfred Nobel his fortune) is detonated, the chemical energy of the nitroglycerine in the dynamite is transformed into the heat energy of the explosion. If we could gather up all the energy of the explosion and measure it, we would find that it is exactly equal to the energy contained in the dynamite.

The second law of thermodynamics says something very profound about the way energy changes its form. It is this law that established the arrow of time in the universe. The second law states that in any closed system, forms of energy will tend to change from those that have greater order to those that have less order. In the long run, the amount of disorder will reach a maximum. The chemical energy in a stick of dynamite is highly organized. The molecules of nitroglycerine in the dynamite are packed into an orderly structure. With the explosion, this ordered form of energy is transformed into a disorderly form: heat. Instead of being a highly organized set of molecules, the heat consists of the random motions of atoms that are in no particular order. During the transformation from an orderly to a disorderly form of energy, however, the dynamite is able to perform work, perhaps blasting a highway through a mountain or carving the foundations for a building out of solid rock.

If we assume that the universe is a closed system, which most physicists do, and recognize that matter and energy are equivalent, then the universe is moving toward a state of maximum disorder—a state in which no work can be done and no life can exist. In the language of thermodynamics, disorder is known as entropy. As the universe expands, the amount of entropy or disorder it contains continually grows. But pockets of greater order can be created. Life itself is a form of matter that is highly organized and thus has very low entropy. According to the second law of thermodynamics, however, the creation of order must be compensated for by the simultaneous appearance of even greater disorder. The amount of disordered energy generated in the manufacture of the stick of dynamite is greater than the ordered energy contained in the dynamite itself, far greater. This disordered energy normally takes the form of waste heat produced when machines are operated or chemical processes take place.

The second law decrees that in any process we must always put in more ordered energy than we get out. That is the reason that no one will ever be able to construct a perpetual motion machine. In the thermodynamic universe, any machine will stop running eventually unless it is supplied with additional ordered energy.

Imagine a record turntable that is attached to a small electric generator, an electric motor, and a battery. The turntable is constructed so that it produces a minimum amount of friction. The generator, motor, and battery are the most efficient possible. If we give the turntable a push, it starts spinning. As it spins, it turns a belt which spins a magnet inside a coil of wire in the electric generator. This produces electricity, which is stored in the battery. The electric generator has a sensor that determines how fast the turntable is spinning. When the turntable's friction causes it to slow to a certain speed, the sensor triggers a switch that causes the energy stored in the battery to flow into the electric motor, turning it on and speeding up the turntable to its original velocity. The sensor then turns off the motor and electricity is again generated and stored in the battery, ready to speed up the turntable the next time it slows.

This is one theoretical perpetual motion machine. The energy we imparted to the turntable with our initial spin is used to generate the energy needed to keep the turntable spinning forever. If this machine worked, there would never again be an energy shortage or concern about depleting the Earth's supply of fossil fuels and other nonrenewable energy sources. We could build machines that always produced at least as much energy as it took to start them running. Once you started your car's perpetual motion engine, it would run forever with no additional gasoline. And if our turntable produced more electricity than was needed to keep it spinning at the desired speed, then we could siphon off some of the excess from the battery to run other machines.

Unfortunately, such a machine will never work. The electricity produced by the turntable will always be less than the amount necessary to accelerate it to its original speed. The disordered waste heat generated by the friction of the spinning turntable, the turning belt, the rotating magnet, the gears of the motor, and the chemical processes in the storage battery will gradually leach away the order of the energy and its ability to do work. The turntable will spin more and more slowly until it stops.

A lump of coal represents a highly ordered form of energy. But when that coal is burned, the gases and other waste products it generates cannot be collected and burned again to produce the same amount of energy as the original lump of coal. The ordered energy of the coal has been irretrievably degraded into less ordered forms of energy. With the burning of that lump of coal, the total disorder in the universe has been increased by a tiny but measurable amount. The second law was formulated in the nineteenth century by scientists trying to understand the operation of the new steam engine. Ever since, engineers have factored it into their designs for machines of all kinds.

The process of creating or maintaining order inescapably degrades more order than it produces. The food we eat to stay alive and healthy is a highly ordered form of energy. The order of this energy is degraded by digestion in the process of fueling our continued existence. Every cell in our bodies is a tiny factory with an energy budget. The fuel for this factory is the molecule adenosine triphosphate (ATP). The food we eat is used to produce this molecule. ATP molecules are like tiny lumps of coal that are burned to provide the energy necessary for the cell to carry on its work.

The price of generating order in our thermodynamic universe is an acceleration in the production of disorder. Whenever order increases, whether in the form of new stars or new life, the total amount of entropy, or disorder, grows more rapidly than it would otherwise. Where will it all end? Scientists can only make educated guesses. If the disorder continues to increase into the future, then billions of years from now the universe will be a place without order or structure of any kind. All matter will have decayed. All energy will be in the form of waste heat, particles of which will move randomly about unable to perform any work. The creativity of the universe will be exhausted. After moving through states of greater and greater disorder, the universe will reach the graveyard of the heat death. (See Figure 8.2.)

There is good reason to believe that the universe, for the most

Journey to the Heat Death

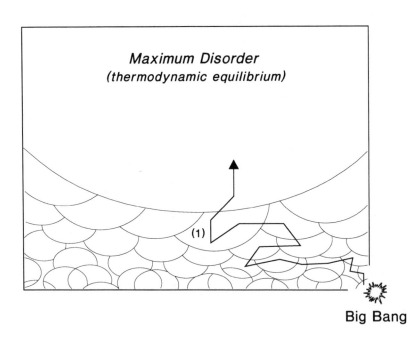

Figure 8.2. If the universe continues to expand, it will move through stages of greater disorder, represented by the successively larger cells, until it reaches maximum entropy or the heat death in which no life or order is possible. We may have already reached position (1) in this process.

part, died this entropy death long ago. We are living in the long, drawn out aftermath. Most of the order in the universe has already dissipated. The pervasive cold cosmic background radiation represents the resulting sea of entropy. The order embodied in the stars and galaxies is insignificant compared to this massive reservoir of disorder.

This theoretical perspective is supported by the comparatively small amount of matter in the universe (even assuming that physicists discover the estimated ninety percent of dark matter that they believe has yet to be observed). Although galaxies such as the Milky Way contain a hundred billion stars and there are billions of galaxies, the galaxies lie on the edge of far vaster areas in which there is virtually no matter at all. It is as if the galaxies were specks of dust floating on the surface of colossal bubbles of emptiness. The universe may be like our stick of dynamite: most of its ordered energy dissipated when it exploded, leaving a few glowing embers and wisps of smoke that are slowly dying away.

FATE OF THE UNIVERSE

Will the universe continue expanding forever? Not necessarily. If a sufficient amount of matter is ultimately found, its mutual gravitational force may be enough to stop the universe's expansion and begin a contraction. After billions of years, the universe that began in a big bang will end in what has been called the big crunch. All matter and energy will again be compressed into an infinitesimally small space. Time may then cease to exist, though some have suggested that the universe will again explode into another big bang. The pulsating universe theory suggests that the universe goes through an endless cycle: big bang, expansion, contraction, big crunch, and big bang again. (See Figure 8.3.)

According to Albert Einstein's general theory of relativity, the amount of matter in the universe also affects the curvature of space-time, since matter warps space-time. If there is enough matter in the universe to halt the expansion, then space-time curves inward on itself and we are living on the skin of a four-dimensional globe. This is the closed universe theory. If there is not enough matter in the universe to stop the expansion, then the curvature is outward and we are living on the surface of a saddle-shaped curved surface. This

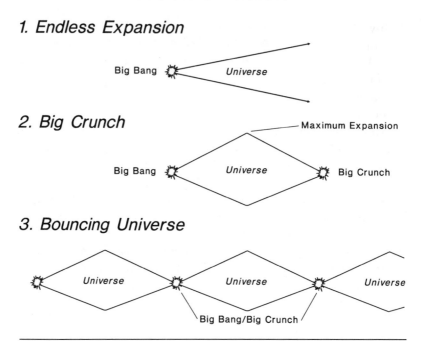

1. Endless Expansion

Big Bang — Universe

2. Big Crunch

Maximum Expansion

Big Bang — Universe — Big Crunch

3. Bouncing Universe

Universe — Universe — Universe

Big Bang/Big Crunch

Figure 8.3. Physicists believe that the universe has three possible fates. If there is too little matter to stop the expansion of the universe through gravitational attraction, then the universe will go on expanding endlessly. If there is sufficient matter to slow and then reverse the expansion, physicists say the universe is closed and it will eventually begin to contract into a big crunch. The final possibility is a variation of the closed universe. At the big crunch the universe rebounds into another expansion. We then have a cycle of big bangs and big crunches.

is the open universe theory. If there is any tentative consensus among scientists, it is that there does not seem to be enough matter to halt the expansion. We appear to live in an open universe.

The expansion and cooling of the universe, which produces the second law of thermodynamics, establish a distinct arrow of time and a clear delineation between present and past. At any moment of thermodynamic time, the universe as a whole is larger and more disordered than it was the moment before. Increasing entropy is something we take for granted in everyday life. As we have seen, an office or home never spontaneously becomes neater. It becomes cluttered and disorganized unless an effort is made to keep it orderly. When a new deck of cards is first shuffled, the ordered arrangement of suits is lost. As the deck is shuffled further, the chance that the cards will again become neatly rearranged according to suits is practically nil, even if the deck is shuffled for a lifetime or a million lifetimes.

As the deck of cards illustrates, the nature of thermodynamic disorder is statistical. The ordered arrangement of a new deck is one way to arrange the cards. But there are an astronomical number of other ways to rearrange the fifty-two cards, a number equal to approximately 1 followed by sixty-eight zeros. The chances of a shuffled deck reproducing its original order are so negligibly low as to be out of the question. If our deck consisted of only two cards, however, the original arrangement would have a fifty-fifty chance of coming up with each shuffle.

Or take a small jar in which a layer of salt is covered by a layer of pepper. If the jar is shaken, the layers of salt and pepper immediately blend. If we are shown a film of a jar of blended salt and pepper being shaken and the pepper and salt suddenly separate into distinct layers, we know that the film is being shown backward. But if we are watching a jar with one grain of salt and one grain of pepper being shaken, we have no way of telling whether the film is being shown forward or backward. The future and past, in that case, are interchangeable.

This is the essence of the second law of thermodynamics. For any large collection of objects, there is a practically infinite number of disorderly ways these objects can be arranged and there are only a few orderly ways. The chances of producing a disorderly arrangement are exceedingly high when compared to the chances of producing an orderly arrangement. In the long run, disorder will relentlessly overwhelm order. Statisticians have calculated that it takes seven shuffles before the orderly arrangement of a deck of cards becomes completely random. The idea of order is subjective in the sense that any arrangement of cards can be termed orderly. But no one arrangement is likely to appear again.[2]

In our macroscopic world—which begins with large molecules like DNA and goes up to objects the size of galaxies and beyond— the probability that atoms will spontaneously order themselves into a coherent form is practically zero. One of the reasons for the existence of the second law of thermodynamics is that the big bang created a universe with vast numbers of particles. It is inconceivable that all these particles could ever spontaneously move in a coherent fashion. If order is to be created, energy or work must be added, and this always creates more disorder than the order it produces. When left to themselves, forms of matter and energy that represent high degrees of order are inevitably degraded into forms that are much more random and probable. Living things die and suns burn out.

The substructure of matter and energy that underlies our macroscopic world remains quantitatively unchanged throughout history. As the first law of thermodynamics states, matter and energy can neither be created nor destroyed; only their form can change. The second law of thermodynamics then states that forms of matter and energy tend to move from those that are more orderly to those that are less orderly. This is a qualitative change in structure. The matter and energy of the universe is constantly being rearranged by thermodynamic time, and this shuffling results in a collection of forms that, as a whole, is more and more disorderly.

The microscopic world of matter and energy is ageless and timeless. Nothing is ultimately created or destroyed. Subatomic particles are merely shuffled and reshuffled. Time has no arrow. Yet the macroscopic world of forms both ages and has a distinct flow of time. Contingent forms of matter and energy are constantly being created and destroyed. The past differs from the future. The macrocosm is filled with changing forms of matter, life, and thought. There is a harsh difference between the two realms. When a living organism dies, its form is destroyed, yet the quantum particles out of which it was made are simply reshuffled back into the environment.

How can order be created in a world ruled by the second law of thermodynamics? The answer rests with the quantum code, the genetic code, and the synaptic code. Before we turn to these codes, consider once more a deck of cards. The odds of shuffling a randomly mixed deck so that the cards separate in numerical order by suit is so small as to be effectively zero. But what if the cards did not slide easily over each other? What if they were selectively sticky? Imagine taking the time and energy to paste small, thin, sticky strips—like Velcro—on the front and back of every card. The front and back of each card has its strip in a specific place that exactly coincides with the strip on the card that precedes it and the card that follows it in an orderly arrangement. (The first and last cards in the deck only have one strip because they do not come between two cards.)

The front of the four of clubs, for example, might have a small sticky strip on its upper right-hand corner. The back of the three of clubs would have its sticky strip on the upper left-hand corner so that if the four of clubs were placed on top of the three of clubs the two cards' strips would exactly match and stick together. The back of the four of clubs might have a sticky strip in the upper left-hand corner. The front of the five of clubs would have a matching strip in its upper right-hand corner. Except for the first and last cards in the deck, each of the cards would have a strip on the front and back, matching those on the cards that it precedes and follows in an orderly arrangement. The strips would be placed in slightly different locations on the cards so that two strips would coincide only for cards in the proper order. If the five of clubs were placed on top of the four of clubs, the two cards' strips would be in the same relative location and would stick together. But if the four of clubs were placed on the three of diamonds, the sticky strips would be in different locations and would not match. (Since this is only a thought experiment, we will minimize the difficulties of actually shuffling such a deck. We will also assume that as they are shuffled the cards retain the same orientation; in other words none of the cards is turned upside down in the shuffling process.)

If this deck were shuffled over and over, with each shuffle there would be a random but fairly good chance that a few cards would come together in the order they would be in if the deck were arranged by suits. If the four of clubs happened to be shuffled on top of the three of clubs, the two cards would stick together during the next shuffle. This would slightly reduce the odds against shuffling the deck into an orderly arrangement. With two cards sticking together, we would now effectively have a deck of fifty-one cards instead of fifty-two. It is somewhat more likely that a deck of fifty-one cards can be randomly shuffled into an orderly arrangement than can a deck of fifty-two.

As the shuffling continued, more cards would stick together, further reducing the effective size of the deck, and the odds. Ultimately, the cards would stick together in two clumps. One clump might consist of two complete suits in proper order along with four cards of the next suit. The other clump would have the remaining cards of the third suit along with the cards in the fourth suit, all in proper order. The deck is now effectively reduced to two cards, which have a fifty-fifty chance of combining in a specified order. After another shuffle or so (it would actually be more like cutting the cards) the clumps of cards would come together so that the bottom card of one clump would be on top of the proper card of the second clump and the whole deck would stick together, arranged in order by suit. With the cards' selective stickiness, reaching this highly ordered arrangement would take a relatively short time instead of millions of years.

But there is one more twist to this example. From the outset, as I shuffle the cards, I have the option of shuffling gently, vigorously, or somewhere in between. If I shuffle vigorously, bending each stack of cards far back as I riffle them together, the bonds between the cards that have managed to stick together are likely to be broken. If I shuffle gently, exerting very little pressure, then the cards that have stuck together will likely stay together. If I shuffle with a force somewhere in between, then some of the clumps of cards will probably stay together while others will come unstuck. This additional element makes it more difficult for the cards to come together in the proper order; but it is still far more likely that they will reach an orderly arrangement than would a deck of non-sticky cards.

Our special deck of cards illustrates in a simple way the mechanism of unified selection. The fundamental codes impart a selective stickiness to matter and energy that permits pockets of order to cumulatively build up as the universe shuffles its way to maximum entropy. The order developed at one step creates new possibilities for further order to be elaborated in successive steps. Each step is affected by the steps that have gone before. The energy required to generate and maintain this order increases the disorder of the universe as a whole. In this way, evolution can temporarily overcome the staggering odds against order emerging spontaneously at the macroscopic scale. If living things could only be created by the spontaneous fusing of gigantic numbers of protons, neutrons, and electrons—with no intermediate steps—the universe would have to be trillions of years old, instead of only fifteen to twenty billion, before even the simplest forms of life would be likely to emerge. We would be back to endlessly shuffling a standard deck of cards, waiting for its original order to reappear.

The engine of unified selection is the expansion and cooling of the universe. Through thermodynamic time, the constant shuffling of tremendous numbers of microscopic atoms and particles produces greater and greater disorder at the macroscopic level. But the stickiness provided by the codes allows a selective clumping of matter and energy that can, step by step, create orderly structures that temporarily resist the general tendency to disorder. But no form can resist forever. Stars may last billions of years but they inevitably burn out. Even black holes may eventually evaporate. Indeed, fundamental forms such as the synaptic and genetic codes eventually succumb. Once every contingent life-form capable of thought dies out, then the synaptic code will disappear. Yet even when all contingent forms of matter and energy reach a maximum of disorder, it would seem that the quantum code will remain, since it determines the very structure of the universe. Only the quantum code is eternal.

It is the laws of the quantum code that generate the mutual gravitational attraction within gigantic clouds of space dust, causing them to contract into densely packed cores that ignite to become stars. Once stars come into existence they become furnaces for cooking protons, neutrons, and electrons into heavier and heavier elements. The subatomic particles within stars stick together in specific ways, the most common of which is for the protons and electrons in hydrogen atoms to fuse to form helium. The quantum code also enables the formation of other heavier elements under the enormous temperatures and pressures within the star and under the even more extreme conditions of a supernova—that is, the explosion of a large star.

Our solar system evolved from a cloud of dust and gas impregnated with heavier elements created by the supernova of older stars. The existence on Earth of carbon and other heavy elements allowed the formation of the large, complex molecules that are essential to life. The rules of the genetic code, which are nested within the quantum code, permitted the clumping of nucleotides into long chains to form the DNA molecules that carry hereditary information. These molecules were incorporated into simple forms of life that, in turn, enabled other forms of life that feed on these simpler forms to evolve. The whole complex, interrelated structure of life began to unfold. The evolution of plants, which harvest the energy of the sun, prepared the way for the evolution of animals that consume these plants, and finally the evolution of animals that prey on the plant-eaters.

The simple information-processing machinery of early life was elaborated into the sophisticated brains of more complex animals. Governed by the synaptic code, the cells in the larger brains of vertebrates and particularly one species, *Homo sapiens*, developed the ability to form unusually complex interconnections that permit the storing and processing of information. Webs of ideas developed. Initially, these ideas permitted *Homo sapiens* to evolve a more complicated social behavior than other primates and made possible the development of rudimentary forms of language and technology. The existence of these technologies and patterns of behavior opened up the potential for a more complex elaboration of the social and economic order, leading eventually to advanced technological societies.

The process by which variations of matter, life, and thought build up their order is, of course, extremely intricate. The variations that come into existence as the codes interact with the shuffling of thermodynamic time are constantly undergoing selection. In our example of the deck of sticky cards, the force of selection was represented by the variable shuffling, from gentle to vigorous. If shuffled gently, the cards that are stuck together tend to stay together. If shuffled vigorously, they will probably come unstuck. If the intensity of the shuffling is somewhere in between, then some cards will probably continue to stick to each other while others will come unstuck. Each shuffle is an act of selection. To survive for another generation, cards that have stuck together must withstand the pressure of shuffling without coming apart. By surviving, a particular clump can grow by adding more cards. If eight or nine cards have stuck together instead of one or two, then even a moderately vigorous shuffle is unlikely to break up the whole group completely and the orderly arrangement of cards in that clump has a better chance of surviving for several generations.

Gentle shuffling is a metaphor for an environment that is favorable to the preservation and accumulation of variations. An example of vigorous shuffling might be the nova of the sun, which would expand its borders outward far enough to engulf the earth and vaporize all the accumulated life forms on our planet.

Unified selection focuses on both the fundamental and contingent forms of matter, life, and thought, and how they are created, persist through time, and change. The mechanism of unified selection is, I contend, variation and selection. Variations are produced as thermodynamic time flows through the quantum, genetic, and synaptic codes, producing an array of unique structures. These forms are then built up or torn down by selection, which is the interaction of the structures with their environment from moment to moment. The environment is the totality of the circumstances in which a structure finds itself. The way the structure responds to the environment depends not only on the nature of the circumstances, but also on the rules of the code, which limit the ways a structure is capable of responding. A DNA molecule is structurally incapable of transforming itself directly into a protein molecule. But over time, DNA has evolved a method for indirectly creating the chains of amino acids that constitute proteins.

A structure may be unable to adapt to its environment. A star that finds itself too near a black hole may be torn apart by the intense gravitational field of the black hole. DNA-like molecules may form on a planet with a fluctuating environment. If the environment becomes overheated, the DNA will break down. In wrestling with a problem, a mind may generate an idea that it then rejects as unacceptable. The idea dies by being forgotten.

In summary, what does unified selection tell us about the nature of time? Through unified selection we find three time barriers that lock us into a present that is constantly collapsing from potentialities into actuality. I call these barriers the uncertainty barrier, the thermodynamic barrier, and the light barrier.

The uncertainty barrier prevents us from simultaneously knowing the precise position and momentum of any quantum particle. Thus the future of that particle is always subject to uncertainty. Unlike the concrete actuality of the present, the future exists in a different realm: the realm of potentialities. As creatures of the present we cannot directly penetrate the future.

The thermodynamic barrier, a product of the evolution of the universe since the big bang, is a barrier to the past. According to the second law of thermodynamics, the universe as a whole becomes increasingly disorderly as time passes. If travel to the past were possible, the state of the universe could be made more orderly instead of less. A perpetual motion machine would be possible because we could always sneak back in time and refuel and repair the machine so that it would continue operating endlessly.

The light barrier also prevents us from traveling to the past. The best way to understand this is to examine the twin paradox that is often used to illustrate the general theory of relativity. In that paradox, one twin takes off in a spacecraft at nearly the speed of light. Since the clocks aboard the spacecraft run slower than those on Earth, the traveling twin ages more slowly than his brother.

As the twin in the spacecraft moves nearer and nearer the speed of light, his clock runs more and more slowly. If he actually reached the speed of light (which Einstein said no object with a rest mass can do because the mass would increase to infinity) then his clock would stop with respect to the Earth. And if the twin could accelerate past the speed of light, then his clock would start to move backward with respect to the twin on Earth and he would be moving into the past.

What is the nature of this strange quantum present that we are trapped in by the three time barriers? In the 1960s physicist John Stewart Bell suggested that there must be instantaneous connections among phenomena with shared wave functions. If two photons are emitted in opposite directions from the same light source, for example, their wave functions become entangled, resulting in a single wave function describing them both. If we collapse the wave function for one of the photons, it instantly affects the other photon, even if it is on the other side of the universe. It is as if the photons were two coins taken from the same roll of quantum coins. The entangled wave function for these two quantum coins might specify that if they are flipped at the same time, no matter how far apart they are, whenever one of them randomly comes up heads the other must come up tails, and vice versa. Careful laboratory experiments have shown that where quantum particles are concerned, this is exactly the kind of thing that happens.

I would argue that the most satisfying way to explain this bizarre result is to assume that the wave function of the universe collapses instantly at every moment of the present throughout the cosmos. Entangled quantum phenomena within this wave function are instantly correlated, but this correlation prevents us from violating the light barrier because it takes the form of random patterns that are useless for things like instant communication.

With the twentieth-century breakthroughs in physics, genetics, and neuroscience, evolution has emerged as the unifying principle behind all change in the universe, on the largest scale and the smallest. This principle has brought with it a new understanding of the nature of time. Evolution through the time frames of the universe is truly the master key to modern science.

Chapter 9

Unified Selection

JUST AS QUANTUM FIELDS PRODUCE SHIMMERING WEBS OF SUBATOMIC particles, the evolutionary field produces the changing forms of matter, life, and thought. This field emerges from a cosmic synthesis of the flow of time with the fundamental codes. As the fire of the big bang expands, cools, and dies away into maximum disorder, it generates an evolutionary field that can build up structures of astonishing complexity.

That metaphor of a dying fire seems bleak. Yet the perfect symmetry of the proto-universe that shattered in the big bang was beautiful but sterile. It was pure potential, the endless possibilities of which would never blossom into reality without a cataclysmic act of creation. In small ways, we too see this principle at work. A clean sheet of paper, a new book, a telescope fresh from the instrument maker all have a certain unblemished beauty. But the promise of each—the literature, the ideas, the discoveries—can never be fulfilled if they are left untouched, though we know that the price of using them will be their more rapid decay. A beautiful package must be unwrapped to be explored. The big bang freed the universe to exhibit its potential, part of which is the human race and other living things. Each of us is a unique creation of that potential and the course of our lives represents the unfolding of a portion of the universe's possibilities.

I have put evolution on a quantum footing by arguing that it proceeds through the constant collapse of the wave function. Out of the many potentialities inherent in the future, one state of the universe collapses into existence at every Planck instant of the present. A single potentiality is selected to become reality from the many potentialities that exist.

The application of quantum principles to the entire universe is audacious and controversial, but it is a direction in which a number of physicists and cosmologists are moving. Jonathan J. Halliwell of the Massachusetts Institute of Technology pointed out this trend. "Even more contentious is the most extravagant extrapolation possible: that quantum mechanics applies to the entire universe at all times and to everything in it. Acceptable or not, this is the fundamental assertion of quantum cosmologists."[1]

This is what I call unified selection. The selection is based on probabilities. The state of the universe at any given moment of the present influences the probable state of the universe at the next moment. The probabilistic influence of the present on the future is what I term the evolutionary field. If, for example, certain members of a species of animals have a trait that gives them an advantage over the other animals, then this structures the evolutionary field for that species so that the better adapted animals are, in the future, more likely to produce more offspring. In other words, in the many possible ways that the world might look in the future, the ones that include more offspring from the better adapted animals have a higher probability of coming to pass than do the others.

The concept of an evolutionary field arises out of the twentieth century's discovery of the mechanism of inheritance, which led to a new formulation of Darwin's ideas, integrating genetics with the process of variation and selection. Genetics not only revealed the unsuspected richness of variations produced by DNA, but also provided fundamental insights into the way the structure of the genetic code constrains the kinds of adaptations that can be produced by natural selection.

Ecology, an important branch of biology, studies how living things change as they interact with each other and their environment under the constraints of the genetic code. The evolutionary field represents the ecology of the cosmos. It is concerned with the interaction of all forms of matter, life, and thought under the constraints of the quantum, genetic, and synaptic codes. The evolutionary state of the universe at any moment in thermodynamic time constrains and channels, but does not completely determine, the changes in the universe at the next moment. Just as the broken symmetry of electromagnetism produces the electromagnetic field, the broken symmetry of thermodynamic time produces the evolutionary field. I argue that it is one of the fundamental fields of nature.

Since the notion of an evolutionary field began with biology, we will first examine its operation in the realm of life, then move to matter and thought.

The reshuffling of genes during sexual reproduction creates a practically infinite variety of genetic combinations, and can even create new genes when mistakes in copying and other errors occur. Mutations, which are changes in the nucleotide sequence, can also be caused by high-energy radiation, such as X-rays, and certain chemicals. Some of these mutations may have no effect on the organism. A few turn out to be beneficial. But many are damaging. For this reason there is great concern about the effects of mutagenic (mutation-causing) chemicals and radiation in the environment. If they affect the reproductive system, the result can be damaged offspring. If they affect other cells of the body, they may damage the genetic control over cell growth and lead to cancer.

For genes to undergo traditional natural selection, their traits must be physically expressed in the body of an organism. This is an elaborate undertaking. A gene must first work together with the other genes of the organism in the still poorly understood processes of generating a whole organism from a single set of genes. An organism's particular combination of genes is called its genotype. The physical characteristics produced by the genes are called the organism's phenotype. For example, the human genotype (set of human genes) produces the human phenotype (the human body with all its complex structures). Genes undergo elaborate interactions as an organism develops from a fertilized egg. If a gene causes difficulties during this period, the organism may never survive gestation, or it may be so weakened that it does not survive long after birth. Once an organism is fully formed, natural selection acts not just on a specific genetic trait but on the organism's genetic traits as a whole. An organism that has greater than average speed, for instance, may not thrive if it has other damaging genetic traits.

FUNDAMENTAL CONCEPTS

Three biological concepts—mosaic evolution, adaptive radiation, and ecology—are fundamental in analyzing the workings of evolution in realms other than life.

Mosaic evolution pictures organisms as being made up of separate pieces, like a mural fashioned from mosaic tiles. Although these pieces are closely coordinated, through history each piece and its underlying genes can experience different degrees of pressure from natural selection and, thus, evolve at a different rate. In mammals, there are dramatic differences in the speed of evolutionary changes in the circulatory system, jaws, and limbs. The mammalian circulatory system has remained very much the same in all species of mammals. It consists of a four-chambered heart connected to an elaborate system of arteries, veins, and capillaries. It has been under less selective pressure than the organs of feeding and movement, organs that must adapt directly to very different ways of life. One need only compare the limbs, jaws, and the digestive system of a dolphin, a cow, and a human being to see the elaborate adaptations to diverse environments of these structures among mammals. Ultimately, natural selection harmonizes the functioning of the separate pieces of the organism—by favoring (with longer lives and more offspring) organisms whose structures work together smoothly. Yet the different evolutionary rates are apparent.

Adaptive radiation describes the rapid proliferation of new species that takes place when an organism enters a favorable and unpopulated, or relatively unpopulated, environment. Through natural selection, the descendants of the initial population of organisms diversify, filling up as many niches as possible in the environment. A niche describes the organism's role in the environment, including what it eats and where it lives. Adaptive radiation occurred when amphibians first began to populate the land. Another important adaptive radiation occurred when the dinosaurs died out, emptying many niches that were rapidly filled by members of a previously minor class of small animals: the mammals. Whole new species of large mammals evolved to take the place of the dinosaurs. These included the ancestors of such modern animals as the elephant, rhinoceros, lion, bear, and whale.

Within ecology the term environment is very broadly defined. It refers to everything that influences the organism, from its molecular structure to the force of gravity. It includes a vast network of interactions—an organism's relationship with others, the terrain it inhabits, the weather, and so forth. The interaction between the environment and communities of different organisms is known as an ecosystem. These interactions are exceptionally complex. It is within an ecosystem that a niche is defined. Niches can be highly specialized. An owl that hunts small rodents at night is in a different niche from a hawk that hunts them during the day. An ecosystem normally has at its base the plants that harvest energy from the sun. Then come the plant-eating animals, predators that feed on the plant-eaters, parasites that feed on the predators, and the microorganisms that feed on all these forms when they die.

One group of biologists—Salvador E. Luria, Stephen Jay Gould, and Sam Singer—observes that ecology would be much more precise if niches could be more rigorously defined:

> But we cannot make a firm distinction between an external environment and the organisms living in it. Organism and environment are not separate entities; one does not precede and determine the other. Interaction and feedback are paramount; organisms structure environments as much as environments permit organisms to live in them.[2]

What is true for life-forms, I would argue, is true for matter and thought. Forms of matter and thought structure their environment as much as the environment structures them. Over time, the distinction between contingent form and environment is blurred. This is a basic characteristic of the evolutionary field. What biologists describe as ecology is, I believe, the application of the evolutionary field to life.

The blurring of form and environment within that field profoundly affects all things. For example, does the climate affect life or life affect the climate? The answer, of course, is both. The climate plays a central role in shaping all forms of life. The Earth's temperature lies in a narrow zone in which organic life, as we know it, is possible. Even within that zone, particular fluctuations such as extremely cold winters or droughts are major adaptive challenges to organisms. The periodic global ice ages have had a decisive impact on the course of evolution. But at the same time that climate influences life, life influences the climate. One of the major environmental concerns today is the greenhouse effect. Modern civilization is powered by fossil fuels such as coal, oil, and natural gas. The combustion of these fuels releases enormous amounts of carbon dioxide. Scientists are concerned that carbon dioxide in the atmosphere will act as an insulator, which will trap sunlight, heat up the Earth's surface, and change the climate. This could lead to melting polar ice caps, rising sea levels, the disruption of agriculture, or other results that we cannot yet foresee.

Green plants play an important role in removing carbon dioxide from the atmosphere. They use carbon dioxide in photosynthesis and release oxygen as a by-product. Some of the greatest concentrations of green plants are found in tropical rain forests, which cluster in a band along the equator, forming a green belt around the Earth. These forests, however, are being rapidly destroyed in the drive for agricultural and industrial development. Their ability to buffer the effects of fossil fuel combustion is eroding.

This is an example of how life may affect a nonliving system: the mixture of gases in the atmosphere and, ultimately, the weather. The atmospheres of planets like Mars and Jupiter also evolve, but apparently without the intervention of life.

I submit that the modern synthesis of Darwinian evolution and genetics, known as neo-Darwinism, has implications far beyond the realm of life. The mechanism of variation and selection operating through a code can be expanded to explain changing forms of matter, life, and thought in the entire universe. I define unified selection as the universal operation of variation and selection through a code.

FIVE PROPOSITIONS

Like Darwin's theory, my ideas about evolution can be grouped under five propositions. First, the universe with all its diversity is not static; it evolves. Second, everything in the universe has a common origin in the big bang. Third, evolution proceeds in a manner that can be rationally understood. Fourth, the mechanism of evolution is unified selection, in which variation and selection, operating in accord with the quantum, genetic, and synaptic codes, create and modify the contingent forms of matter, life, and thought. Fifth, Darwinian evolution must be integrated with quantum physics, cosmology, thermodynamics, and symmetry to develop a grand synthesis that seeks to provide a model for all evolutionary change.

This last point is perhaps the most important. I argue that the universe collapsed into existence at the big bang, generating a thermodynamic pulse that has been collapsing the potentialities inherent in the big bang into the present ever since. The future does not exist as anything but potentialities and the past is a long string of former "presents." (See Figure 9.1.)

Although the evolution of the wave function of the future

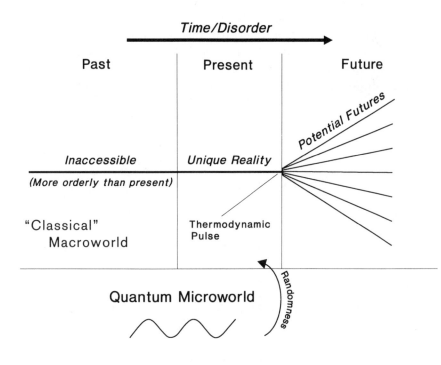

Figure 9.1. The thermodynamic pulse from the big bang collapses many potential futures into a single definite state of the present. The past is inaccessible because the second law of thermodynamics states that the universe must always move into states of greater disorder. Meanwhile, quantum randomness leaks from the microworld to the macroworld.

appears to be linear, the present universe is a complex, nonlinear place that amplifies quantum randomness and is thus essentially indeterminate. The mechanism of unified selection employs the variation and selection in a particular way. Variations are associated with the future potentialities. The odds that each of these potentialities will come into existence shifts over time, like the changing odds on a horse before a race. The odds are influenced by the changing state of the present.

Selection is identified with the collapse of the wave function, when one of the potential universes actually does come into existence. As the universe continually collapses into existence, the state of the universe at every moment in the present becomes the grist for the next round of evolution. There is a constant feedback process. (See Figure 9.2.)

Take the example of the American Civil War. In 1860, two contradictory potentialities existed: that the North would force the South to reunite with the Union or that the southern states would remain independent. The probabilities for each of these potentialities shifted as decisions were made in the present that reflected chance as well as purpose. When Robert E. Lee chose to lead the Army of Virginia rather than accept the position of head of the Union forces, the probability that the South would succeed in-

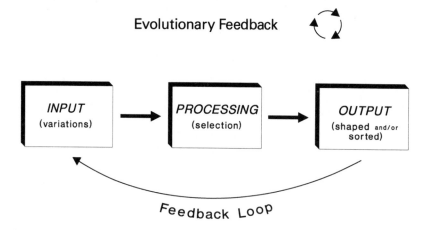

Evolutionary Feedback

Figure 9.2. The process of evolution has a continuous feedback loop in which those organisms and objects that successfully navigate the selection process become the variations for the next stage of evolutionary sorting and shaping.

creased. When Abraham Lincoln appointed Ulysses S. Grant as his commanding general, the probability that the South would succeed declined. A vast number of actions in the present shifted the odds on what would happen in the future, until the final collapse of multiple future potentialities into a single actuality: the South was defeated.

Symmetry principles are extremely important in unified selection, because it is the hidden and broken symmetries that have caused evolution to occur and forms to diverge. The aim of my theory of unified selection is to reconstruct the symmetries of life and thought, just as physics is seeking the primal force in which all matter and energy was once united. The three codes provide the structures on which evolution works its changes.

Nearly three-quarters of the matter in the universe is hydrogen. Most of the rest is helium. Less than four percent of all matter that we can detect consists of the heavier elements essential to life. The big bang model explains the fusing in the hot early universe of protons and electrons to form hydrogen atoms and the subsequent fusion of some of these atoms to form helium. Since then, additional helium and essentially all the heavier elements have formed in the cores of stars. The big bang model has been further strengthened by the finding that there are only three families of matter. This, again, means that there seem to be no extra superheavy families of matter lurking around and the composition of matter in the universe is consistent with the big bang theory.

The general theory of relativity predicts that the universe is either expanding or contracting, although Einstein initially resisted this interpretation. Georges Lemaître synthesized general relativity and the early astronomical evidence for expansion. He suggested that the universe began explosively from a primeval atom. An important part of Lemaître's argument was based on the observations of astronomers early in this century, who discovered a pronounced shift toward the red end of the spectrum in the spectral lines of the light from other galaxies.

Edwin Hubble, working at the Mount Wilson observatory outside Los Angeles, realized that this red shift was a kind of Doppler effect. The most common example of the Doppler effect occurs with sound. The horn of a car has a particular sound if the car is standing still. But if you stand on the sidewalk with the honking car traveling in your direction, the sound waves reaching your ears are being compressed by the relative motion of the car. This produces waves of a higher frequency and a higher pitch. But as the car speeds past you, the sound shifts to a lower pitch than you would hear if the car were standing still. This is because the relative motion of the car going away from you is stretching out the sound waves. (See Figure 9.3.)

Hubble concluded that the shift of the spectral lines toward the red or lower-frequency end of the spectrum is an example of the same phenomenon. Light waves from faraway galaxies and stars are being stretched out because they are speeding away from the Milky Way, our galaxy. In one of the greatest advances in the history of

The Doppler Effect

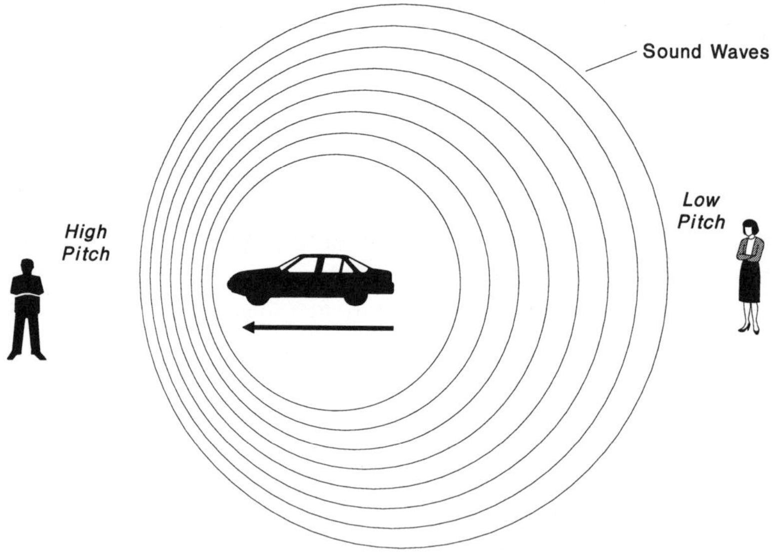

Figure 9.3. Sound waves generated by a moving car are compressed in the direction of its motion and stretched out as it recedes. This has the effect of increasing the frequency of the sound to an observer in front of the car and decreasing it to a person whom the car has passed. The person in front hears a higher-pitched sound than would have been the case if the car were stationary, while the person behind hears a lower-pitched sound. The same principle operates with the red-shifting of light from distant stars and galaxies. The light waves from a star moving away from the Earth are stretched out and have a lower frequency. We measure this as a shift toward the red or lower-frequency end of the spectrum of starlight.

astronomy, Hubble was able to make a rough correlation of the red shifts with relative speeds and distances of the receding galaxies. Science now had the tools to map the structure of the universe. The speeds at which distant galaxies move away from us are remarkably fast: from thousands of miles per hour to substantial fractions of the speed of light. The farther away a galaxy is, the faster its speed of recession. Only galaxies that are close enough to the Milky Way to have gravitational ties to it are not receding.

The red shift was critical evidence for the expansion of the universe. The geometry of the expansion explained the link between greater speeds of recession and greater distances from Earth. Imagine a huge balloon the size of a large asteroid. Drawn on the balloon's surface are three points labeled Milky Way, Galaxy 1, and Galaxy 2. The point labeled Milky Way is ten miles from Galaxy 1 and 100 miles from Galaxy 2. Now imagine that the balloon is inflating at a rate that doubles its size every hour. After an hour, Galaxy 1 will be twenty miles from the Milky Way and Galaxy 2 will be 200 miles away. Although the balloon is expanding at the same overall rate, the difference in distances between the points means that the speed of recession from the Milky Way of Galaxy 1 is ten miles per hour while the recession speed of Galaxy 2 is 100 miles per hour.

The evolving universe is therefore an expanding universe.

THE IDEA OF EVOLUTION

Although biologists and, later, physicists came to accept an evolutionary model of change, the acceptance of the evolution of thought—the continuous change of ideas over time—has been less focused. Historians of thought have often employed the general concept of evolution to trace the transformation of ideas through recorded time. Einstein entitled his history of the physics (written with Leopold Infeld) *The Evolution of Physics: From Early Concepts to Relativity and Quanta.* Many thinkers, including G. W. F. Hegel, Karl Marx, Herbert Spencer, and Pierre Teilhard de Chardin, have incorporated explicitly evolutionary elements in their ideas. These interpretations, however, have been dominated by notions of inevitable progress and cosmic design, rather than the opportunistic workings of variation and selection. Some thinkers have rejected evolution in favor of views that are more static. Plato, with his doctrine of eternal, unchanging forms, is often cited as an example. Yet Plato's philosophy may have been more a reflection of his preoccupation with fundamental forms, under the influence of the mathematical thinking of his day, than a categorical rejection of contingent forms.

Unified selection is opportunistic; it takes as its grist whatever is available at a given historical moment. Science has found no evidence of a larger purpose or design in the universe. Unified selection cannot be termed either progressive or regressive. It simply combines and recombines matter and energy into changing forms according to the rules of the codes. Sometimes this produces greater complexity. Sometimes complexity is broken down. Whenever there is a local increase in order, it is at the price of greater disorder in the larger universe. In an open universe that expands forever, the overall direction of change is toward maximum disorder.

No two ideas, living things, or forms of matter are exactly alike. Every one of them is custom-made by a unique historical sequence of steps. Each is the physical manifestation of one of the endless number of ways that matter and energy can be combined in accordance with the rules of the codes. In this sense, everything that has ever existed or will ever exist is inherent in the structure of the codes, just as everything that has ever been or will ever be written is inherent in the structure of language. The works of Shakespeare are both consistent with and inherent in the alphabet and structural rules of English. His works are one of the immense number of ways that the letters of the alphabet can be combined into understandable forms. Before the fact, it would have been impossible to predict that his works would ever be written in this particular way. Their actual creation was the result of both the unique set of historical circumstances that produced Shakespeare and his culture, and the contingent process of variation and selection that Shakespeare went through in composing them.

In an interview not long before his death, the renowned physicist Richard Feynman objected to the suggestion that great complexity of matter, life, and consciousness mysteriously brings forth completely new principles of change:

> It's certainly true that when things become complex we use new principles to help us analyze things. For example, in chess, bringing the pieces toward the center of the board increases their general strength. This is a principle which is not contained explicitly

in reading the rules of chess, but which can be understood in terms of the rules of chess in an indirect fashion. The principle is obviously a consequence of only those rules and of nothing else. Yes, indeed, there are wonderful principles, ideas of valence, sound, pressure, and many other organizing principles, which help to understand a complex situation. But to add that they're not contained in the fundamental laws is a misunderstanding. The fundamental laws have everything in them. It's just a question of finding convenient methods for analyzing complex systems.[3]

Although it is analytically useful to classify the genetic and synaptic codes as fundamental forms, they are also the products of evolution. If their rules should evolve further, then the potential kinds of life and thought would also change, just as a modification in the rules of chess would change the total set of potential games that could be played. In contrast, the quantum code appears to have existed for as long as the universe. Every form of matter, life, and thought is an inherent variation in the rules of the quantum code. The challenge of science is therefore twofold: first, to discover the complete rules of the quantum code (and the genetic and synaptic codes as well) and, second, to understand the steps that produce from these rules the complex and changing forms of matter, life, and thought that populate the universe.

I argue that within all evolution there is a common mechanism of evolutionary change: unified selection. Unified selection, I believe, is the mechanism that produces the diversity of forms in the macroscopic world. It operates throughout the three realms of existence—matter, life, and thought—to build up and break down complexity. It is fueled by thermodynamic time.

SHAPING AND SORTING

Unified selection unites matter, life, and thought in a common evolutionary process. It unites artificial and natural selection. There is no distinction between selection by human beings and natural selection. Humans are completely immersed in nature. Their works are just as much the product of nature as are the works of all other living things.

In addition, unified selection unites shaping evolution and sorting evolution in a single evolutionary process. Reproduction, which is a type of sorting, is the dominant mode of evolutionary change for living things. The environment does not act on the genes directly, but on the physical traits they express in the organism. If these traits have adaptive advantages, then the organism and the underlying genes reproduce and survive. If the genetic traits are maladaptive, then the organism is less likely to have offspring and the genes may disappear. Neither the environment nor the organism can act directly on the underlying genes. If greater speed would be advantageous to an organism, for example, the organism or its environment cannot tinker directly with its genes to construct a different genetic endowment that results in more speed. Reproductive evolution only works on populations, sorting out the individuals whose chance genetic endowment has produced greater speed. Reproductive evolution produces evolutionary change in populations, not in individuals.

Shaping evolution, as I define it, does produce evolutionary changes in the individual. An animal goes through developmental stages from infancy to adulthood. Although these are programmed by the genes, their actual expression in the organism varies depending on its interaction with the environment. The same genes may express themselves in more than one way, depending on the environment experienced by the developing organism. Experiments have shown, for example, that if the eggs of certain lizards are incubated in a normal environment, then the resulting offspring have a passive temperament. If the eggs are incubated in an unusually warm environment, however, the offspring have an aggressive temperament.

If an animal lives in an environment in which explosive speed is important, it may well extensively develop the muscles in its hind legs. Although this muscular development cannot be directly inherited by its offspring, it is a product of the direct interaction of the animal and the environment. The environment may directly modify the animal in negative ways. The animal might lose an eye or a limb. Again, these modifications are not inherited by the offspring. Yet over the course of time the animal changes through this kind of shaping evolution. It may become stronger or weaker as it interacts directly with the environment. Its condition at any moment is a variable—a variation—that affects whether it will survive and for how long.

Shaping and sorting evolution are complementary. For example, an individual organism with a highly adaptive genetic endowment may nonetheless have a difficult time surviving because of the effects of shaping evolution in the form of damage done by accident, disease, or predators.

By focusing on modification through reproduction, Darwin simplified evolution. Most complex forms of life can be divided into species, which reproduce only among themselves. Dogs cannot reproduce with cats, although both mammals once had a common ancestor. Reproductive evolution permits the drawing up of clear evolutionary trees with clear branching patterns, because once organisms like dogs and cats have diverged, they never recombine. The branch of life that contains dogs may give rise to new species, but it will never again merge with the branch that contains cats.

In practice, analysis based on reproductive evolution is more difficult than it might seem on the surface. Aside from the perpetual controversy over the sequence and timing of divergence among organisms (for example, did the chimpanzee or gorilla split off first from the common ancestor leading to human beings, and how long ago did these divergences take place), even the simplest organisms present special difficulties. Although one-celled organisms sometimes exchange genetic material, they generally reproduce by simply dividing and cloning themselves. Since they do not consistently interbreed, it is difficult to divide them into species, and no adequate species classification has ever been drawn up for organisms such as bacteria.

Yet the greatest challenge to traditional evolutionary thought, and one of the strongest arguments for the importance of shaping evolution, has come with the advances of modern genetics. Through genetic engineering, the reproductive barrier between species has been breached even in complex animals. Geneticists have already inserted human genes into bacteria so that the bacteria produce human insulin and other products. We are reaching the point at which the genes of any organisms, no matter how different, can be directly combined to produce a new life-form. This wreaks havoc with evolutionary trees. It violates the rule of endless divergence. With genetic engineering, separate evolutionary branches containing dogs and cats may, indeed, be able to be merged to produce new animals. In the development of future species of plants and animals, shaping evolution may well become as important as reproductive evolution— and much more important in human beings.

Traditional biology often ignores the implications of genetic engineering by categorizing it as another example of artificial selection, which is thought to be outside the main body of evolution. But combining the basic genetic endowments of vastly different species is far different from interbreeding varieties of wheat. It makes the distinction between artificial and natural selection untenable. Ignoring shaping evolution becomes impossible.

Genetics is also overcoming the generation barrier in evolution. Instead of waiting many generations for evolutionary modifications to emerge, these modifications can be directly introduced into individual organisms. An organism that began as a plant can become part animal through the insertion of specific genes. A radical genetic transformation can take place during the life of a single organism, and this transformation is inheritable by the organism's offspring. If the genome (the total set of genes) of an organism is genetically engineered so that the organism can no longer reproduce with other members of its species, then an organism that was born into one species can die as part of another. This is another instance in which shaping evolution will play as important a role as reproductive evolution in unified selection.

The traditional evolutionary tree is rapidly becoming obsolete. It should be replaced by an evolutionary network in which branches diverge and merge. This network is much more tangled than the branching tree, but it is a better representation of the reality of both shaping and sorting evolution.

When examined from the perspective of the universe as a whole, shaping evolution is the dominant mode of evolution and reproductive evolution is the exception. Other than life and thought, very few forms of matter reproduce. A star or planet evolves, but it does not give birth to other stars or planets. Clays and crystals are exceptions to this rule. They have structures that are highly organized and can even grow by reproducing their organization in a regular way. A number of scientists suspect that clays and crystals may have had a role in the origin of life.

Although it does not generally reproduce, nonliving matter does evolve directly. Stars go through cycles that we are beginning to understand. Galaxies change over time. All these contingent forms are produced by the flow of thermodynamic time through the quantum code. The environment in which a contingent form of matter exists directly modifies it. If a smaller galaxy comes close to a larger galaxy, the gravitational force of the larger galaxy may warp its shape and structure. The tremendous gravitational force of black holes may alter the form of nearby stars. The outcome of any evolutionary process depends on both the internal structure of the form (star, galaxy) and the external environment. As in all evolution, there is a large measure of unpredictability, as the quirks and randomness of history play themselves out.

Biologists have recognized the similarities between the evolution of life and the evolution of the universe. They nevertheless stress the differences in the two processes and argue that biological evolution is more complex. Yet is it fair to say that the evolution that produced life on Earth is more complicated than the evolution that produced the entire universe? Is the quantum code less complex than the genetic code? (The genetic code, after all, evolved out of the quantum code.) And what about the chemical evolution that preceded the emergence of life? Surely a process that produced molecules of DNA must have been highly complex.

One problem with making too sharp a distinction between the realm of life and the realm of nonliving matter is explaining the transformation of nonlife to life. Did evolution through variation and selection spring into existence with the emergence of the first DNA molecule? Or is life the product of a more universal process of variation and selection through the codes in which shaping and sorting evolution interact? Clearly, unified selection takes the latter position.

WHAT ARE THE FORMS?

A major hurdle in applying evolution to the world of matter is defining the forms that evolve. The definition of forms is somewhat subjective, even when trying to classify living things. If we ran a film of the evolution of life on Earth that covered a million years a second, the seemingly solid differences among species that we observe at our time scale would melt away as organisms rapidly changed and diversified.

Galaxies, stars, and planets appear to be reasonably self-evident forms in the realm of matter. But what about clusters of galaxies, swarms of asteroids, and solar systems? And on Earth, do rocks, clouds, and grains of sand evolve? In my opinion they do, though not, of course, through reproduction. The evolution of matter generally occurs through the direct interaction of the environment with the object's structure.

Unified selection studies not only the ways one form changes into another but also the persistence of forms through time. How long must a structure last before we consider it to be a form? The answer seems to depend on the perspective of the observer. Physicists study elementary forms of matter that may exist for just a few trillionths of a second before decaying. Biologists study successful forms of living things, such as bacteria and starfish, that use life's strategy of reproduction to persist relatively unchanged for millions or even a few billion years. Astronomers study stars that often last for many billions of years.

We have seen that there is an inherent uncertainty in making the distinction between the observer and the observed when we study the nature of electrons and other phenomena of the quantum world. There is a similar ambiguity when we try to carve out a form to examine with respect to its environment. Every form is intimately coupled to its environment, so intimately that the distinction between form and environment tends to fade away. Singling out any form for analysis is thus somewhat arbitrary. In addition, we are in the paradoxical position of being ourselves forms of nature embedded in the environment. We can, for example, study the evolution of human beings in an environment that includes all other living things. Or we can group human beings with all other forms of life and study the evolution of all life with respect to the changing environment provided by the surface of the Earth.

In a real sense, the only true form is the form of the universe as a whole. This contingent form changes as the structure of the matter, energy, space, and time it contains is rearranged. At any moment, the universe has a single, evolving structure because it had one beginning. If current theories are correct, the universe had a particular form at the big bang—perfect symmetry—in which gravity, electromagnetism, and the strong and weak forces were united into one field. The fact that the universe is now so immense and diverse makes it difficult to grasp that at any given thermodynamic moment it has a contingent form of staggering complexity. Assuming the universe continues expanding forever, we also know its final form: perfect disorder, in which no work is possible, orderly structure on the macroscopic scale disappears, and elementary particles simply bounce around aimlessly.

After the big bang, as the universe expanded, it underwent a kind of mosaic evolution. The conglomerations of matter and energy scattered throughout the cosmos were each subject to different selective pressures, due to the accidents of history. Many of the conglomerations condensed into galaxies of different shapes and sizes. The galaxies themselves became a mosaic of star systems, evolving in different ways. Our particular star system, which formed about five billion years ago, contains planets. Recent space probes have shown that the other planets and moons of our solar system, although they possess no apparent life, have undergone an amazingly rich diversification.

The Earth, which is 4,000 miles in diameter, evolved into three basic layers: a core of molten metal that is about 2,200 miles in diameter is surrounded by a lighter mantle roughly 900 miles thick. Atop the mantle is the surface of the planet, or crust, which averages only about six miles thick. All three layers interact, but the core and the mantle have evolved slowly with a relative minimum of diversification. The matter on the surface of the Earth has diversified rapidly, forming an atmosphere, oceans, continents—and life. Life can thus be seen as one element in the mosaic evolution in the crust of the Earth.

There is a misconception that changes in the realm of matter are simply processes that rearrange atoms and molecules, like the shuffling of our original, nonsticky deck of cards. Richard Dawkins, best known as the author of *The Selfish Gene*, commits this error in his otherwise excellent book on complex design in evolution, *The Blind Watchmaker*. He writes:

> Complicated things, everywhere, deserve a very special kind of explanation. We want to know how they came into existence and why they are so complicated. The explanation, as I shall argue, is likely to be broadly the same for complicated things everywhere in the universe; the same for us, for chimpanzees, worms, oak trees and monsters from outer space. On the other hand, it will not be the same for what I shall call "simple things," such as rocks, clouds, rivers, galaxies and quarks. These are the stuff of physics. Chimps and dogs and bats and cockroaches and people and worms

and dandelions and bacteria and galactic aliens are the stuff of biology.[4]

Dawkins rests his explanation on a distinction between single-step selection and cumulative selection. In single-step selection, order may be produced by simple shuffling or by more complex processes such as sieving—an example would be the stripes of lighter and heavier pebbles on a beach produced by the sieving action of waves—but that order is not used as the basis for further change. Cumulative selection, epitomized by the reproduction of living things, uses each generation of selection as the starting point for the next.

Dawkins, it seems to me, greatly underestimates the role of cumulative selection (his term for step-by-step selection) in shaping the forms of matter. Cumulative selection plays a pivotal role in the evolution of galaxies. The evolution of the Earth in all its diversity, including life, is the product of the mosaic evolution of the Milky Way galaxy through cumulative selection. Within galaxies, stars are formed in nurseries of dense gas and dust. The stars forge heavy elements that impregnate the galaxy when larger stars explode as supernovas. These heavier elements combine and recombine in a complex process of chemical evolution that on Earth, at least, led to an environment in which life was possible, and then to life itself.

Stars evolve through variation and cumulative selection. No two stars are exactly alike. They do not reproduce, but they change over time through an interaction of their structure with their environment. After a large star undergoes a supernova, its remaining matter may form a pulsar—a spinning, incredibly dense core of solid neutrons, perhaps no more than six miles in diameter, that sends powerful pulses of radiation into space like a cosmic lighthouse.

Clouds and rivers are part of the complex weather cycle that continuously alters the form of the Earth. Even a wave washing pebbles on the beach is simply one brief episode in a long-term process of erosion that pulverizes rock into sand and soil, and shapes the topography of continents.

Reproducing forms can be analyzed in relative isolation. We can examine the genealogical line of an organism and over the generations note the changes in form in the descendant caused by natural selection. Nonreproducing forms cannot be seen in isolation. It is the interaction of these forms that builds layers of cumulative selection. The existence of one form of matter serves as the basis for the evolution of greater complexity in an altogether different form of matter. For example, when a large star creates heavy elements and ejects them into space in a supernova, these elements form part of another gas cloud that condenses into a solar system. A planet in that solar system, which is permeated with these heavy elements, develops an atmosphere through the venting of gases from its hot interior. The atmosphere makes sophisticated chemical reactions possible among the heavy elements, and so on—possibly ending with the evolution of some sort of life-form.

In this example, different forms of nonliving matter have interacted to build layers of complexity and new forms of matter. Complex molecular structures and the forms they generate would be impossible if the universe consisted solely of the hydrogen and helium produced in the big bang. Stars, planets, atmospheres, oceans, and other forms of matter have cumulatively built up the complexity that we now observe, even though none of these forms reproduces.

In traditional biology, populations, not individuals, evolve. No creature was ever born an amphibian and later in life evolved into a dinosaur. If it was born an amphibian, it died an amphibian. Yet the form of one group of amphibian descendants was altered over many generations until it emerged as dinosaurs. In unified selection, the individual does evolve through the direct interaction of its structure and the evolutionary field. In living things a large measure of the changes that take place over a lifetime is built into their internal structure. A human being moves from embryo, to infant, to adolescent, to adult, to old age in accordance with a built-in genetic program that itself evolved in the distant past.

Most forms of matter do not have a central set of instructions equivalent to DNA. They are shaped by the matter and energy available, the rules of the quantum code, and the pressure of the environmental field. An ocean can be squeezed out of existence over millions of years when two crustal plates collide. A planet can be burned to a cinder by the supernova of its star. A star can be destroyed in a gravitational collision with another star in the central region of a galaxy, where the population density of stars is a million times greater than it is in the galactic suburbs that our solar system inhabits.

Mainstream biology has been torn in recent years by controversies over whether genes are fundamental units of evolution, or species, or something in between. The Darwinian belief that organisms undergo selection based on their degree of success in adapting to the environment has been vigorously challenged. On one side are those who believe the real actors in evolution are the selfish genes, and that the body is just a gene's way of making more genes. On the other side are those who believe in group selection: that local populations of organisms and entire species are also units of selection. Unified selection contends that all these forms—genes, individual organisms, local populations, and species—play a distinctive role in evolution, both by serving as units of selection and by shaping the evolutionary field.

THE SCIENCE OF CHAOS

Complicated systems can have a disproportionate impact on evolution. The classic example is the weather, which is a system so complex that small fluctuations can be magnified into enormous results. The stir of the air caused by a butterfly fluttering its wings in a Yucatán jungle can theoretically be amplified into a hurricane in the Gulf of Mexico.

The weather is an example of a nonlinear system. When described mathematically, such systems are found to have variables that are interconnected in complicated ways. When one variable changes, all the others change. For example, the weather is determined by many variables, including temperature, humidity, barometric pressure, wind speed and direction, and so forth. But changing any one of these variables—temperature, for instance—changes all the others. There are complex feedback relationships among the variables that can lead to the huge amplification of small fluctuations. Nonlinear systems are chaotic and the study of chaotic systems is the emerging science of chaos.

Scientists and mathematicians find it difficult to solve nonlinear equations. They are more successful in handling linear systems, in which a change in one variable does not change the others in complicated ways. For example, if we fire a cannon, it is fairly easy to calculate the trajectory of the cannonball if we know its weight, the explosive force of the gunpowder, the angle or elevation of the barrel, and the air resistance. If we use a bit more powder the next time we fire, the cannonball goes only slightly farther because all the other variables have stayed basically the same (air friction is a nonlinear variable, but its effect is so small that it can for practical purposes be ignored). This is an example of a linear system. Fortunately, many important systems—the orbits of planets, for example—can be simulated with substantial accuracy by linear equations and science has made great progress in understanding them. Many other systems, such as the weather and the economy, are nonlinear, made up of many interconnected variables. This is why experts have such a hard time accurately determining what will happen to interest rates or what the weather will be more than two or three days from now.

Nonlinear systems such as the weather and the brain can amplify slight fluctuations at the quantum level to the macroscopic level. (See Figure 9.4.) A cosmic ray striking the DNA of an organism, for example, can cause a mutation that alters the course of a species' evolution. Quantum randomness is continually leaking

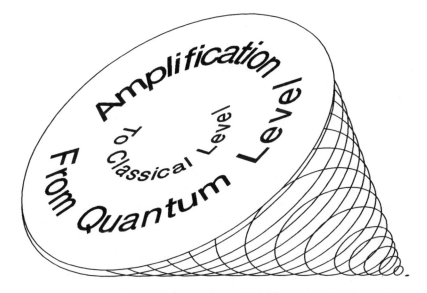

Figure 9.4. The brain's nonlinear operations at the molecular level offer the perfect opportunity for amplifying quantum randomness into the mind itself. The macroscopic universe is not deterministic because quantum randomness leaks into it through complex nonlinear systems such as the brain.

into the macroscopic or classical world, making it impossible in principle to predict the future with certainty. The collapse of future potentialities into the single actual state of the present has an inherently random element.

Complex systems that are sensitive to initial conditions can reflect underlying quantum uncertainties. Although the brain and the weather are two such systems, complexity need not be so dramatic. Take a coin, for example. If I push a coin along a smooth tabletop, I can predict almost exactly where the coin will stop—that is, if I know its starting position and how much force I have exerted on it. The coin behaves like a linear system: the harder I push it, the proportionally farther it slides along the table. The most accurate description of the moving coin, however, includes the nonlinear element of the friction between the coin and the table. But on a smooth tabletop the effect of friction is relatively small and does not prevent a linear model of the sliding coin from predicting with great accuracy where the coin will stop.

But when we flip a coin and allow it to land on our tabletop, we have a much more complex system. No linear approximation can predict precisely for any given flip which side of the coin will land face up, heads or tails. We can only predict the probabilities for a large number of flips: half the time the coin will end up heads and the other half it will end up tails. The flipped coin is extremely sensitive to initial conditions. If we built a machine to flip the coin so that we could accurately measure the position and momentum with which the coin began its tumbling flight, and we flipped the coin over and over again with the same settings for position and momentum, we still could not accurately and consistently predict whether the coin would land heads or tails on any given flip.

What causes this uncertainty? A determinist like Pierre Laplace would say that it results from our ignorance of the precise initial conditions of the flip. All our measuring devices contain a margin of error, and this margin of error is exponentially amplified by a system that is sensitive to initial conditions so that we quickly lose the ability to make accurate predictions. Nevertheless, the determinist would add, if we could somehow know the initial position and momentum of the coin with *infinite accuracy*, then we could predict exactly whether the coin would end up heads or tails.

I would argue, however, that our inability to predict the outcome of an individual coin flip is built into the quantum structure

of the universe. Even if we could build machines that were successively more accurate in measuring the initial position and momentum of the coin, we would eventually reach the quantum level and
the Heisenberg uncertainty principle, which forbids us from knowing the simultaneous position and momentum of a quantum phenomenon. I contend that adding this incredibly tiny uncertainty to
the sensitivity to initial conditions of the flipped coin would be
sufficient to prevent us from predicting precisely how an individual
coin would land. Thus, in my view, a flipped coin truly reflects the
quantum randomness that underlies reality.

Complex systems that are sensitive to initial conditions provide
a striking example of how quantum uncertainty leaks into the macroscopic world. The brain and the DNA molecule are examples of
such systems. Two identical DNA molecules, as they divide, will
accumulate mutations at different rates because of quantum uncertainties accumulating at the molecular level. Thus we can never
predict with complete accuracy the future course of evolution. Similarly, even if nature could construct two identical brains and put
them in an identical environment, quantum fluctuations in their
synaptic processing would lead them over time to generate different
ideas and behaviors.

This is the basis of free will. Our past environment and decisions do not completely determine our future behavior, although
they may make the probability of certain behaviors more likely than
others. No one, including ourselves, can predict precisely how we
will respond to a particular set of circumstances in the future.

Among living things, the most complex system we know is the
human mind and its expression through language, ideas, behavior,
and culture. Through variation and selection, minds have created
an extravagant array of new forms of matter, life, and thought.
Biologists have tended to distinguish natural selection from human
beings' artificial selection, leaving the implication that human beings are somehow outside of nature. Unified selection combines
nature and artificial selection, viewing human beings as a product of
nature and human activities as eminently natural.

The age-old distinction between artificial and natural selection
was promoted by Darwin. He was aware that human beings were a
product of nature, but he was also firmly convinced that natural
selection operated without predetermined purpose or plan. His major opponents were the creationists, who believed that nature was

the result of a religious design laid out at the beginning of time (which some religious authorities estimated to be only a few thousand years ago). After spending so much effort eliminating purpose and design from his scheme, there are indications that Darwin hesitated to bring it back with human beings as its agents.

The evolutionary field is nothing more than the sum total of the interacting quantum fields evolving through thermodynamic time. It is a probability field. The shape of the field at any given moment influences the probabilities that future scenarios will collapse into actuality.

Using the concept of the evolutionary field, we can better understand human purpose and free will. Pound for pound the human brain generates the strongest evolutionary field we know of in the universe. It can change the face of our planet, and perhaps other planets, too. It is capable of taking action that strongly shifts the probabilities that one set of future scenarios rather than another will come to pass. If, for example, human beings decide to undertake over the next several centuries to make Mars habitable (a plan that is being seriously discussed by NASA), then the probability of those future scenarios in which Mars is habitable becomes much more likely. Human beings might take action in the present seeking to keep this probability high until one of these scenarios actually collapses into existence and Mars becomes habitable. The outcome is never absolutely certain, however. A multitude of unforeseen events can thwart this purpose. Yet the human brain, more than any other animal's brain, is capable of sustaining a high probability that his or her future scenario will actually come to pass. This is the meaning of purpose in unified selection: the identification of one or more future potentialities (scenarios) whose probability of actually coming into existence one seeks to increase.

Both the purpose and the means by which one accomplishes that purpose have an element of uncertainty. This is the basis of free will. The brain is made up of billions of cells that can be influenced by the probabilistic functions of such mechanisms as the NMDA receptor. Quantum fluctuations make it impossible to know our own minds with certainty. We cannot be certain of what our purposes or goals will be a year from now. And if we seek to accomplish a purpose, the ends we choose may surprise us. The varying strategies and ideas that the brain generates through its stream of consciousness cannot ever be completely anticipated. The mind is always capable of novelty through recombining old elements or producing new ones. Our selection from this stream of ideas is also unpredictable. Attacking the same problem at two different times can easily result in two different strategies.

The quantum fluctuations that rule out complete certainty within our minds are also found at the heart of the universe. In the spring of 1992 George Smoot and his team of scientists announced that they had detected the cosmic fossils of these fluctuations. If, as the big bang theory contends, the very early universe was smaller than an electron, then it was subject to the same fluctuations as any quantum particle. These fluctuations would cause the fabric of the universe to be grainy rather than smooth. Using satellite data, Smoot and his team detected the first evidence of these primal ripples in space-time. The evidence takes the form of variations in the temperature of the cosmic microwave background radiation, an electromagnetic echo of the big bang that fills the universe. These same fluctuations presumably created different densities in the distribution of matter in the early universe. Areas of higher density would have condensed gravitationally to evolve into the galaxies and stars we see today.

Unified selection is a synaptic model that forces us to give up some of our most cherished notions of reality. If the present flashes into existence trillions of times per second as the wave function of the universe collapses from potentiality to actuality, then space-time resembles a cosmic television screen. Human beings and every structure in the universe are changing quantum patterns on the screen, just as the picture on an actual television consists not of real objects but of shifting patterns of glowing dots. This analogy makes the uncertainty principle easier to grasp. If an electron is not an object but a pattern across a screen, then when we pin down its exact position at any moment all we will see is a single glowing dot. We lose the overall pattern and thus cannot calculate its momentum. Yet if we take enough time to observe the electron pattern as it moves across the screen, we can calculate its momentum but it no longer has an exact position.

With unified selection, we have a natural way to reunite purpose with evolutionary theory. Purpose emerges from the synaptic code and the models that the brain constructs as it probes the universe. Synaptic models are the vehicles by which the mind contemplates the glory of creation.

The Thought Era

Concepts, like individuals, have their histories, and are just as incapable of withstanding the ravages of time as are individuals.

—SØREN KIERKEGAARD

Mind: The Marketplace of Ideas

THE MIND IS THE MARKETPLACE OF IDEAS AND THERE HAS BEEN NO busier marketplace than the mind working within the courtyards of science. The success of science at penetrating the mysteries of the origin of the universe—one of the greatest achievements of the twentieth century or any century—is a classic example of the variation and selection of ideas at work. Take one of the outstanding problems of biology today: the origin of life. Scientists have created many models to explain this mystery and these models are now contending for supremacy, just as different species of animals might compete for dominance in a particular niche.

The theories are wide-ranging. Some argue that RNA evolved first, since it is capable of synthesizing both itself and proteins. DNA, the argument goes, evolved later as a more stable carrier of the genetic information. Other theorists believe the earliest forms of life were self-replicating units of crystalline clay. These clay structures became the structures on which the early nucleic acids and proteins formed complex molecules. Once these molecules could reproduce on their own, the replicating forms of clay became extinct. Still others believe that life was seeded on the earth by the amino acids and other molecules contained in comets and meteors. Scientists continually perform experiments and gather data to help them make a choice among these and many other theories.

A similar process of variation and selection goes on in the debate over the origin of matter. Physicists and astronomers are puzzled that there is any matter at all, since matter and antimatter were presumably created in equal amounts after the big bang and should have annihilated each other. Yet several of the Grand Unified Theories that seek to unite electromagnetism, the strong force, and the weak force hint at subtle broken symmetries in the early universe that may have left a slight excess of matter over antimatter—enough to produce the stars and galaxies we see today.

Similarly, there is a debate about the origin of thought and consciousness. Neuroscience, however, unambiguously points to the evolutionary breakthrough that made both possible: the evolution of the neuron in animals roughly half a billion years ago and the subsequent evolution of elaborate networks of intermediate neurons between the input neurons and the output neurons.

In all these debates, the evolution of ideas proceeds in the same general way. First the ideas must be acquired through individual creativity or learning from others. Then the ideas are either remembered or forgotten. If they are remembered, then the mind may modify them. Finally, the ideas are communicated to other minds, where the process begins again. Each mind has an evolving population of ideas and behaviors.

This evolution of thought is a part of a never-ending river of ideas. This river was fed by an ancient outpouring of ideas: the rapid evolutionary explosion of knowledge that occurred nearly three thousand years ago among the ancient Greeks.

That intellectual and cultural flowering set an agenda that Western civilization and ultimately world civilization have been following ever since: the application of the rational spirit, epitomized by logic and mathematics, to every aspect of existence. Its triumph is symbolized by the pervasive presence in the modern world of computers, the mightiest logic machines yet invented. The computer is indispensable to fulfilling the Greek agenda at its deepest level: reducing reality to its fundamental components and fathoming the rules by which these components combine to create the cosmos.

The discovery of the quantum code, which is intimately linked to the big bang, also exposed facets of reality so bizarre that they challenge the underpinnings of the rational spirit. Paradoxically, just as we are reaching the culmination of the Greek agenda, our concept of reason itself is being forced to evolve. The strangeness of quantum reality has robbed us of our safe assumptions. Space is not flat but curved in four dimensions. Strict determinism has been overthrown by the statistical nature of the subatomic world. And logicians have proved that all logical systems are incomplete. We now live in a world in which space and time are non-Euclidean, causality is non-Newtonian, and logic is paradoxical and non-Aristotelian.

The problem in the twentieth century is that much of our progress, including science, was built on the assumed certainties of Greek logic and mathematics. Those certainties have collapsed, leaving a profound uncertainty. The collapse came from two directions. First, quantum mechanics revealed a contradiction, the wave-particle nature of matter, at the heart of physics, the most rigorous of the sciences. Since formal logic holds that permitting a single contradiction permits one to prove anything (and makes traditional logic useless), the compromise was to formulate the principle of complementarity to paper over the paradoxes of quantum physics.

At the same time the queen of the sciences—mathematics— which had rigorously purified Greek syllogistic logic into formal logic, discovered that even within the citadel of logic itself (assuming it to be correct) one could not formulate a completely consistent, self-contained, noncontradictory system. Thus the dream of a perfectly logical science built on a perfectly logical mathematics collapsed.

But neuroscience will help us rebuild our confidence, constructing our system on the principle of association, which allows us to link any ideas or emotions no matter how absurd or contradictory they may seem, rather than the more rigid law of contradiction, which states that a proposition cannot simultaneously be true and false. The brain is not logical but associative. Any two concepts that can be represented in the brain as a pattern of synaptic connections that fire an impulse, such as the concepts true and false, can be associated with a third concept even though the two concepts are logical contradictions. This is the source of our imagination. It is easy for us to imagine elephants that can fly or mice that can talk. We can also imagine propositions that are both true and false.

Much of what we see in the everyday world falls into a gray area rather than the cold, hard clarity of logic.

The principle of association is not the simple stimulus and response system of the behaviorists. It is constructed out of infinitely subtle and diverse associations generated by the mass of intermediate neurons in the brain. Within these neurons we represent the environment by creating maps and models.

This new evolutionary system built on unified selection will allow us to comprehend far better the complexity and contingency of the universe, as well as its order. The law of contradiction has led to all sorts of false distinctions and unnecessary exclusiveness in both our ideas about the categories of thought and categories of human beings. The exclusiveness of race, religion, and class are some of the worst of these.

The unsettling nature of many scientific discoveries in this century has intensified a difficulty that has dogged the rational spirit since the time of the Greeks: the tendency of reason to lead to skepticism, fragmentation, alienation, and despair. As with any powerful creation of the human mind, reason cuts two ways. The history of the rational spirit is a history of the tension between the constructive and destructive potential of reason.

In trying to understand where the human race is going, we must understand from where we have come. The cultivation of reason by the ancient Greeks and the relatively recent unearthing of the quantum code at the core of physics are two deeply interrelated leaps in human history. Greek philosophy and its unique point of view permeate modern science.

THE ROAD TO REASON

The Greeks were among the first recorded thinkers to begin setting aside myths and traditions in their search for the origin of all things. Among their leading thinkers, the conviction evolved that the universe, rather than being chaotic and unknowable, was a "kosmos" (the Greek word for an ordered whole) and that through reason the mind could understand the innermost mysteries of creation. The conviction that the universe is built from a few basic principles that the mind can grasp is one of the greatest ideas in human history. It is central to the evolution of what has come to be known as Western civilization.

Like the origin of life, the explanation for the origin of this idea around the sixth century B.C. is a mystery, lost in the bubbling variations of history. The idea did not appear to originate on the mainland of Greece, which was convulsed by outside invaders. Instead it surfaced in Ionia, a string of Greek colonies along the shores of Asia Minor across the Aegean Sea from the mainland. If history operates according to the rules of unified selection, then this idea arose through the complex evolutionary process of variation and selection. In this process, the fundamental form of the synaptic code, operating in the minds of individuals, interacts with the contingencies of chance, circumstance, and design. Just as the rise of the mammals depended on the fortuitous extinction of the dinosaurs, the rise of Western thought was a fortunate accident and might not have happened at all, or at least might have followed a significantly different path.

What were the variations present in the Ionian culture of that era from which the notion of an ordered universe might have been selected? Ionia was swept by the currents of the rich Mediterranean world without being dominated by any one civilization. The cultures of Europe, Asia, and Africa had made fragmentary advances in both speculative philosophy and mathematics. The prosperous Ionian polises or city-states had evolved a system of government based on the rule of law rather than the whims of despots. Perhaps early thinkers wondered whether the cosmos as a whole was similarly governed: by laws of nature rather than the caprices of the gods. The Ionian city-states did not have a strong priestly class that discouraged the dissemination of knowledge because it sought a monopoly on wisdom. And it was chiefly the Ionian Greeks who stumbled upon another of the human race's greatest inventions: the phonetic alphabet.

The term "phonetic" honors the seafaring Phoenicians, whose alphabet the Ionian Greeks borrowed. The Greeks made a momentous modification, however, by taking five Phoenician consonants for which there were no equivalents in spoken Greek and converting them to the vowels a, e, i, o, and u. These five vowels (along with two others the Greeks added) plus the Phoenician consonants constituted mankind's first fully phonetic alphabet. It could unambiguously translate spoken language into written form using a limited number of vowels and consonants (twenty-six, later reduced to twenty-four).

This highly abstract system has been followed by all major European languages and is strikingly different from languages such as Chinese that are more pictographic (in which, for example, the word for "sun" is rendered with a stylized picture of the sun) and may have thousands of symbols. Human language, as we have seen, is one of the most powerfully synaptic subcodes, and the Greek alphabet, which breaks down the infinite diversity of language into a few vowels and consonants, not only served as a vehicle for widespread literacy among the citizens of Ionia, it was also a compelling model for those early Ionian thinkers who sought to reduce the diversity of the natural world to a few basic principles: an alphabet of nature.

The first of the Ionian Greek thinkers was Thales of Miletus, who flourished around 585 B.C. Thales and those that followed him were materialists. They looked for the unifying principles of nature among various kinds of matter: earth, air, fire, and water. This was a radical break from the traditional cosmic explanations of the ancient world, which usually focused on myths, superstitions, the will of gods, or other supernatural causes. The poetry of Homer was an example of traditional explanation.

The philosophers debated the nature of the fundamental substance. Anaximenes, also of Miletus, argued that the substance was air. Heraclitus of Ephesus said it was fire. Empedocles, a citizen of a Greek colony in Sicily, chose pluralism and taught that the fundamental elements were water, air, fire, and earth.

Leucippus of Miletus, the founder of the atomist school, took a different approach. He and his disciple, Democritus of Abdera, contended that there were an infinite number of units that they called "atoms" (Greek for indivisible). These atoms, which were too small to see, were thought to be the fundamental units of matter. They had many different sizes and shapes. As they moved through the void, they combined and recombined into the shapes of the various objects we see. Reality, said Democritus, consisted of atoms and void. Inspired by the atomists and later philosophers who were influenced by them, the Roman poet Lucretius would write in his great work, *On the Nature of Things*, of a universe created by atoms falling and sometimes swerving together in the void.

Another revolution of thought was begun by Pythagoras and his followers. He was a native of Samos, an island located not far from the coastal town of Miletus, but he migrated to Italy where he founded a kind of religious community devoted to studying his doctrines. Aristotle wrote that the Pythagoreans, "who were the first to take up mathematics, not only advanced this study, but also having been brought up in it they thought its principles were the principles of all things." They believed that of the principles of mathematics, "numbers are by nature the first, and in numbers they seemed to see many resemblances to the things that exist and come into being—more than in fire and earth and water (such and such a modification of numbers being justice, another being soul and reason, another being opportunity—and similarly almost all other things being numerically expressible). . . ."[1]

Although Aristotle preferred logic to mathematics as the primary organizing principle, the idea that mathematics is the language of nature has proven to be one of the most fruitful and powerful legacies of the Greeks. In modern science, the universe is indeed made of numbers.

The influence of the Greeks goes far beyond logic and mathematics. The *Dialogues* of Plato employ reason to explore the deepest human concerns. The works of Aristotle mix both induction and deduction in broadly applying the rational spirit. His works include treatises on physics, astronomy, meteorology, metaphysics, ethics, politics, rhetoric, and aesthetics. There are lengthy biological treatises that demonstrate careful observation of animals and plants. There are shorter works on such subjects as sense and the sensible, memory and reminiscence, youth and old age, sleep and sleeplessness, and dreams.

Aristotle had created an enormous pool of ideas that could be tapped by later generations as they adapted to the contingencies of history. With the revival of classical learning in the West during the Renaissance, Greek ideas spread rapidly, accompanied by other pivotal advances virtually unknown to classical civilization, including the development of printing and the formulation of the scientific method.

The Greek agenda or program was to apply the rational spirit, using the tools of logic and mathematics, to every field of knowledge and every aspect of human existence. This rationalization of human life, with varying degrees of success, has proceeded rapidly since the Renaissance and is the hallmark of modern civilization.

We live and work by the clock, an instrument that rationalizes time. By applying the rational spirit to tools, we have created technology. By applying it to trade, we have created economics. By applying it to government and large organizations, we have created the bureaucratic style of management and the ubiquitous administrative state. By applying it to number, quantity, and space, we have vastly expanded the domain and power of mathematics. By applying it to the natural world, we have created modern science. By applying it to logic, we have created new forms of reasoning that transcend the syllogism. Among these improvements is the scientific method, a momentous advance in inductive reasoning. Scientists test hypotheses in controlled experiments that can be duplicated and confirmed—or falsified—by anyone who wishes to make the effort. The emblem of our rational age is the supreme logic machine: the computer.

REASON'S COMPETITORS

The rational age has not been an easy one. There are other forces in the human soul that compete with reason: mysticism, emotionalism, irrationalism, sensualism, egoism, authoritarianism. These forces at times enrich the rational spirit and at other times threaten to overwhelm it. History is filled with societies organized on nonrational principles. The competition with the rational spirit is further evidence that the human mind is not fundamentally rational but associative, and can build all kinds of strange and elaborate networks of ideas using the principle of association. Human sacrifice, for example, in many ancient societies, including the Aztecs and the Mayas, was a central ritual associated with success in war and the fertility of the soil.

Rationalism itself has been perverted to serve the cause of destruction and genocide. It has played a part in the rising sense of alienation in the modern world. Nevertheless, the rational spirit of the Greeks has survived the contingent circumstances of history—though at times just barely—and spread. With the aid of the computer, modern science is playing a leading role in the quest to complete the Greek agenda through mastery of the quantum code of matter and energy, the genetic code of life, and the synaptic code of thought.

Twenty-five hundred years after Thales gazed at the stars above the shores of Asia Minor, his dream of subsuming nature's boundless diversity under the operation of one basic principle has come close to fulfillment.

Ironically, the very success in achieving this staggeringly ambitious agenda has sown the seeds of reason's transformation. The relentless application of systematic analysis to logic itself has exposed major gaps in its foundations. And the discovery of the quantum code, the foremost of the codes and the key to the large-scale structure of the universe beginning with the big bang, has revealed features of reality so peculiar that they are hard to understand logically. Science is facing the twin difficulties of the fundamental incompleteness of logic and contradictions at the heart of quantum mechanics.

The problem with Aristotle's formulation of logic was that it was a linear system. The key to its linear nature is that the whole is simply the sum of its parts. Like a wave, it can be broken down into its constituents and then added up again. Modern physics and neuroscience have shown that we need a nonlinear logic.

Just as linear equations are an oversimplification of dynamical systems yet are useful for revealing certain features, formal logic is an oversimplification of thought yet is useful for revealing certain features. The heart of its oversimplification is that it tends to group things into clear-cut categories, when in the actual world things are grouped into categories that are fuzzy, messy, overlapping. Being clear-cut is usually an arbitrary, human-imposed quality. The shortcoming of logic flows from its most fundamental principle: the law of contradiction, which forbids a proposition from being true and false at the same time. This law is built into the logic gates of every computer. If one grants that things can be both true and false, then the whole superstructure of logic collapses. This is why, to save the logic of quantum mechanics, Niels Bohr had to formulate his principle of complementarity stating that though an electron or other quantum entity may behave sometimes like a wave and other times like a particle, it can never be both at the same time.

We have found that the operation of the brain is not logical but associative. The brain has no hierarchy of logic gates and operators like a computer has, although the brain can simulate, somewhat clumsily, this kind of thinking as one subset of its operation. In addition, emotion is alien to logic. A deductive system has no place for love, hate, or fear. But the associative principle can easily link ideas and emotions. In the human brain, logical conclusions often have emotional overtones as in, for example, the judgment that Nazi racial theories are not only logically incorrect but despicable and horrifying.

Linear logic leads to vast oversimplifications of our interrelationship with the world that we see every day. The simple, logical categories that we learn in school are quickly overwhelmed by messiness of a real world that demands street savvy. History is overly logical, and those of us who live through events that are written about by historians (or journalists, who write the first draft of history) are invariably struck by how much of the subtle interplay, uncertainty, chanciness of events, role of personality quirks, and general ambiguity felt by those with first-hand experience is left out. The clear-cut structure of our history, our education, our books, our language itself will have to be modified in the nonlinear age. The oversimplifications will give way to a more realistic, fractal picture, with variation and selection operating at all levels. In fractal geometry, which is one of the disciplines of nonlinear dynamics, a shape maintains the same jagged form no matter how much it is magnified. Similarly, unified selection operates at the quantum level as well as the level of stars and galaxies. (See Figure 10.1.)

It is interesting to note that recent research indicates a reason that shapes in the real world so seldom come with smooth surfaces and straight lines. The rough edges of the fractal shape, it seems, are superior to smoother geometries in damping out unwanted fluctuations and vibration. The scaling down to nearly the quantum level saps the strength of these fluctuations. The vibration produced by the beating heart, for example, might tear apart the circulatory system were it not for the endlessly branching shape of the blood vessels, from arteries to capillaries. Just as some systems promote the amplification of quantum fluctuations to the macroscopic level, the fractal seems to promote the suppression of macroscopic fluctuations to the quantum level.

The ancient Greeks were not supermen and superwomen. Their lives were like ours, filled with achievements, setbacks, cooperation, rivalry, rationality, and strong emotions. What they produced through the variation and selection of ideas was a series of contingent forms of mathematics, logic, philosophy, and the arts that have been reproduced and modified over the centuries. Why did they

**Fractal
Evolution**

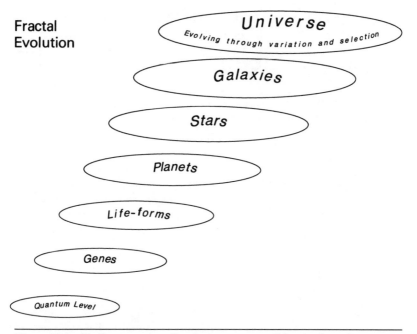

Figure 10.1. Similar processes of evolution occur at all levels, from the universe as a whole to the quantum level.

generate so many forms of such importance? In part, because the domain of rational thought was sparsely populated when they discovered it, like the dry land that amphibians found nearly empty of animals when they crawled out of the water 350 million years ago. Just as amphibians spawned many different species of life, the Greeks generated many different species of thought. There was a burst of intellectual niche-filling that has only been equaled in the last two centuries.

As the Greeks quickly discovered, these niches included the niche of skepticism. Reason can be turned on itself to cast doubt on its own ability to know and understand the world. If we conclude that nothing is truly knowable, then we become prisoners of our own minds, alienated in a meaningless world. Indeed, alienation and meaninglessness have had an important effect on twentieth-century thinking.

Skepticism was one of the earliest tools of reason for challenging dogma and false opinion and forcing individuals to think through their ideas. In the *Apology* of Plato, Socrates employs skepticism, with a generous dollop of satire, in defending himself against the charge of impiety. He relates how the oracle at Delphi said that no one was wiser than he. Yet realizing his limitations, he determines to prove the oracle wrong:

> Accordingly I went to one who had the reputation of wisdom, and observed him—his name I need not mention; he was a politician whom I selected for examination—and the result was as follows: When I began to talk with him, I could not help thinking that he was not really wise, although he was thought wise by many, and still wiser by himself; and thereupon I tried to explain to him that he thought himself wise, but was not really wise; and the consequence was that he hated me. . . . So I left him, saying to myself, as I went away: Well, although I do not suppose that either of us knows anything really beautiful and good, I am better off than he is, —for he knows nothing, and thinks that he knows; I neither know nor think that I know.[2]

The debate over the nature of knowledge has gone on ever since. It is one of the deepest issues in philosophy. René Descartes believed that everything we think we know is subject to doubt except the consciousness of our own thoughts. His theory of knowledge came down to the following: I think, therefore I am. The argument over knowledge was taken up by John Locke, David Hume, Immanuel Kant, Søren Kierkegaard, and many others. The arguments go something like this: I seem to know what my senses tell me, but my senses can be fooled by illusion or illness. And what is it that I am perceiving through my senses? Not objects directly but sensations from objects that travel through my nerves to my brain. So all I really know is a set of nerve impulses. How can I objectively verify that these nerve impulses are providing me with accurate information? Whatever I do to try to confirm the accuracy of my knowledge simply generates more nerve impulses in my brain. How do I know these new nerve impulses are any more accurate than any others?

These arguments and many others like them have never been settled. The inability of logic to definitively prove that knowledge is possible has been a source of disillusionment and uncertainty about the fundamental soundness of rational systems of thought. Of course few of us pay attention to such debates. Nevertheless, they damage the faith in the rational order of many perceptive and influential people. The disillusionment has been clearly visible in modern art and literature. It has been intensified by the failure of rational societies in this century to prevent the two bloodiest wars in history. The failure of logic to provide a bulwark of certainty in a world filled with uncertainty has led some thinkers to conclude that truth is unattainable and life is meaningless.

The answers to the puzzle of the nature of knowledge are being revealed as we look more deeply inward to the structure of the mind. We have used the laws of thought that Aristotle taught us to examine the foundations of matter and life. Now as we turn our attention to the key to thought itself—the synaptic code—we begin to see the answers. Unified selection shows how the Greek system of linear dynamics and rigid logic must be replaced by a system modeled on the mind, which is nonlinear and associative rather than mechanically logical. Minds have used and will continue to use logic as a powerful tool of thought and discourse. But insights come from many other places as well and we must learn more about those places as we study the brain.

In summary, logic has revealed three major failings. First, as Austrian logician Kurt Gödel proved with his incompleteness theorem, it cannot be used to construct a fully consistent, self-contained system of thought. Second, logic is incapable of analyzing emotion. Emotional states are completely foreign to the rigors of logic. Yet we know that emotion is inextricably involved with being human. Third, logic cannot prove that anything exists outside the human mind. The challenge to logic of David Hume and others remains unanswered. All we directly perceive are sense impressions. No one has been able to logically prove that anything exists outside of our minds. The real world that we perceive may be a dream or an illusion. Logic is helpless against rigorous solipsism.

The conclusions of modern science and unified selection are that we must give up our desire for complete certainty, coherence, predictability, and completeness and accept the fact that reality is often uncertain, unpredictable, contingent, messy, and ambiguous. This does not mean that we should give up clarity or rational analysis, but rather that we should recognize that there is more to thought than reason and logic. Wisdom comes from a dialogue between clarity of analysis and the richness and ambiguity of interconnection. This is why art, with its novel juxtaposition of images, feelings, ideas, and behaviors, so often transcends logic and appeals to the fundamentally associative nature of the mind. Physics, through quantum mechanics, has confronted uncertainty and incompleteness. We must be able to hold opposite conclusions in our mind simultaneously and realize that since our minds are organized on associative principles, we do this with an ease that perhaps we refuse to admit.

In an odd way, the discoveries of science and mathematics have brought us back to the insights of common sense, which intuitively seems to recognize the slipperiness and uncertainty of rational categories. This shock of reality is experienced by every academically trained professional when he eventually faces the ambiguities of the real world, ambiguities that the neat categories of his training have not prepared him to face. Dealing with these ambiguities must be learned, but the more definite wisdom of science and logic can be exceedingly useful in this process. They can serve as a focus for integrating and organizing what would otherwise be complete chaos. This is comparable to the role that the word plays in language, serving as a concrete focus for innumerable associations and interrelationships. The classical logic of the Greeks enriched by the modern insights of symbolic logic has served us well, and will continue to serve us in many contexts in the future. But the discoveries of neuroscience and physics have brought a new logic into the world, a nonlinear, associative logic.

Unified selection has revealed a universe in which a definite present and past stretch into a future that exists only in potential. The future can never be precisely predicted as the classical physicists, heirs to the Greeks, hoped. It can only be estimated. It is this potentiality of future states that gives the universe its ambiguity. But the present is far less ambiguous than the future and this is why Aristotle's principle of contradiction (the idea that a proposition cannot be both true and false) did not seem unreasonable. It is true that in the present a photon can be manifested as either a particle or a wave but not both simultaneously. In the future, however, prior to measurement through the collapse of the wave function, a photon can be simultaneously a particle and a wave and the principle of contradiction fails.

The final irony, perhaps, is that the Greeks anticipated this, too. They lavished much of their philosophical attention on the distinction between being and becoming, what is and what will come to be. Nature, according to Aristotle, is continually transforming potentiality into actuality. A block of marble cannot be analyzed in isolation. Its potentialities must be considered. And one of those potentialities is that it will be carved into a statue. When a sculptor performs this task, he is actualizing this potential. This is very similar to the view put forward in this book, in which future potentialities become a single actuality with the collapse of the wave function.[3]

While hopes for unassailable logical systems have run aground, this aspect of Greek philosophy seems more relevant than ever. Quantum mechanics has given a new formulation to the ancient debate over being and becoming. Being is the realm in which uncertain potentialities have collapsed into comparatively unambiguous actuality. It is the realm of the present and past. Becoming is the realm of the unmeasured wave function, brimming with overlapping potentialities. The probabilities that any one of these potentialities will actually come into existence is constantly changing. Potentialities exist in the realm of the future, which is far more ambiguous than the present and past. In 1861 it was unclear who would win the Civil War. There were many possible outcomes, all overlapping in the realm of future potentialities. Today there is no doubt about which army surrendered.

In studying the macroscopic world of the present and past, a logic based on the principle of contradiction is valuable. But such a logic is nevertheless incomplete in describing the universe as a whole (with its extension in thermodynamic time) because it does not apply in the contradictory world of the future. Even in the present and past it must be applied with caution and not categorically because the nature of future potentiality makes any concrete categories delineated by logic inherently fuzzy and unstable.

Quantum mechanics has taught us a valuable lesson about future potentialities. They are not discrete and independent of each other. Rather than being subject to the either-or choices of the law of contradiction, they overlap and interfere with each other. Understanding how this overlapping and interference works is vital to understanding how the probabilities evolve that finally lead one of these potentialities to collapse into reality. This is a fitting challenge for the next two thousand years.

Chapter 11
Evolutionary Burst

SOMETIMES IT PAYS TO BE STUPID.

With our huge cerebral cortex, our unique abilities with language, our powerful sense of consciousness, and our rapid mastery of the quantum, genetic, and synaptic codes, human beings can hardly help feeling that they are lords of the Earth.

We forget, however, that we are a comparative newcomer on the scene of living things, having existed in our present form for only about a million years. We consider dinosaurs to have been a failure, yet they ruled virtually unchallenged for more than 100 million years.

Our big brains provide us with superb adaptability, but also risk getting us into trouble. We have built weapons of mass destruction and industrialized so fast that we have risked upsetting the climatic balance. We should pause to think that many of the most successful species of life have taken just the opposite evolutionary path that we have: evolving small brains instead of large ones.

In his 1973 essay, "The Evolutionary Advantages of Being Stupid," biologist E. D. Robin pointed to many species that derive large advantages from small brains. The freshwater turtle has survived virtually unchanged for 200 million years. Its small brain requires relatively little oxygen and is capable of functioning normally with virtually no oxygen in the blood, deriving all the oxygen it needs from other bodily processes. The turtle can survive underwater dives of more than a week. Other small-brained animals, such as the diving iguana lizard, can remain submerged for more than four hours. In contrast, the brainy and intelligent bottle-nosed porpoise has a maximum dive time of only about five minutes.[1]

These cautionary thoughts are perhaps in order as human beings prepare to move rapidly down the path of even greater intelligence. If intelligence is not used prudently, it can lead to dangers and instabilities. Yet despite the dangers, the promise of the age of unified selection is overwhelming. We are heading into a revolution in understanding matter, life, and thought that will take us far beyond the magnificent achievements of even the ancient Greeks.

This book has provided a framework with which to contemplate the tremendous challenges ahead of us. Unified selection with its variation and selection has been identified with the potentialities of the future and the collapse of the wave function through the thermodynamic pulse. Evolution has been reformulated as a search for hidden symmetries and an understanding of the processes that break the symmetries.

What are these symmetries? First there is the original oneness of the big bang, when all particles and forces were combined into a single unity. Then there is the breaking of the symmetry or unity between matter and the forces, followed by the successive splitting of the forces into gravity, the strong force, the weak force, and electromagnetism. Next there is the genetic symmetry between all life on Earth. Every living thing shares the genetic code that was present in our common ancestor—the first form of life—that emerged billions of years ago. Since then species have emerged, evolved and split into daughter species. Mammals, birds, and reptiles, for example, had a common ancestor millions of years ago. A species is often defined as a population of organisms that can mate with each other to produce offspring. Evolution breaks this reproductive symmetry. With the synaptic code, we have the symmetry of the synapse, which is shared by all multicellular animals. There even seems to be a deep symmetry between thought and development. In the young organism, NMDA receptors are deployed to tune senses, such as vision, to the environment. Once the senses are wired during the critical early period, the receptors are no longer active. But in organisms such as human beings, which continue to learn and remember, the NMDA receptors remain active in key areas such as the hippocampus of the brain. Learning is an extension of development.

Underpinning all of this are the quantum, genetic, and synaptic codes. Each of the codes offers enormous opportunities for applying its knowledge in the form of new technologies.

By understanding the quantum code, we are able to shield ourselves against the harshness of nature. Using this code has allowed us to communicate with each other and organize ourselves far more effectively than ever before to pursue worthwhile ends, if we choose. From the perspective of material well-being, most members of modern societies are far more fortunate in this respect than even the most privileged members of past societies. The good fortune of everyone has increased substantially.

Through understanding the genetic code, we are compensating more and more for the bad fortune of illness. Knowledge of genetics leads to greater control over other disasters in the biological realm (crop failures, plagues). It may also lead to the strengthening of our genetic endowment, giving us a greater measure of physical well-being.

Understanding the synaptic code will give us a better chance to cure the mental illnesses and diseases that afflict millions of people as well as enhance our mental powers and well-being. We are beginning an era of synaptic engineering. The benefits of understanding these codes could provide the maximum good fortune to all members of society and allow them to achieve truly happy lives. But as Aristotle might observe, without a just society and the exercise of temperance and courage by its citizens, the knowledge gained by understanding the codes can be perverted, resulting in general misery.

From an evolutionary standpoint, the three basic human needs are learning, feeding, and mating. If we strip away the environmental complexities that face most living things—for example, those that require self-defense for survival—and imagine a completely benign environment, these would be the three essential tasks. In many ways, advanced societies have diminished the complexities and rigors of the natural environment. People with poor eyesight or chronic illnesses no longer die of hunger and neglect. Some think learning is a luxury for intellectuals. Yet learning is a necessity. Human beings are born helpless with a minimum of the instincts that allow automatic adaptation to the environment. To survive, they *must* learn; this is why infants and young children are such efficient learning machines. In a technological age, this learning must continue far beyond childhood. Individuals and societies make a serious mistake when they focus their energies on feeding and mating and ignore learning.

For the first three billion years or so after the Earth became habitable, its life was dominated by simple blue-green algae. Then, some 600 million years ago at the beginning of the Cambrian period, there was an evolutionary burst of living forms that produced in a few million years a huge number of complex invertebrate animals. No such explosion of diverse living things had ever occurred before or ever occurred again.

The causes of this explosion are not known for certain. Somehow conditions for animal life became more favorable and whole new niches in the environment opened up for population by new species.

The Cambrian period was the great period of creativity in the evolution of life on Earth. We are now living through the great evolutionary burst of thought. With the emergence of *Homo sapiens* into consciousness some 250,000 years ago—only yesterday in geological time—a new niche is being explosively filled: the niche of mind. We are seeing an accelerating adaptive radiation of ideas. The complexity of these ideas rivals anything that has so far been produced on Earth.

Ecologists use an exponential growth formula to estimate the population growth of organisms under a variety of environmental conditions. A simplified version of the formula is $I = (b - d)N$, where "I" is the rate of increase in the number of individuals in the population, "b" is the average birth rate per individual in the population, "d" is the average death rate per individual, and "N" is the number of individuals in the population at any given moment. This formula is used to show the potentially tremendous increase in numbers of living beings if the maximum number of offspring are produced and all those offspring survive to reproduce at the maximum rate.[2]

For example, if a pair of house flies began breeding in April under these assumptions, the formula calculates that by August that single pair would have more than 191 quintillion descendants. The fact that we are not suffocating in house flies indicates that relatively few of the fly offspring survive to breed. If the survival rate (b − d) increased only a little, the population of house flies would jump dramatically.

The concepts in this formula can be used to help understand the tremendously rapid rate of increase in knowledge. (See Figure 11.1.) By some estimates, human knowledge now doubles every five years or less. Clearly the survival rate of ideas has increased. With widespread literacy and new information-processing technologies, the limitations of individual memory and paper-and-pencil analysis are far less a factor today in inhibiting the growth of ideas than in earlier times. We forget less, therefore "d," the death rate for ideas, has declined. In addition, the average birth rate per individual for

The Flowering of Thought

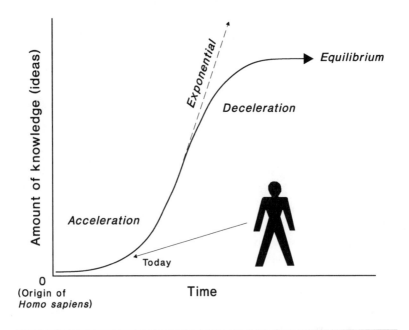

Figure 11.1. Human knowledge and power is increasing exponentially. The human race is at only a very early stage of an enormous burst of achievement.

ideas, "b," has undoubtedly risen. With increased levels of education and technology, and increased numbers of scientists, authors, and others to generate new ideas, more ideas than ever are being created per individual.

With the value of $(b - d)$ increasing, it is no wonder that ideas are growing just as the formula predicts: exponentially. Barring an international crisis or some natural catastrophe, there is no sign that this growth will level off. With this burgeoning thought comes rapid growth in both technology—the source of which is ideas—and the complexity of civilization.

Every fundamental breakthrough in the study of matter, life, and thought opens new frontiers for the growth of ideas. In this environment of explosive growth, it is difficult to predict the new forms of matter, life, and thought that will be developed, and how they will transform civilization.

Yet there are many dangers, not the least of which is overpopulation of the Earth, particularly if science finds ways to extend our life spans. There is another cautionary note that we should keep in mind. The lesson of Earth's history is that species are fragile and eventually become extinct.

As primates evolved over the last several million years, they adopted an evolutionary strategy of adaptability and flexibility, rather than specialization. With one major exception, that strategy has had only modest success. Most branches of primates have died out, and of the few that remain, many have relatively small populations and are endangered. Other species that rely more heavily on instinct than on brains, such as birds and insects, have been far more successful. We, of course, are the spectacular exception to the somewhat disappointing evolutionary history of primates. Nevertheless, it is too soon to call human beings an unqualified success. Our tenure as the Earth's preeminent species has been brief. We may not have staying power.

Thus, perhaps, the human race should move quickly, while we have the technological power, to establish itself in colonies beyond Earth or risk a disaster that will destroy or severely damage either our species or our society, and thus our ability to explore other worlds. Such a disaster could be environmental, biological, astronomical, or cultural. Many experts felt that plagues in the advanced countries were a thing of the past, yet AIDS proved them wrong. What if an AIDS-like disease suddenly became highly contagious? Although we probably have the ability to eventually cure such a disease, we might not be able to find the cure before massive damage is done to the species and our highly interconnected modern society.

We have discovered the quantum, genetic, and synaptic codes. But might there not be others? Could there be different codes underlying different forms of life and thought on other worlds? (See Figure 11.2.)

One source of despair in the modern world is the realization that we are only a petty life-form on a small planet in an insignificant solar system in the backwater of one galaxy out of billions. But the principle of amplification—the idea that small causes can lead to large effects—should act as an antidote to this. Life on Earth, insignificant as it may seem, is capable of influencing the destiny of the solar system, and perhaps the galaxy itself, through nonlinear amplification. We have the potential to use the knowledge we have accumulated to spread our life-form and its civilization beyond the earth. There is no certainty that this will happen. Indeed, at any time our species may be suppressed by social and environmental circumstances and move toward extinction. Yet the process of amplification provides a means for realizing an unlimited destiny, whether humanity is the only form of life and thought in the galaxy or one form among countless others.

Humanity has nearly completed the circle. The intelligence that enabled science to fathom the quantum code of matter and the genetic code of life is beginning to fathom the synaptic code of the mind. Since *Homo sapiens* emerged on the planet, biological evolution has had little influence on our fate. Our success has been dominated by the evolution of ideas. Those ideas have organized matter and life in a stunningly rapid cultural evolution. This latest epoch of the Earth's history must truly be called the Thought Era.

Yet self-awareness sets us apart from our fellow creatures and nature itself. We divide ourselves into hostile communities, interest groups, regions, and nations. We segregate our ideas into separate specialties and systems.

As we experience the revolutions of the Thought Era, civilization may one day be threatened by the fragmented and limited nature of its outlook. Unified selection does not guarantee progress, only the imperatives of adaptation and change. Both extinction and survival are consistent with its rules.

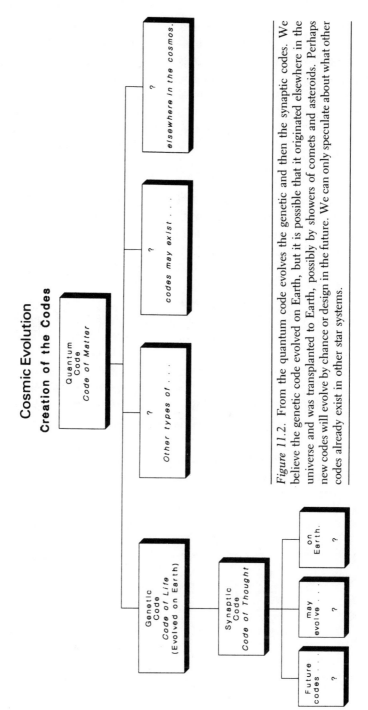

Cosmic Evolution
Creation of the Codes

Quantum
Code
Code of Matter

?
Other types of . . .

?
codes may exist . . . .

?
elsewhere in the cosmos.

Genetic
Code
Code of Life
(Evolved on Earth)

Synaptic
Code
Code of Thought

Future
codes . . .
?

may
evolve . . .
?

on
Earth.
?

Figure 11.2. From the quantum code evolves the genetic and then the synaptic codes. We believe the genetic code evolved on Earth, but it is possible that it originated elsewhere in the universe and was transplanted to Earth, possibly by showers of comets and asteroids. Perhaps new codes will evolve by chance or design in the future. We can only speculate about what other codes already exist in other star systems.

Yet the essence of unified selection—unity in diversity—provides a lesson that can aid in our survival, an antidote to the fragmentation of the age. This unity is before our eyes at every moment, if we could only see it. The root of nearly every word we speak can be traced back, mind to mind, to ancient peoples. All forms of knowledge have sprung from the same source: the synaptic code. Our bodies are marked by the common evolutionary heritage we share with all life. All matter is descended from the big bang.

Unified selection places us in the evolving present, on the frontier of change. Each of us is physically and mentally unique in the universe. We spin out variations that are shaped by the unique circumstances of our lives. At the same time, we select among ideas and other creations, and in doing so shape the world around us. The quantum nature and complexity of the world restore to us a large measure of freedom of action. We know of nothing in the universe that is more breathtaking than our minds.

The existence of each one of us is a miracle of amplification: we began our existence as a microscopic fertilized egg that was amplified through the information contained in forty-six DNA molecules into a full-grown human being made up of trillions of cells. Earth, too, can be considered a fertilized egg whose living embryo may grow and develop into a far-flung civilization inhabiting and exploring many solar systems. Amplification offers hope that our existence as a species and as individuals may have more meaning than we dreamed.

The Earth is our birthplace. Soon, however, we may be capable of moving beyond it and exploring our metropolis, our mother city, the Milky Way.

Notes

INTRODUCTION: ARIZONA NIGHTS

1. Quoted in Heinz R. Pagels, *Cosmic Code* (New York: Simon & Schuster, 1982), p. 3.

2. Dennis Flanagan, *Flanagan's Version* (New York: Vintage Books, 1988), p. 9.

3. In recent years there has been a greater interest in broadening the scope of Darwinian evolution. Richard Dawkins has coined the term "meme"—the neural equivalent of a gene—to describe ideas and behaviors that propagate and evolve in human brains. See Richard Dawkins, *The Selfish Gene* (New York: Oxford University Press, 1989), pp. 192–194. Dawkins, however, is opposed to applying the principles of biological evolution to most nonliving things. See Richard Dawkins, *The Blind Watchmaker* (New York: W. W. Norton, 1987), pp. 1–13. I shall discuss his objections further in Chapter 9. For an example of a philosopher applying Darwinian analysis to the evolution of thought, see Stephen Toulmin, *Human Understanding* (Princeton, N.J.: Princeton University Press, 1972).

NOTES

CHAPTER 1. THE QUANTUM CODE

1. A. Zee, *An Old Man's Toy* (New York: Macmillan, 1989), p. 207. For a similar example see Stephen Hawking, *A Brief History of Time* (New York: Bantam, 1988), pp. 71–72. See also David H. Freedman, "The New Theory of Everything," *Discover* 12, 8 (August 1991): 54.

2. Malcolm W. Browne, "Rival Scientists Decide Universe Is Composed of 3 Types of Matter," *New York Times*, 13 Oct. 1989, p. 1. Michael D. Lemonick, "The Ultimate Quest," *Time*, 16 April 1990, p. 50. The Stanford and CERN physicists discussed their findings more dispassionately in Gary J. Feldman and Jack Steinberger, "The Number of Families of Matter," *Scientific American* 264, 2 (February 1991): 70.

3. Browne, "Rival Scientists."

4. Aristotle, *Metaphysics*, trans. by W. D. Ross, in Great Books of the Western World, 2d ed., vol. 7 (Chicago: Encyclopaedia Britannica, 1990), p. 504.

CHAPTER 2. SOUL OF THE UNIVERSE

1. Pierre S. Laplace, *A Philosophical Essay on Probabilities* (New York: Dover, 1951), p. 4. This essay was originally published in 1819.

2. Werner Heisenberg, "The Physical Content of Quantum Kinematics and Mechanics," in John Archibald Wheeler and Wojciech Hubert Zurek, eds., *Quantum Theory and Measurement* (Princeton, N.J.: Princeton University Press, 1983), p. 83.

3. Léon Rosenfeld in Wheeler and Zurek, eds., *Quantum Theory*, p. ix.

4. Ibid., p. viii.

5. Pagels, *Cosmic Code*, p. 45.

CHAPTER 3. THE GENETIC CODE

1. Erwin Schrödinger, *What Is Life?* (New York: Macmillan, 1947), p. 61.

2. Horace Freeland Judson, *The Eighth Day of Creation* (New York: Simon & Schuster, 1979), pp. 47, 49–50.

3. James D. Watson, *The Double Helix* (New York: Atheneum, 1968), p. 15.

4. Judson, *Eighth Day of Creation*, p. 109.

5. Christopher Upham Murray Smith, *Elements of Molecular Neurobiology* (New York: John Wiley, 1989), p. 59.

6. Ernst Mayr, *The Growth of Biological Thought* (Cambridge, Mass.: Harvard University Press, 1982), p. 715. Despite the truth of Mendel's insight, some scholars argue that Mendel's experiment was too perfect. They claim he may have ignored breeding results that were inconsistent with the 3:1 ratio.

CHAPTER 4. REVOLT OF THE BRAIN

1. Daniel L. Klayman, "Weeding Out Malaria," *Natural History* (October 1989): 18.

2. Quoted in Stephen Jay Gould, "Darwin and Paley Meet the Invisible Hand," *Natural History* (November 1990): 8.

3. Srisin Khusmith and Yupin Charoenvit, et al., "Protection Against Malaria by Vaccination with Sporozoite Surface Protein 2 Plus CS Protein," *Science* 252 (3 May 1991): 715.

4. Jean Marx, "Many Gene Changes Found in Cancer," *Science* 246 (15 December 1989): 1386. See also Natalie Angier, "Gene That Checks Cell Growth May Be Key to Many Cancers," *New York Times*, 23 April 1991, p. C1.

5. Robin Marantz, "Dr. Anderson's Gene Machine," *New York Times Magazine*, 31 March 1991, p. 30.

6. Jeremy Cherfas, "Sex and the Single Gene," *Science* 252 (10 May 1991): 782.

7. A. H. Handyside, E. H. Kontogianni, et al., "Pregnancies from Biopsied Human Preimplantation Embryos Sexed by Y-specific DNA Amplification," *Nature* 344 (19 April 1990): 768.

8. Osamu Sugawara, Mitsuo Oshimura, et al., "Induction of Cellular Senescence in Immortalized Cells by Human Chromosome 1," *Science* 247 (2 February 1990): 707. See also Deborah Erickson, "Seeking Senescence," *Scientific American* 264, 4 (April 1991): 18.

9. Erickson, "Seeking Senescence," p. 18.

10. Richard Dawkins, *The Selfish Gene*, p. 23.

11. Jared Diamond, "The Cost of Living," *Discover* 11, 6 (June 1990): 62.

CHAPTER 5. THE SYNAPTIC CODE

1. Gordon M. Shepherd, *Neurobiology*, 2d ed. (New York: Oxford University Press, 1988), p. 192.

2. Eric R. Kandel, James H. Schwartz, and Thomas M. Jessell, eds., *Principles of Neural Science*, 3d ed. (New York: Elsevier Science Publishing Co., 1991), p. 328.

3. Quoted in Shepherd, *Neurobiology*, p. 40.

4. Ibid., p. 65.

5. Kandel, et al., *Principles of Neural Science*, p. 126.

CHAPTER 6. LEARNING, MEMORY, CONSCIOUSNESS

1. Eric R. Kandel, ed., *Molecular Neurobiology in Neurology and Psychiatry* (New York: Raven Press, 1987), pp. viii–ix.

2. Kandel describes his work with *Aplysia* in Kandel, et al., *Principles of Neural Science*, pp. 1009–1019.

3. Geoffrey Montgomery, "Molecules of Memory," *Discover* 10, 12 (December 1989): 46.

4. Daniel L. Alkon, "Memory Storage and Neural Systems," *Scientific American* 261, 1 (July 1989): 42.

5. Elizabeth A. Debski, Hollis T. Cline, and Martha Constatine-Paton, "Activity Dependent Tuning and the NMDA Receptor," *Journal of Neurobiology* 21, 1 (January 1990): 18.

6. Ronald E. Kalil, "Synapse Formation in the Developing Brain," *Scientific American* 261, 6 (December 1989): 85.

7. Marcia Barinaga, "Is Nitric Oxide the 'Retrograde Messenger?' " *Science* 254 (29 November 1991): 1296. See also John Garthwaite, "Glutamate, Nitric Oxide and Cell–Cell Signalling in the Nervous System," *Trends in Neurosciences* 14, 2 (1991): 60.

8. Larry R. Squire and Stuart Zola-Morgan, "The Medial Temporal Lobe Memory System," *Science* 253 (20 September 1991): 1380. See also Philip J. Hilts, "A Brain Unit Seen as Index for Recalling Memories," *New York Times*, 24 September 1991, p. C1.

9. Kandel, et al., *Principles of Neural Science*, p. 15.

CHAPTER 7. SKIN OF A LIVING THOUGHT

1. James Goldman and Lucien Côté, "Aging of the Brain," in Kandel, et al., *Principles of Neural Science*, p. 977.

2. *Towne* v. *Eisner* 245 U.S. 425 (1918).

3. Max Delbrück, *Mind From Matter?* (Palo Alto, Calif.: Blackwell, 1986), pp. 256–258.

4. Lynn A. Cooper and Roger N. Shepard, "Turning Something Over in the Mind," in Rodolfo R. Llinás, ed., *The Workings of the Brain* (New York: W. H. Freeman, 1990), p. 121.

5. The organization of language in the brain is discussed in Kandel, et al., *Principles of Neural Science*, pp. 843–848.

NOTES

CHAPTER 8. TIME FRAMES

1. P. C. W. Davies and Julian Brown, eds., *Superstrings* (London: Cambridge University Press, 1988), pp. 181–184.

2. Gina Kolata, "In Shuffling Cards, 7 Is Winning Number," *New York Times*, 9 January 1990, p. C1.

CHAPTER 9. UNIFIED SELECTION

1. Jonathan J. Halliwell, "Quantum Cosmology and the Creation of the Universe," *Scientific American* 265, 6 (December 1991): 82.

2. Salvador E. Luria, Stephen Jay Gould, and Sam Singer, A *View of Life* (Menlo Park, Calif.: Benjamin/Cummings, 1981), p. 714.

3. P. C. W. Davies and Julian Brown, *Superstrings*, p. 205.

4. Richard Dawkins, *The Blind Watchmaker* (New York: W. W. Norton, 1987), p. 1.

CHAPTER 10. MIND: THE MARKETPLACE OF IDEAS

1. Aristotle, *Metaphysics*, pp. 503–504.

2. Plato, *The Republic and Other Works* (New York: Anchor Books, 1973), p. 451.

3. Hans Christian von Baeyer, "Picture This," *The Sciences* (January/February 1991): 48.

CHAPTER 11. EVOLUTIONARY BURST

1. Cited in Harvey B. Sarnat and Martin G. Netsky, *The Evolution of the Nervous System*, 2d ed. (New York: Oxford University Press, 1974), pp. 3–4.

2. William T. Keeton and James L. Gould, *Biological Science*, 4th ed. (New York: W. W. Norton, 1986), pp. 924–925.

Bibliography

Adair, Robert K. *The Great Design: Particles, Fields, and Creation.* New York: Oxford University Press, 1987.

Aristotle. *Metaphysics.* Great Books of the Western World. 2d ed. Vol. 7. Chicago: Encyclopaedia Britannica, 1990.

————. *Posterior Analytics.* Great Books of the Western World. 2d ed. Vol. 7. Chicago: Encyclopaedia Britannica, 1990.

Asimov, Isaac. *Asimov's New Guide to Science.* New York: Basic Books, 1984.

Bolter, J. David. *Turing's Man.* Chapel Hill, N.C.: University of North Carolina Press, 1984.

Changeux, Jean-Pierre. *Neuronal Man.* New York: Oxford University Press, 1986.

Churchland, Patricia Smith. *Neurophilosophy.* Cambridge, Mass.: MIT Press, 1986.

Cohen, I. Bernard. *The Birth of a New Physics.* Revised and updated edition. New York: W. W. Norton, 1985.

BIBLIOGRAPHY

Coveney, Peter, and Roger Highfield. *The Arrow of Time*. New York: Fawcett Columbine, 1990.

Darwin, Charles. *The Descent of Man*. London: Murray, 1871.

———. *On the Origin of Species by Means of Natural Selection*. London: Murray, 1859.

Davies, Paul. *Cosmic Blueprint*. New York: Simon & Schuster, 1988.

———. *Other Worlds*. New York: Simon & Schuster, 1980.

Davies, P. C. W., and Julian Brown, eds. *Superstrings*. London: Cambridge University Press, 1988.

Dawkins, Richard. *The Blind Watchmaker*. New York: W. W. Norton, 1987.

———. *The Selfish Gene*. New York: Oxford University Press, 1989.

Delbrück, Max. *Mind From Matter?* Palo Alto, Calif.: Blackwell, 1986.

Dennett, Daniel. *Consciousness Explained*. Boston: Little, Brown, 1991.

Drexler, K. Eric. *Engines of Creation*. New York: Doubleday, 1986.

Edelman, Gerald M. *Neural Darwinism*. New York: Basic Books, 1987.

———. *The Remembered Present*. New York: Basic Books, 1989.

Edelman, Gerald M., W. Einar Gall, and W. Maxwell Cowan, eds. *Synaptic Function*. New York: John Wiley, 1987.

Eimas, Peter D., and Albert M. Galaburda, eds. *The Neurobiology of Cognition*. Cambridge, Mass.: MIT Press, 1990.

Einstein, Albert, and Leopold Infeld. *The Evolution of Physics*. New York: Simon & Schuster, 1938.

Fabian, A. C., ed. *Origins: The Darwin College Lectures*. London: Cambridge University Press, 1988.

Ferris, Timothy. *Coming of Age in the Milky Way*. New York: Doubleday, 1988.

Flanagan, Dennis. *Flanagan's Version*. New York: Vintage Books, 1988.

BIBLIOGRAPHY

French, M. J. *Invention and Evolution*. London: Cambridge University Press, 1988.

Fritzsch, Harald. *The Creation of Matter*. New York: Basic Books, 1984.

Gardner, Howard. *The Mind's New Science*. New York: Basic Books, 1985.

Gleick, James. *Chaos*. New York: Viking Penguin, 1987.

Grant, Verne. *The Evolutionary Process*. New York: Columbia University Press, 1985.

Gribbin, John. *In Search of Schrödinger's Cat*. New York: Bantam, 1984.

––––––. *In Search of the Big Bang*. New York: Bantam, 1986.

––––––. *In Search of the Double Helix*. New York: McGraw-Hill, 1985.

Hawking, Stephen. *A Brief History of Time*. New York: Bantam, 1988.

Heilbroner, Robert L., and Lester C. Thurow. *Economics Explained*. New York: Simon & Schuster, 1987.

Herbert, Nick. *Faster Than Light*. New York: New American Library, 1988.

––––––. *Quantum Reality*. New York: Doubleday, 1985.

Hey, Tony, and Patrick Walters. *The Quantum Universe*. London: Cambridge University Press, 1987.

Hoffman, Antoni. *Arguments on Evolution*. New York: Oxford University Press, 1989.

Jantsch, Erich, ed. *The Evolutionary Vision*. New York: American Association for the Advancement of Science, 1981.

Jensen, U. J., and R. Harré, eds. *The Philosophy of Evolution*. New York: St. Martin's Press, 1981.

Johnson, George. *In the Palaces of Memory*. New York: Knopf, 1991.

Johnson-Laird, Philip N. *The Computer and the Mind*. Cambridge, Mass.: Harvard University Press, 1988.

BIBLIOGRAPHY

Judson, Horace Freeland. *The Eighth Day of Creation*. New York: Simon & Schuster, 1979.

Kandel, Eric R., ed. *Molecular Neurobiology in Neurology and Psychiatry*. New York: Raven Press, 1987.

Kandel, Eric R., James H. Schwartz, and Thomas M. Jessell, eds. *Principles of Neural Science*. 3d ed. New York: Elsevier, 1991.

Keeton, William T., and James L. Gould. *Biological Science*. 4th ed. New York: W. W. Norton, 1986.

Kline, Morris. *Mathematics in Western Culture*. New York: Oxford University Press, 1953.

Kneale, William, and Martha Kneale. *The Development of Logic*. New York: Oxford University Press, 1975.

Laplace, Pierre S. *A Philosophical Essay on Probabilities*. New York: Dover, 1951. Originally published in 1819.

Llinás, Rodolfo R., ed. *The Biology of the Brain*. New York: W. H. Freeman, 1989.

———. *The Workings of the Brain*. New York: W. H. Freeman, 1990.

Luria, Salvador E., Stephen Jay Gould, and Sam Singer. *A View of Life*. Menlo Park, Calif.: Benjamin/Cummings, 1981.

McNeill, William H. *Plagues and Peoples*. New York: Doubleday, 1976.

———. *The Rise of the West*. Chicago: University of Chicago Press, 1963.

Mayr, Ernst. *The Growth of Biological Thought*. Cambridge, Mass.: Harvard University Press, 1982.

Mill, John Stuart. *On Liberty*. London: Penguin, 1974. Originally published in 1859.

Moravec, Hans. *Mind Children*. Cambridge, Mass.: Harvard University Press, 1988.

Pagels, Heinz R. *Cosmic Code*. New York: Simon & Schuster, 1982.

———. *Dreams of Reason*. New York: Simon & Schuster, 1988.

———. *Perfect Symmetry*. New York: Simon & Schuster, 1985.

BIBLIOGRAPHY

Pais, Abraham. *"Subtle Is the Lord . . ." The Science and Life of Albert Einstein*. New York: Oxford University Press, 1982.

Penrose, Roger. *The Emperor's New Mind*. New York: Oxford University Press, 1989.

Penzias, Arno. *Ideas and Information*. New York: W. W. Norton, 1989.

Plato. *The Republic and Other Works*. New York: Anchor Books, 1973.

Re, Richard Noel. *Bioburst*. Baton Rouge, La.: Louisiana State University Press, 1986.

Renfrew, Colin. *Archaeology and Language*. London: Cambridge University Press, 1987.

Restak, Richard M. *The Brain*. New York: Bantam, 1984.

———. *The Brain Has a Mind of Its Own*. New York: Harmony Books, 1991.

———. *The Mind*. New York: Bantam, 1988.

Richards, Robert J. *Darwin and the Emergence of Evolutionary Theories of Mind and Behavior*. Chicago: University of Chicago Press, 1987.

Rosenfield, Israel. *The Invention of Memory*. New York: Basic Books, 1988.

Sarnat, Harvey B., and Martin G. Netsky. *The Evolution of the Nervous System*. 2d ed. New York: Oxford University Press, 1974.

Schrödinger, Erwin. *What Is Life?* New York: Macmillan, 1947.

Shepherd, Gordon M. *Neurobiology*. 2d ed. New York: Oxford University Press, 1988.

Shepherd, Gordon M., ed. *The Synaptic Organization of the Brain*. 3d ed. New York: Oxford University Press, 1990.

Sherrington, Charles S. *Man on His Nature*. New York: Penguin, 1951.

Silk, Joseph. *The Big Bang*. Revised and updated edition. New York: W. H. Freeman, 1989.

BIBLIOGRAPHY

Smith, Christopher Upham Murray. *Elements of Molecular Neurobiology*. New York: John Wiley, 1989.

Spiegel, Rene, and Hans-J. Aebi. *Psychopharmacology*. New York: John Wiley, 1981.

Toulmin, Stephen. *Human Understanding*. Princeton, N.J.: Princeton University Press, 1972.

Watkins, J. C., and G. L. Collinridge, eds. *The NMDA Receptor*. New York: Oxford University Press, 1989.

Watson, James D. *The Double Helix*. New York: Atheneum, 1968.

Weinberg, Steven. *The First Three Minutes*. Updated edition. New York: Basic Books, 1988.

Weiner, William J., and Christopher G. Goetz, eds. *Neurology for the Non-Neurologist*. 2d ed. Philadelphia: J. B. Lippincott, 1989.

Weizenbaum, Joseph. *Computer Power and Human Reason*. New York: W. H. Freeman, 1976.

Wheeler, John Archibald, and Wojciech Hubert Zurek, eds. *Quantum Theory and Measurement*. Princeton, N.J.: Princeton University Press, 1983.

Wills, Christopher. *Exons, Introns, and Talking Genes*. New York: Basic Books, 1991.

Zee, A. *An Old Man's Toy*. New York: Macmillan, 1989.

———. *Fearful Symmetry*. New York: Collier Books, 1986.

Glossary

Amino acids   The molecular units that make up proteins.

Amplification   The nonlinear response in which a small input produces a large output.

Antimatter   Elementary particles that are identical with the particles of ordinary matter except for the opposite electrical charge. The electron is a particle of ordinary matter and has a negative charge. The positron is its antimatter equivalent and has a positive charge.

Atom   The basic unit of a chemical element such as hydrogen or oxygen, consisting of a nucleus surrounded by one or more electrons.

Axon   The long projection from the central area of a neuron that is used to signal other cells.

Big Bang   The cosmological model in which the universe begins in a microscopic state of enormous density and temperature and then explosively expands to form, over billions of years, the universe we inhabit today.

GLOSSARY

Bosons   Elementary quanta or particles that carry the four fundamental forces. An example is the photon, which carries the
electromagnetic force.

Cerebral cortex   The outer, heavily folded layer of the brain.

Chaos   The discipline that seeks to uncover regularities in apparently random or complex events.

Cosmology   The study of the origin and structure of the universe.

Dendrite   The branching projection from the neuron that receives
signals from other cells.

Determinism   The doctrine that all events, in principle, are completely predictable on the basis of prior causes. A web of
ironclad cause and effect stretches back to the beginning of
time.

DNA (deoxyribonucleic acid)   The molecule whose structure carries the genetic information necessary to reproduce an organism.

Doppler effect   The shift in the apparent wavelength of light or
sound generated by a moving body.

Electromagnetism   The fundamental force, combining radiation
and magnetism, that affects all particles with electrical charges.

Electroweak theory   The quantum theory that unites the electromagnetic force and the weak force.

Enzyme   A protein or other substance that acts as a biochemical
catalyst, affecting the rate of a chemical reaction.

Evolution   The theory that the forms of matter, life, and thought
change over time.

Fermions   Elementary particles or quanta that are the smallest units
of matter. Electrons and quarks are fermions.

Gene   The basic unit of heredity, found on the DNA molecule.

General theory of relativity   Albert Einstein's theory of gravity,
space, and time.

Gluon   The messenger particle that carries the strong force.

Grand Unified Theories (GUTs)   A class of theories seeking to
unify electromagnetism, the strong force, and the weak force.

Graviton   The messenger particle that is thought to carry the force of gravity.

Gravity   The fundamental force of attraction between all matter in the universe.

Intermediate vector boson   The messenger particle that carries the weak force.

Leptons   The class of lighter particles of matter that includes electrons.

Molecule   The smallest unit of a chemical compound that retains the characteristics of that compound.

Natural selection   The mechanism for biological evolution proposed by Charles Darwin in which species gradually change as individual organisms with inheritable traits that better adapt them to the environment produce more offspring than others in a population.

Neuron   The basic information-processing cell in the brain and nervous system.

Neurotransmitter   A chemical that is used to transmit signals in the brain and nervous system.

Neutrino   An electrically neutral particle with little or no mass that interacts very weakly with matter.

Neutron   An electrically neutral particle, composed of quarks, found in the nuclei of many atoms.

Nonlinear dynamics   A discipline studying phenomena in which inputs are disproportional to outputs. This may involve amplification, in which a small input produces a large output, or suppression, in which a large input produces a small output.

Particle accelerator   A machine designed to accelerate streams of subatomic particles and then smash them into a target as a means to study their structure.

Photon   The messenger particle that carries the electromagnetic force.

Planck time   The briefest instant of time in quantum mechanics, equal to about 10^{-43} second.

Planck's constant   The fundamental unit of quantum mechanics. Associated with the quantity of action.

Proton A positively charged particle, composed of quarks, found in the nuclei of atoms.

Quantum chromodynamics The theory of the strong nuclear force, which is carried by gluons, and its interaction with quarks.

Quarks Elementary particles of matter that make up, among other things, protons and neutrons.

Receptor A protein structure in the cell that is sensitive to a certain type of signal, such as a neurotransmitter or hormone.

Red shift The shift toward the red end of the spectrum of the spectral lines of the light from a star or other object moving away from Earth. It is due to the Doppler effect.

RNA (ribonucleic acid) A molecule used to translate the genetic information contained by DNA into proteins.

Strong force The fundamental force felt between particles in the nucleus of the atom.

Superstring theories A class of theories seeking to unify all fundamental forces—gravity, electromagnetism, the strong force, and the weak force—using the idea that the basic constituents of reality take the shape of tiny strings rather than points.

Symmetry The idea that whenever something is changed or transformed, there remains an invariant quantity. Often this involves a fundamental unity between two seemingly different objects or phenomena.

Synapse The information-processing link between neurons.

Uncertainty The doctrine that events are based on probabilities, rather than strict cause and effect.

Uncertainty principle The postulate formulated by Werner Heisenberg that there are pairs of attributes, such as position and momentum, the precise values of which for any quantum phenomenon cannot be measured simultaneously.

Wave function The mathematical procedure used to calculate the probabilities that a quantum system will be found in a specified state.

Weak force The fundamental force that acts to produce certain types of radioactivity.

Index

INDEX

INDEX